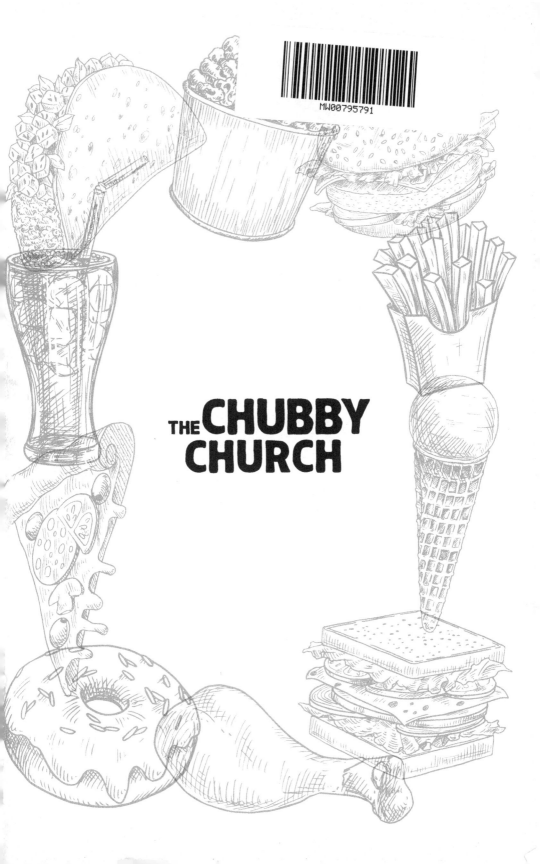

THE**CHUBBY**
CHURCH

BOOK 1

THE CHUBBY CHURCH

A CALL TO BREAK FREE OF WEIGHT & EATING BONDAGE

JENDAYI HARRIS

Emotional Fitness Trainer

WHOLE & FREE
PRESS

© 2019 by Jendayi Harris

ISBN: 978-0-9971867-0-3 (paperback)
      978-0-9971867-4-1 (hardback)
      978-0-9971867-1-0 (mobi ebook)
      978-0-9971867-2-7 (epub ebook)
      978-0-9971867-3-4 (audio)

Library of Congress Control Number:

Classification: LCC RC552.E18 | DDC 616.8526–dc22

Front Cover: Vanessa Mendozzi & Sunil Kargwal
Back Cover: Najdan Mancic
Interior: Wordzworth
Editors: Sarah Hayhurst & Bree J. Schuette

Printed in the United States of America.

Published by:
Whole & Free Press
P. O. Box 371391
Denver, CO 80237

DEDICATION

With Great Love To:

My Source, my All,
Words cannot express my love and gratitude.

To My Mothers:

Joann, Thank you for your incredible generosity, and for being
my one and only biological mom. I love you immensely.

Lorianne, Thank you for seeing the vision,
believing in me, and encouraging me without fail.

Debbie, Thank you for laboring with me
to get to the front line of my ministry.

My grandmothers, *Josephine* and *Ada,* I cherish you.

In Loving Memory and Honor:

My grandfather, *Ellis E. Harris, Senior,* Thank you
for filling the gap. You were my favorite eating buddy.

DISCLAIMER

Jendayi Harris, Whole & Free Press, Next Level Therapy, Llc.
Disclaimer for The Chubby Church Book Contents.

This book, its content and any linked material are presented for informational purposes only and are not a substitute for medical advice, diagnosis, treatment, or prescribing. Nothing contained in or accessible from this book should be considered to be medical advice, diagnosis, treatment, or prescribing, or a promise of benefits, claim of cure, legal warranty, or guarantee of results to be achieved. Never disregard medical advice or delay in seeking it because of something you have read in this book. Neither Jendayi Harris, nor Whole & Free Press, nor Next Level Therapy Llc is a medical doctor or other licensed healthcare practitioner or provider. Consult with a licensed healthcare professional before altering or discontinuing any current medications, treatment or care, or starting any diet, exercise or supplementation program, or if you have or suspect you might have a health condition that requires medical attention. The United States Food and Drug Administration has not evaluated any statement, claim, or representation made in or accessible from this book or any linked material. The content of this book is not guaranteed to be correct, complete, or up-to-date. The Chubby Church e-book especially may contain links to other resources on the Internet. These links are provided as citations and aids to help you identify and locate other Internet resources that may be of interest, and are not intended to state or imply that Jendayi Harris or Next Level Therapy, Llc or Whole and Free Press recommends, endorses, supports, sponsors, or is in any way affiliated or associated with any person or entity associated with the linked material, or is legally authorized to use any trade name, registered trademark, logo, legal or official seal, or copyrighted symbol that may be reflected in the linked material. If you would like to communicate with us, please email *info@wholeandfreepress.com*.

Note: All references to diabetes refer to type 2 diabetes, not type 1 diabetes.

Disclosure: Remember to consider all advice with a medical doctor. The author and any affiliation with this book are not held liable for health recommendations.

TABLE OF GOODIES

Download Your Free
Call to Weight & Eating Freedom Action Plan
www.WholeNFreeHealth.com

INTRODUCTION

We're going over a mountain, from a place of bondage to a place of freedom. Like the children of Israel, we'll move out of our weight and eating Egypt to our weight and eating promised land—as illustrated in Scripture. In this quest, you can't go halfway and win: you've got to go the whole way.

Each of *The Chubby Church* books represents half of the mountain we're to conquer. Let's walk through how this journey to win the weight and eating battle is structured.

Book 1: *A Call to Break Free of Weight & Eating Bondage* starts with us leaving our bondage behind, and then we ascend to the top of the mountain to gain our freedom. We're laying a foundation for freedom. This book covers the basics of body care, soul care, and spirit care.

Book 2: *A Call to Win the Weight & Eating Battle for Good!* descends down the other side of the mountain to reach the promised land. We're aiming for total victory to manifest our weight and eating freedom, health corrections, and lifestyle changes. We will reach and embrace wholeness and enjoy our promised land.

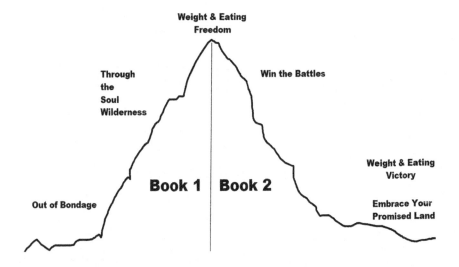

Out of Bondage

The children of Israel cried out to God to deliver them from the harsh conditions of enslavement by the Egyptians. They were desperate, and their desperation made them willing to change and embrace something different.

Are you desperate?

As they humbled themselves, God gave grace to be led by a chosen deliverer, Moses. Even though the Egyptians in our case may resemble chocolate-chip cookies or chips, God has heard our cry. Praise the Lord!

After hundreds of years of enslavement, the bondage expiration date came due.

How long have you struggled with weight and eating?

It's time for this struggle to end in your life.

Moses was as ready as anyone could be, given the circumstances. He said, "Yes, God," in spite of all of his own insecurities, like his lack of confidence in speaking, to lead the people out of their bondage.

The Israelites only had to obey and say, "Yes," when it was time to put blood on the doorposts, collect goods, or cross the Red Sea. And, they did.

There was no turning back.

If they turned back, it would've been an early death sentence.

Pharaoh and his cohorts were blind to God's truth. Pharaoh only saw red when it came to God's people. As an oppressor, he was ruthless, without an iota of mercy in his enslavement of the Israelites. Pharaoh refused to let God's people go, even after ten plagues.

Ten.

Plagues.

How much has your health or life been plagued by body image, medical threats, and eating struggles?

For Pharaoh, it took his firstborn son to die in order for him to let the people go. And when he did finally release them, he attempted to pursue them again.

Relentless.

How relentless has food temptation been in your life? Or the desire to diet? Binge? Criticize your body? Hide from mirrors? Or base your happiness on numbers on the scale?

Every Israelite had a decision to make. Do I trust the man of God leading us? Do I leave everything I've known and go? Or do I risk death?

At the moment of commitment, each thought, I either cross the Red Sea now or I'll be bound, killed, or drowned.

Freedom was the only life giving alternative to bondage.

In one of the greatest miracles ever reported, the Red Sea parted, and the Israelites were free. A shout of victory could be heard in the heavens.

To be set free from weight and eating bondage, we cry out. It's time to move forward and get out of this place of turmoil with food, body image, eating, and weight.

In the first few chapters, we'll do that as we lay the foundation for freedom in body, soul, and spirit. In the next chapter, we'll complete a quiz to check how much weight and eating bondage grips us. I'll share more of my story to help you connect with your own weight and eating story. We'll cover the basics of body, soul, and spirit functions and how they relate to holistic healing.

We'll make a conscious decision to get free from weight and eating bondage for good—for life. And we'll complete **The Call to Weight & Eating Freedom Action Plan** to help us persevere up and over the mountain. Join others and download your plan online at *www. WholeNFreeHealth.com*. This commitment to freedom must be front and center as we move out of bondage and into our personal promised land.

Through the Soul Wilderness

The wilderness was a transition time from bondage to freedom. The Israelites had developed a bondage mindset across generations. I'm sure it was tough to eat the same food every day, wear the same clothes, and be around the same people.

Bondage was broken in the physical realm—they were away from Pharaoh and they were free from harsh physical labor. But, a sense of bondage lived in their hearts and minds. This was evidenced by their golden calf, complaints, and rebellion.

God delivered perfect instructions for living. But their longings for bondage overcame them. They didn't understand.

While they wanted to inherit the promised land flowing with milk and honey, or silk and money in modern terms, and slim and mobile in ours, many couldn't get there because their bondage mentality hadn't been broken. They weren't willing to do what was required to attain their freedom.

The goal of our wilderness is to root out the spirit of bondage based in fear, doubt, bad habits, and rebellion. We do so with deeper understanding—in body, soul, and spirit.

In the same way, if we drop weight with the latest diet fad, the bondage will still be alive on the inside, and we'll be challenged again. That's why 90 to 95 percent of people who lose weight regain it and then some.[1] The soul wasn't addressed. Bondage still lives. Idols weren't demolished. Instructions weren't obeyed.

We'll face our truth on why we use food, like others use liquor or cigarettes.

Freedom comes with an investment of time to work on our mindsets, character, identity—it's the soul work, the body work, and the spirit work that takes change, sacrifice, and shifts.

We'll walk through freedom strategies for body, soul, and spirit. We'll need to understand how we got here, and why, and the chains jerking us backward and keeping us stuck in the wilderness.

Chains like Body Neglect, The Dieter's Mindset, Emotional Eating, and Going It Alone. If we're unwilling to break the chains, chances are we'll be stuck in weight and eating bondage for life.

To counteract the chains, we'll Habitize Body Stewardship, Adopt the Freedom Mindset, Enact an Emotional Strength Training Plan, and Supersize Our Power Source.

We'll also gain an understanding of our soul's psychology in weight and eating bondage. You'll learn the psychological reasons that you self-protect with weight in Chubbology. We'll understand the *Inner Glutton* and our personal Grubbology. This insight helps us find the hidden reasons we sabotage progress, eat like there's no food supply, and beat ourselves up over the damage.

Win the Battles

Those who made it through the wilderness were confronted with the giants that inhabited their promised land. Out of a team of twelve scouts, only Joshua and Caleb believed they'd win. With God they knew they would take down the giants. But doubt paralyzed the rest of the Israelites. It was difficult for many to move beyond the wilderness to press through to the promised land.

The purpose of giants is to grow into the identity of who God says we are and what God says we can do. We defeat giants so that we can stay free. If giants overran the land, then the Israelites would be subject to future enslavement. There was no way to skip the battles. They had to not only be fought, but won.

When we know who we are, there's no giant too big. When we understand who God is, we know we've already won.

We'll deal with the seven behaviors that keep this stronghold in place. With a strategy to win the battles we face, we can defeat them. To win these battles is to win the war.

Like the seven enemies the Israelites had to face, we'll have seven battles, too. They are compulsive overeating, food addiction, fleshy fasting, body shame, isolation, unclean eating, and generational yokes. When we go after our enemies and take a rightful position as a warrior of the Most High God, we can be like Caleb and Joshua—zealous to overcome.

Embrace Your Promised Land

The Israelites experienced peace and rest for many years as they enjoyed the promised land. I want you to see this through, until you have the life in Christ promised to you of health and wholeness in body, soul, and spirit.

In the promised land is where you'll experience your heart's desires. You get to enjoy all of the desires you've cultivated on why you wanted weight and eating freedom. Your victory is calling. And there's significant rewards for those who work for it and believe for it.

So today, I'm asking you, on behalf of the Lord, to commit to your freedom and to cultivate your desire to be free—no matter what ups and downs you face on the journey.

Freedom is bigger than weight and eating because on the journey to freedom from weight and eating a more abundant life in Christ will be gained.

We'll find antidotes for specific obstacles, unexpected treasures, and ruts along the way for you to embrace wholeness and defeat this stronghold for life. In Book 2, we'll review how to embrace and love your whole self, discern the red flags of recapture into weight and eating bondage again, be encouraged as you restore your health over time, and embrace the whole and free you.

Why I Relate to Moses

I flipped on the television to the Daystar network. The anointed Bishop T. D. Jakes of The Potter's House Church in Dallas was preaching. The next thing I knew I jumped out of bed and started praising God like never before.

Overtaken by the glory of His presence in my bedroom, I fell to my knees with my arms spread wide.

"Hallelujah!" all of my heart, mind, and soul yelled out, in adoration. "Hallelujah! Hallelujah! Hallelujah!" A hundred times.

The Lord had spoken to my spirit. He said, "You are called to lift the bondage off the people and establish the kingdom of God."

My soul vibrated as glory intensified in the atmosphere. A powerful surge of His Spirit moved through me, and it held my arms in the air. TV church was still on in the background, but a full on revival was happening right there in my bedroom in Denver, Colorado.

I felt the call. I felt it in every fiber of my body. I was called to lift bondage! My purpose of why I was here on the earth, why I had read countless books on psychological growth, and why I went through deep healing and agonizing pruning to heal my past, my character, personality, and my pain like my life depended on it. Why I've been trained in a wide variety of areas in life like health, business, finance, family, single life, and marriage. And why I have testimonies for days on end.

Now it all made perfect sense why anyone would have to do that depth of soul work. It was because I'm on a mission to equip the body of Christ with practical and psychological wisdom. I'm to provide practical strategies and advice to do life in Christ well.

I knew my calling would manifest itself as an author to write books that help free people from their bondages—all kinds of bondages. But

I had to start by overcoming my own biggest, hardest, most grueling, and primary battle—the one I call Weight and Eating Bondage.

This inkling to write was already in me. But like when the Lord called Moses to free the children of Israel out of their Egypt, I too felt incredibly inadequate, flabby, and not good enough. I relate to Moses because I'm far from perfect, but my answer is always, "Yes, God!"

As you turn the pages of this book, know that I deeply care and resonate with the struggle with food, body image, weight gain, dieting, and binge eating.

I know what it's like to feel absolutely hopeless that my weight would ever change, that my mind would be forever held hostage by its obsession with my next meal, or wonder if I'd ever really like kale. I know what it's like to be a slave to food, a slave to cultural body image, a slave to the scale's report, and a slave to fear.

You too are an overcomer by the blood of the Lamb and the testimony of Jesus Christ (Revelation 12:11). Are you willing to do what it takes to overcome your weight and eating battle for good? Will you commit to your freedom? Just go ahead and tell the Lord, "Yes!"

Soul Freedom Author & Teacher
Emotional Fitness Trainer
Lover of the True and Living God
Friend of the People

xoxoxo

Additional resources to help you in your journey, such as courses and book clubs, can be accessed online at *www.WholeNFreeHealth.com.*

CHAPTER 1

DOES GOD CARE ABOUT MY WEIGHT & EATING?

"Cast all your care upon Him, for He cares for you"

−1 PETER 5:7

Next time you see someone with a nice body who looks like he or she just walked out of the Garden of Eden, think to yourself, I look like that under here.

I sn't the picnic today?" One church goer said to another, "This sermon is lasting an eternity. Doesn't pastor see he's over his twenty nine minutes? We need to get to the picnic already," she said.

She knew full well just a couple hours ago she filled up on bacon, eggs, and jelly laden biscuits for breakfast. But her brain snapped photos of all-you-can-eat chili, sweet tea, apple pie, and hamburgers, causing her food obsession to overtake her patience.

"He'll be done soon. Are you here for God or the picnic?" the church neighbor responded with irritation as the sermon wrapped up. Before another word could roll off his tongue, she— unbeknownst to herself—got up and smooshed his face with the side of her ridiculously large purse, complete with an encased New King James study Bible inside, as she pushed her way through the aisle to be first in line for char grilled Angus.

He rubbed his battered cheek as he quietly murmured, "Glutton."

Have you ever stood perplexed, as you looked around while people pigged out at the church picnic, thinking, *What's wrong with this picture?* Have you felt like this hungry church goer? Or wondered in the back of your mind if God cares about your weight?

For years, I struggled with my own bondage to weight and eating without thinking about the bigger picture. I needed more insight than worldly diet advice telling me to eat cottage cheese and work out.

I had no idea I had a god named McNuggets, accompanied by worship practices that included fries and hot mustard sauce. I was a slave to feel good food and the health consequences thereof.

I emotionally ate and ate and ate. I loved the Lord, but my mind was fixed on donuts.

I battled diet after diet, ate fast food three times a day, and lost and gained weight several times. How frustrating to win in other areas of life but feel like a loser in the weight and eating battle, over and over again.

Then one day, in much agony over weight and eating struggles after losing less than expected on a thirty day juice fast, I parked my car and laid my head on the steering wheel.

This time you'll need to do things My way.

Tears streamed down my cheeks as the Holy Spirit whispered. My diet shenanigans needed to retire. I faced a problem my education, knowledge of health, and understanding of Scripture alone couldn't solve.

You'll get permanent instead of temporary.

I listened to that still, small voice. Permanent sounded much better than the dramatic up and down weight woes I experienced for the past decade.

I replied, "Was my fast in vain?"

I needed to understand if my thirty day juice fast was pleasing to the Lord. I had, after all, lost some of the weight I'd gained during the past year of marriage.

What is it about marriage that makes one want to eat?

In that moment I realized the juice fast wasn't one of pure motive, but rather my motive was to lose marital weight. *Ugh*, I had my answer. The fast wasn't a true fast but another diet.

"I repent," I said. The turmoil years of dieting had on my emotions and weight felt like a churning of my intestines, but the word *permanent* gave me peace. "Lord, help me in this."

It was time I allowed the Lord to have this locked part of my heart. I hadn't invited Him into this part of my craziness because I thought I solved it three years ago with health knowledge. To approach Him, begging for help in weight and eating struggles, again, seemed futile and beneath His time.

Three years prior, I learned about the body and helped many others lose weight with whole food nutrition and proper detox protocol. *I'm trained as a board certified health coach*, I thought. *What was this? Why was I back to square one and a half? How did I gain weight again?*

Confused, I confessed, "I will go your way, Lord."

At that moment, something released in my heart. His Spirit welcomed the opportunity to free me into whole and free health.

Freedom, Yes, Freedom

For many years of my life, most of my heart and mental energy was spent trying to figure out what I wanted to eat or the weight I needed to lose. In 2004, I was fifty pounds overweight from eating fast food three times a day, yet I wondered why I had symptoms of weight gain, disgusting greenish black fungal issues on my skin, irritable bowel syndrome, moodiness, depression, fatigue, bad acne, psoriasis, and asthma.

But worst of all, a tormented mind harassed me like a pre-teen who wants a cell phone. It drove me to think I needed to lose weight, even at times when I didn't. At that time, my mind demanded fatty, sugary, doughy foods and took my focus from God and His plan for my life.

The Lord led me to holistic nutrition, allowed me to lose over fifty pounds, and delivered me from traditional fast food.

A miracle of the modern age.

Yet, along the way, I somehow regained the weight because the problem wasn't just the food. In fact, I'll share with you in Chapter 3 how I regained the pounds by eating organic cookies and snacks.

Three times, I've lost and gained significant poundage. So, I'm not sure if I'm an expert on weight gain or weight loss at this point, but either way, I'm happy to help.

My body reflected my soul. And I now know it was my soul weight that really needed to get lost. Soul weight is our brokenness, grief, financial anxiety, anger, and insecurity.

Yes, our inner transformation allows for body revelation.

Through the Holy Spirit, I found the path to freedom from the bondage of weight and eating. As I learned to seek physical, emotional, mental, and spiritual health, I was able to win the battle for good. "With God all things are possible" (Matthew 19:26b).

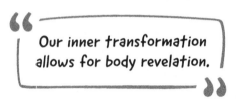

Our inner transformation allows for body revelation.

Are You Ready to Win the Weight & Eating Battle for Good?

Are you, too, a Jesus lover who struggles with weight and eating? Have you tried diet books, pills, or personal trainers only to gain more weight? Do you struggle with emotional eating, overeating, or sugar addiction? Are you wondering why God just won't help you with your weight even after you've prayed a hundred times?

I call this struggle: weight and eating bondage. It's a complex issue that I've simplified to help you move out of bondage to your promised freedom in Christ.

Let's make sure you're in the right place.

WEIGHT & EATING BONDAGE QUIZ

Mark each statement below that resonates with you:

1. I feel out of control with certain foods, ingredients, and/or drinks. ☐

2. I often overeat and stuff myself with food. ☐

3. I undereat, skip meals, and often neglect my nutritional needs. ☐

4. I have poor health. ☐

5. I've had surgery to help me lose weight. ☐

6. I don't like my body. ☐

7. I often criticize and obsess about certain body parts. ☐

8. I avoid looking at myself in mirrors. ☐

9. I always want to lose weight, but I don't get any lasting results even when I try. ☐

10. I often work out but then eat poorly after my workout. ☐

11. I exercise primarily to lose weight. ☐

12. I fast with the main motive of losing weight gained from poor eating. ☐

13. I often obsess over my health and weight condition. ☐

14. I fear getting a disease. ☐

15. I frequently crave sugary, salty, fatty, or floury foods. ☐

16. I eat quickly—a full plate is gone in less than five to ten minutes. ☐

17. I am considered overweight or obese. ☐

18. I've been diagnosed with an eating disorder. ☐

19. I've gained and lost weight over twenty pounds more than once in my life. ☐

20. I feel my weight blocks me from living my best life in Christ. ☐

Total Score:

_____

**Any statement marked is a sign
you're reading the right book.**

This book is for the chronic dieter, the fast food junkie, and the binger. The man or woman threatened with heart disease or diabetes because of eating habits. It's for the woman who got gastric bypass years ago only to gain it all back and then some. The guy obsessed with his leg muscles. And for the person scared they'll get cancer again if they don't change their eating habits.

And you don't have to be chubby to read this book. Plenty of skinny fat people are popping lots of pills and chomping on bottomless bags of chips. Many are normal weight but in weight and eating bondage.

Whatever your story, I'm glad you want to do something about it.

There's no condemnation here, and this isn't about shaming you because of the candy bar you ate yesterday. It's about you emotionally, mentally, and spiritually maturing into a person who can stand fully in love for who God made you to be. It's about freedom from that little god in your belly who demands your attention and takes you away from being emotionally and physically available to what matters.

Again, inner transformation brings body revelation.

So, the next time you see someone with a nice body who looks like they just walked out of the Garden of Eden, think to yourself, *I look like that under here*, because the physical body you want is already there, waiting to be revealed.

Thankfully, we don't need false weapons of liposuction, diet potions, or a will power ax to win the battle. What we need are solid strategies, mindsets, skills, and principles for health. No matter what your size or how long you've struggled with weight and eating, victory is yours!

Please don't just read this book: read it through quickly, then read Book 2, and study them both. You'll have the principles to become the best version of yourself on the inside, which in turn will manifest on the outside.

Why God Cares About Our Weight & Eating

Our God is deeply personal. He cares about the smallest details of our lives. He's intentional. The universe was built with a purpose. He created this planet and created man on it for a reason.

Our God loves.

And He loves intimately, securely, and jealously.

He wants no other gods before Him.

I felt my weight and eating was beneath Him earlier in my walk, but that was before I knew better.

The Lord wants us to use our faith muscles in the area of our skinny jeans. Why? Because He cares.

God Cares About Your Heart

How much of your heart is consumed by ice cream?

The Scriptures say, "You shall love the Lord your God with all your heart, with all your soul, with all your mind, and with all your strength [body]. This is the first commandment" (Mark 12:30).

The heart is the most precious thing any human has to offer. It's valuable. It's to be loved, honored, held closely. When the heart is enslaved to anything other than God, it won't receive the peace fully possible by Him since He is not only the Creator of it and died for it, but He is love (1 John 4:8).

Desiring food over God is the oldest tempter in the book. Adam and Eve were tempted first by food and failed. Jesus was also tempted and prevailed.

God Cares About Your Love for Yourself and Others

Are your poor eating habits rubbing off on your children or grandchildren? His second greatest commandment is to love your neighbor as you love yourself (Matthew 22:37–40). How we care for and feed our bodies affects how we love ourselves and others.

7

God Cares About Your Walk

How can overcoming weight and eating bondage empower you spiritually? As we gain freedom, we become a more spiritual man. A carnal Christian is driven only by the lust of flesh (taste buds), the lust of the eyes (delicious commercials telling us to go order more burgers), and the pride of life (1 John 2:16). A spiritual man or woman is driven by love and truth.

God Cares About Your Health

Do you sense your health destiny may end up in a hospital bed? Mental, emotional, and physical health is at jeopardy from those who suffer with weight and eating issues. His desire for us is to prosper in health (3 John 1:2). It's also to visit the sick in the hospital, not to eat our way there.

God Cares About Your Freedom

Do you feel tormented by your food, weight, eating, and body thoughts? Christ makes us free, but we've got a role to play to work out our salvation (Philippians 2:12). We're to stand fast therefore in the liberty by which Christ has made us free, and do not be entangled again with a yoke of bondage (Galatians 5:1). We're to lay aside every weight that easily ensnares us (Hebrews 12:1).

God Cares About Your Victory

How long have you struggled with weight and eating? There's no testimony of freedom without a testimony out of bondage. We're called to overcome, even the internal warfare we battle. We're to be overcomers by the blood of the Lamb and the testimony of Jesus Christ (Revelation 12:11).

God Cares About His Temple

Could you use more energy to fulfill God's call on your life? Your body is a temple of the living God (1 Corinthians 3:16–17). We're to steward it well because we're needed to work the harvest. He said to them, "The harvest truly is great, but the laborers *are* few; therefore, pray the Lord of the harvest to send out laborers into His harvest" (Luke 10:2). Perhaps the laborers were lured away by Papa John's?

> " God cares about your weight and eating because He cares about you. "

My point is that God cares about your weight and eating because He cares about you. So, "Cast all your care upon Him, for He cares for you" (1 Peter 5:7). Every detail of your life matters—especially your struggles. As David said, "What is man that You are mindful of him?" (Psalm 8:4a).

What's Been Missing?

Clearly, why you haven't succeeded before isn't because God doesn't love you or want you to succeed. It's not because you're born to be fat or inherit disease.

The world misleads us on this topic of weight and eating just like with most other things. The world says being a size two is successful and worthy of love. Not true! You're loved no matter your shape and size.

This isn't about being a size two or having a thirty four inch waist. It doesn't mean you have to start a crash diet today or give up cake forever. It's not my mission to be the food police. And, for the record, it's not the size of a person that determines their freedom. Some of us are naturally bigger than others and naturally carry more weight.

It's also not all about being overweight or obese. Plenty of church folks are a normal weight but are still not paying adequate attention to proper nutrition and take diet induced blood pressure, cholesterol, or diabetes medications. No matter what your state of health or shape, you're so much more than your body shape and size!

I believe that freedom is being emotionally, spiritually, physically, and mentally healthy and engaged with life. See, the world says, "Diet, diet, and diet some more," yet dieting gets you big, bigger, and the biggest you've ever been in your life!

Because diets don't look at the deeper root cause but only symptoms. Which, as a result, leads you on the search for another diet. This is soul extortion from the father of lies. It's demoralizing to go on and off diets, to win and lose the weight battle over and over again.

The world is deceptive, but the biggest deception is who you really are as a kingdom son or daughter. The real you isn't chubby, nor is the real you subject to torment in thinking you're not healthy enough, good looking enough, or saved enough.

> " Modern day battles for believers are an internal warfare of sorts. "

Weight and eating struggles don't mean that you're defective or a piglet. It means God wants to show you His powerful love. Weight and eating freedom is a measurement tool of how much you're growing in the fruit of the Spirit (Galatians 5:22).

You're blessed because you will see your growth and transformation from the inside to the outside. And, you're not alone. We've all got something to overcome, right?

Battles were gruesome back in the day when the Israelites had to defeat real giants with arrows. Modern day battles for believers are an internal warfare of sorts. We battle enemies of our own soul's mind, will, and emotions as well as spirit and body.

Once you're in agreement with unhealthy living, hating your body, abusing your body with food, hanging out on the hamster wheel of dieting, or absolute inertia from making a change out of obesity, there's nothing more for Satan's helpers to do. You've lost, and they've won because the lies are internalized. In other words, you believe what you repeat in your head several times a day, even if it's a lie.

No more will you be subject to these destructive lies. God is our victor, and yes, He requires your will to surrender to His, your understanding to come into agreement, and for you to *want to* put this thing under your feet.

As we move through the material, you'll become equipped with knowledge, wisdom and understanding, practical application, and real strategies to win for life. "[You] can do all things through Christ who strengthens [you]" (Philippians 4:13), so this is a battle you've already won in Him. You cannot fail with these principles.

What to Expect

This isn't a diet book. Diet books only work for a limited time. I'm interested in your complete freedom and wellness for life. Unlike weight loss books that give specific diet guidelines to follow or make you feel like it just takes your willpower to *shape up and honor God, you bad, bad Christian, you*, this book does neither. This book offers no shame and certainly no unrealistic rice cake diet or any diet at all for that matter.

I have no stones to throw.

The promise in this book is weight and eating freedom. This is an "I want to take my life and health out of lies and into the truth and appreciate my body and self as God intended" type of book. I want you to be free at any weight. I outline the exact thinking, skills, and understanding to get you there, but take it one day at a time with God. You can trust the Holy Spirit to help you synthesize this material to work for you.

I hope you get that it isn't about looking great in swim trunks or a bikini, but about being healthy for the glory of God, the goodness of God, and His good plan for your life. "For we are His workmanship, created in Christ Jesus for good works, which God prepared beforehand that we should walk in them" (Ephesians 2:10).

Remember, Christ said He's overcome the world. You're unstoppable in Him. I know there's a testimony of overcoming weight and eating bondage that's gripped your life so strong that it will bring you to your knees in gratitude when you overcome it.

You may cry with real thanksgiving, as my clients have, that you have been set free by the power and anointing of the Holy Spirit. I cried on my knees several times in gratitude and awe that I was F-R-E-E, even though I don't have a fitness model body. In fact, I have strategically optimized cushioning, compliments of my African American heritage.

I'm ready to get to some stats and facts. But if you're ready to rejoice now and receive your victory in advance, please do, but after your dance off for the Lord, come right back and finish this book!

REFLECTION QUESTIONS

1. What did the weight and eating bondage quiz reveal to you?

_____

_____

2. Why else do you believe God cares about your weight and eating freedom?

_____

_____

3. Why do you care about your weight and eating freedom?

_____

_____

PRAYER

Lord,

Please help me read The Chubby Church books to gain what I need to gain for my growth. Help me to grow in body, soul, and spirit and to understand it deeply. Help my weight and eating freedom to be permanent. Cut off every chain, hindrance, and bondage in my life. Take me fully through this journey, Lord, and finish this work unto completion.

In Jesus' name,
Amen!

CHAPTER 2

ARE YOU A MEMBER
OF THE CHUBBY CHURCH?

*"You shall love the Lord your God with all your heart,
with all your soul, and with all your mind"*

−MATTHEW 22:37

We know deep down we're digging
our graves faster with a knife and fork.

H ow can we truly love God with all of our heart, soul, and mind if we use all of our heart, soul, and mind to meditate on food and weight? Everyone knows by now that certain food choices will lead you to heaven faster. So, why are we choosing them? Why is it so difficult to control?

I believe it's because America and the church are on a highway to obesity and disease. The Centers for Disease Control and Prevention report that one half of the American population will be obese by 2030.[1] In 1980, 15 percent of American adults were obese, and in 2016 that number was 38.9 percent.[2,3] I wish stocks doubled like that—but people, not so thrilling. It's already the case that more than a third of us are over-weight and a third are obese. Researchers estimate the growing obesity figures will result in up to an additional $66 billion dollars in health care expenditures, 7.8 million new cases of diabetes, 6.8 million new cases of stroke and heart disease, and more than 500,000 new cancer diagnoses per year.[4]

Bondage is expensive.

Yet we know that you don't have to be obese to be in bondage to poor food choices, binge eat, or obsess about weight.

The Standard American Diet (notice its acronym S.A.D.) is an eating disorder in and of itself. Currently, most Americans eat less

Bondage is expensive.

than 12 percent fruits and vegetables and 60 to 70 percent processed or highly processed foods.[5, 6] This leaves many in a state of slavery to food temptation, be inactive, overeat, or drive the body to be thin. And it's far from God's instructions to eat mostly plants for food (Genesis 1:29) and later after Noah's flood to eat meat, birds, and fish if we desired to (Genesis 9:3).

Our lack of quality macronutrients (proteins, complex carbohydrates, and fat), combined with a severe micronutrient malnourishment (vitamins and minerals), are contributing to extensive health prayer requests and an abundance of medication, robbing Americans of the energy needed for quality of life.

The abominable practices of the food and drug industry are pushed by the media to tempt you. Then the media has the nerve to tell you that you're fat and to get on the latest diet pill. Not only that, but in the Body section, I'll explain the habits we need for better health. And it's not move more and eat less that solves our weight issues. That's the industries' way of putting their lack of responsibility on us.

With a focus on health, not weight, we can correct our eating from human engineered foods to God created foods to take back our health in body, soul, and spirit. We're a part of a weight obsessed culture that places self-worth on thinness, shame on fatness, and blames us—the child sized consumers compared to the dominating giants of industry.

Chubby Church Stats

I was shocked to discover this faint pulse is especially alarming in the spiritual arena. One study discovered the most obese group amongst all religious groups was fundamental Christians—led by Baptists with a 30 percent obesity rate.[7] Young adults who faithfully attended Bible study on a weekly basis increased their likelihood of obesity by 50 percent.[8]

Another study found that people who attended church were more likely than non-church members to be 20 percent overweight and have both higher cholesterol and blood pressure numbers.[9]

While it's my hope you obey the Scriptures to assemble at church and grow in His Word at Bible study, these findings beg the question, why aren't we talking about this?

We can't disregard the fact that weight and eating bondage is being ignored in the church.

A woman shared her heart around a ministry program she just went to when she said, "I feel sad that all of the ministers were so overweight and obese that they could hardly walk to the pulpit without being out of breath."

> Spiritual knowledge is no match for the wounds of the soul.

"Why does it make you sad?" I asked.

"Because, it's hypocritical," she said.

I asked, "Why do you think it's hypocritical?"

She said, "I expect people who preach about God to care about their bodies and be healthier. It clearly shows a lack of belief and a total lack of temperance."

While I'm not a fan of judging anyone else and certainly people are various shapes and sizes, this woman had a point—the exact point I would like to make in this book. Spiritual knowledge is no match for the wounds of the soul nor is health knowledge or any other knowledge about what we *should* do. Look at your local doctors or nurses: they know health, don't they? Yet, we can see they look just like the statistics, too.

The soul matters.

It needs healing as our mind, will, and emotions affect our choices—for good or for evil—in spite of what we know. And certainly, in spite of what we don't know (Hosea 4:6).

Can you agree that we may know what to do for our health—eat vegetables, drink water, and exercise, but we don't do it? This is why previous weight loss attempts have been limited. Too many address weight and eating from a one or two dimensional physical perspective, such as, "How many calories should I eat?" or, "How long should I do cardio to lose weight?"

> **The body, soul, and spirit operate together.**

When we as believers struggle with weight and eating, it's much more than the physical. A traditional diet book can help in a limited way because it only addresses a part of the problem. The body, soul, and spirit operate together. We can't look at only the body and attempt to force it into better health and weight without looking at the motivations driving the soul.

Body manipulation is all those attempts you've made in the past to lose weight by working out and eating only lettuce for breakfast.

Manipulation is unsustainable.

We need to address psychological and spiritual aspects of weight and eating with fresh perspectives on the physical, too.

Your weight matters to God. But it's not His fault you're unhappy with your body. You create your life and body with the choices you make. And sadly, like I said, it's extremely difficult to make sound choices when your food supply is engineered to get you addicted to it. So, we must take responsibility, but we cannot do it in our own strength. We need God's strength in this abundant yet deceptive environment.

Jesus was fed in a specific way for Him to choose wisely in life. Mother Mary fed him curd and honey so He will know how to reject evil and receive good (Isaiah 7:15). Samson's father and mother were instructed not to feed him grapes, beer, or wine in the womb as it would affect his strength and who he would become (Judges 13:4,14).

We all know Daniel's powerful diet that caused him to refute the attacks of the Babylonian king (Daniel 10:2–3). And John the Baptist's father, Zacharias, was instructed by an angel of the Lord, Gabriel, that John would never drink wine or beer as he was called to prepare the way of the Lord (Luke 1:15).

Nazarite vows or not, our eating matters.

Lord, Help Me to See What I Don't Want to See

To come into reality and talk about this is the first step to being free. We must come out of denial. We can pretend all we want that our eating habits don't matter, our body isn't important, or our weight doesn't reflect our soul, but we know deep down that we're digging our graves faster with a knife and fork.

Denial is the psychological phenomenon of being unable to see or admit the truth staring you in the face. Webster's dictionary calls it an unconscious, defense mechanism characterized by refusal to acknowledge painful realities, thoughts, or feelings.[10]

People who walk in denial have an invisible shield of protection from truth and reality. They continually live in a state of fantasy and victimization caused by avoiding making real changes.

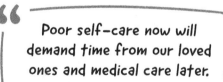

Poor self-care now will demand time from our loved ones and medical care later.

They aren't truly alive or engaged with life. They're like a zombie on *The Walking Dead*—blind that eating habits, food choices, and body criticisms create an unhealthy reality.

And when in denial, we live in a vacuum and can't see that our actions and inactions affect others in big and small ways. There's always an elephant in the room. We can't continue to be selfish by mismanaging our health. And poor self-care now will demand time from our loved ones and medical care later.

A Secret Struggle

Weight and eating bondage is a secret struggle. Believers know gambling, drunkenness, and promiscuity are biblically unacceptable behaviors, but because weight is taboo and everyone likes a nice church spread, myself included, millions go without the real healing and help they need. We seem to ignore Scriptures that warn about care of the body and the sanctification process of the body, soul, and spirit.

My hope is for the eyes of the church to open to this very real bondage happening in plain sight. Every single day, a good and well meaning believer may suffer with weight and food obsession. But he or she cannot begin to express the struggle to a pastor, who may very well suffer from the same bondage.

We cannot help what we haven't healed.

It's an unrecognized form of bondage the enemy has used to keep people back from receiving the joy God has for them. Would you agree, it's difficult to live your best life when you're caught up in chronic health issues stemming from weight and eating obsession?

At church everyone's busy trying to look good, wearing sharp suits or Spanx™ to tighten up that gluttony secret. Seriously folks, Spanx™ can only do so much. Eventually, we need to decide to deal with the way we use food to cope with life, hide in our emotions, and protect ourselves with that extra layer of chub.

It's time to let go of denial—the denial of thinking that another diet is the answer or that it's God's fault you're in the chubby suit you've created. It's time to accept that poor food choices create problems for you, your family, your purpose, and your health destiny. The fact of the matter is only you can decide to do something about it.

To break out of denial one of my favorite bold prayers is, "Lord, help me to see what I don't want to see."

This prayer will help you grow like a wildflower. Often, we shut down from addressing reality. Be bold, look in the mirror and accept the good, the bad, and the ugly so we can work out our salvation with Christ and change our destiny for our best potential and for His greatest good purposes in our life. Free will is the most powerful force on the earth. Our wills completely submitted to God's will for our lives is the secret to our freedom.

REFLECTION QUESTIONS

1. Why do you think this issue isn't discussed openly at church?

_____

_____

2. How does it reflect on us spiritually to mistreat our bodies?

_____

_____

3. How have you been in denial about your weight and eating bondage?

_____

_____

PRAYER

Father,

I lean on your Word, to ask and it will be given to me, seek and I will find, knock and the door will be opened to me. Thank you for opening the door that I've knocked on. Thank you, heavenly Father, for this journey that I'm embarking upon.

May I experience your wisdom and increase as a direct result of this weight and eating revelation. Pour liberally on me with your love and truth and may the words jump into my heart and create permanent soul freedom so that I can take full benefit of your kingdom of heaven on earth. I give you all the glory, honor, and praise!

In Jesus' Name, Amen.

• CHAPTER 3 •

WELCOME TO BURGER KING

My Story

"Looking unto Jesus, the author and finisher of our faith"

−HEBREWS 12:2A

I realized I had a problem when I was a slave to the Burger King.

Before we dig into things, I'll share the details of my story with you for three reasons. First, when we connect to our stories, we lay a stronger foundation for lasting change. Second, my story is used throughout this book to help you apply the principles. And third, it's easier to connect more dots in your own story when you hear and can relate to someone else's story. So, here it goes.

For over three months in 2003, I couldn't break free from Burger King's chocolate-chip cookies, which really put a dent in my perpetual diet. I was trapped in a vicious cycle. It happened like this; on the drive to work at my new job as a financial advisor, I stopped at Burger King and got a cookie or two at 8 a.m. Don't tell my kid nephew this, but yes, I ate cookies for breakfast. On the way home from work, I'd get another one at around 8 p.m. Some days, I went for a lunchtime cookie fix, too.

Perhaps a job on *Sesame Street* would have been better suited because I was the biggest cookie monster on the block.

Besides the ooey, gooey, chocolatey taste bud party and the intoxicating aroma, I had no consciousness of why I ate the cookies. *Sure, I thought, I deserve these, I'm stressed.* But no real answers came to mind—only excuses. Did I even want an answer? Not really. A part of me liked eating those cookies, a rather large part. I enjoyed my daily worship routine as I pulled up to the drive through window.

"Welcome to Burger King. Can I take your order?," said the worker.

At 230 calories a pop and with a desire to lose weight, I wanted to stop this cycle but found myself answering that question every single day. Out of the burger kingdom temptation called. I wanted to serve the King of Kings, not the Burger King. I needed deliverance from a cookie! Finally, a new commute from an office move got this cookie demon off my back. But my cookie freedom only lasted a little while.

Victory at Last … So I Thought

My cookie stops turned into fast food meals three times a day, which fast tracked me to a two week sick leave from work for bronchitis, amongst a host of other strange things happening to my body. I did what any twenty something year old would do: I went home to mama who lived about ninety minutes away for a reprieve.

It was there that a life changing moment came in the restroom. I saw a book in my peripheral vision entitled *Natural Cures They Don't Want You to Know About. Who is they?* I certainly wanted to know. I coughed uncontrollably as I leaned over to pick it up. Intrigued, I thumbed through it. As I skimmed the pages that talked about nutrition, I thought, *Could I be sick because of my diet?*

Barely able to breathe, I hobbled down the hall to my bedroom with my eyes fixed on the book. The book's wisdom invited me into a sense of God's presence.

I sat on the bed, and for a moment I enjoyed the sunlight through the window as the warmth embraced my face. I didn't recall the last time I had sat in the sun. I couldn't remember the last time I read a book.

Where have I been? Eighty hours of work a week was likely the culprit. *Oh yeah,* I realized as though a light bulb glowed over my head, *I'm sick because I'm a workaholic and maybe my diet.* At that time to think I was a food addict was incomprehensible despite the obvious signs. Denial is a doozie.

As I read, I reflected on my health. My air supply randomly cut off, it took me at least an hour to get out of bed in the morning, and I wheezed in between every other word. Not feeling too healthy. Not to mention the extra poundage I carried around. I longed for my energetic lean runner's body from college weight loss efforts.

I was beyond out of control.

The lines struck me as I read: "But once the food is processed and put in a box or a can, you're going to have to eat 100 times more to get the same nutritional value; nutrition is virtually wiped out. So, in addition to having the poisons put in your system from the chemicals not even listed on the label, the food you are getting has almost no nutritional value."[1]

Unbelievable, I thought. I hadn't known anything about nutrition. *Could this be true?* It was about dinner time. On a mission of truth ... or camouflaged addiction, I drove to my favorite fast food establishment. *Is fast food empty food with no nutritional value?* I should know. I ate it three times per day for weeks on end.

"I'll take the nuggets and fries meal with sweet and sour sauce, please." With an ear to ear grin, I picked up my experimental meal. As a fast food junkie, I relaxed into my daily worship practice and ate on the way back to mom's house. And twenty-three minutes later, I was hungry again. My brain seemed to want more nuggets. My stomach felt empty. But my belly could've been mistaken for a round pool float.

It was December 28, 2004. The sacred date of my last traditional fast food meal.

I read. All night. Amazed.

But, when I rose the next day, panic set in. *What in the world was I going to eat?!* I had to go to the dreaded grocery store.

25

Oh, God. I thought, as I stared at the bright tomatoes, carrots, and green vegetables I didn't know existed. Bewildered, red nosed, and hacking, I thought, *I could live off chicken soup this week. But what would I eat next week? Grapefruits.* I was clueless as my diet was 100 percent processed foods with a dismal array of cooking skills.

My journey over the next few months astounded me and my colleagues. I went from fast food junkie to whole-clean-slow foods and lost fifty pounds.

My strange symptoms disappeared and were replaced by a vibrant glow so bright my colleagues and their spouses signed up to learn about health from me. Overnight I had a health coaching business. It felt amazing to support people in such a meaningful way. I read incessantly about health, whole foods, and nutrition. A natural passion awakened.

I thought I'd never have a weight problem again.

Never say never.

The Return of the Cookie Demon

My diet had transformed to eat healthier, organic, whole foods until a new relationship. Turns out my *inner glutton* was in remission during my health revelation. The threat of falling in love when I met my fiancé sparked deep insecurities. Love felt worse than tight underwear on backwards in a work meeting—awful.

Naturally, I made regular trips to buy large, organic, chocolate-chip cookies from Whole Foods Market. Sounds healthier, doesn't it? Certainly, but no less fattening nor less insulin spiking.

When I became engaged, it got worse. My insecurities around closeness made me eat more. And I didn't hide it either. Before a long drive my mother made homemade cookies for my fiancé and me. There were forty freshly baked, chocolate-chip cookies for us to share. By the time we drove the two-and-a-half-hours to Maryland from New Jersey, the cookies were gone! Like Houdini. Not a crumb in sight. The cookie-to-person ratio was an embarrassing 35:5, for each one he ate, I ate seven.

After marriage, the obsession morphed into a full-on compulsion. I ate whole boxes of cookies, now from a local bakery. By this time I knew all about health, food, and weight loss. I taught whole foods nutrition classes and coached people. I lost fifty pounds, not once but twice!

First, I did it with exercise in college. *Aha!* I thought at the time, *I could just work out every day to slim down.* Only after the slim down, I went back to being too busy to exercise.

Second, I lost it with body detoxification and healthy clean eating. *Aha!* I thought, *I could heal my body through nutrition and cleansing.* After some time, the pounds boomeranged back. *Hmm, maybe there's more to this eating and exercise thing.* I admit, I'm not always the sharpest pencil in the box.

As the baked goods frenzy amplified, so did my waistline. I gobbled cookies and prayed for weight loss at the same time. I was at a standstill, unable to solve the problem of weight and eating in my life.

I worked a twelve-step process. I'd go to the store, get cookies, eat

> Things didn't change until I wanted freedom from soul bondage more than I wanted the weight to fall off, and more than I wanted the object of my false comfort.

cookies, feel bad, feel bloated, feel unhealthy, feel sad, feel demoralized, feel ashamed, feel lonely, and then had the audacity to go get and eat more cookies to feel better! I was entrapped. I'd eaten enough chocolate-chip cookies to last not only my lifetime but that of four generations after me, too.

Things didn't change until I wanted freedom from soul bondage *more* than I wanted the weight to fall off, and *more* than I wanted the object of my false comfort (cookies).

It was more than body weight I was wearing. I wore soul weight. I wore the weight of my past. I wore the weight of my sin. I ate my fears, anger, grief, lust, and insecurities.

I knew about health, I relied on the Lord, but no matter what I knew was right for me, my health knowledge was no match for the holes in my soul. I worked with God to find answers to heal my mindset, my fear of releasing weight for good, and the emotions underneath the compulsions.

These answers led me to permanent weight release, more energy, soul freedom, and a healthier, happier body and mind. The results of this weight and eating freedom only make the evidence of weight and eating bondage more obvious.

> "Health knowledge was no match for the holes in my soul."

What Weight & Eating Freedom Is Like

Whether your cookie shows up as ice cream, potato chips, tortilla chips, chocolate, soda, coffee, cake, bread, pizza, or cookies, like me, freedom can begin.

The benefits of weight and eating freedom keep giving. It's a blessing to eat a piece of cake and not the whole cake. And when I do overeat, I provide myself compassion instead of berating myself, which used to lead me to eat more. I can now enjoy my body as weight fluctuates with hormones or age.

What a joy it is to fit comfortably into an airline seat or easily bend down to pick something up. How nice it is to see my feet when I look down or play airplane with a child with ease. I appreciate the freedom of not judging myself when I want to eat real food.

I fully appreciate who I am and know that I am more than how much I weigh. I know God loves me as I am. I can come to Him as much as I want or need for help to stop eating, choose better, or repent for messing up. I can trust Him always to lead me to truth. I am free to be me, and I am so much better in Him.

This soul freedom allows me to be honest with myself, as well as others, about what I think, how I feel, and what I need. I value myself just as much as anyone else. I'm no longer a doormat or a bulldozer. I matter. I believe I can handle life because I have Jesus Christ as my life partner. He's my unequivocal best friend. And He will sustain, help, and protect me at all times. This is true freedom. This is security. This

> **"Nothing tastes better than the whole and free you in Christ."**

is soul safety. God uses weight and eating struggles to free us not only in body, but in soul and spirit.

I wanted you to get a taste of what my freedom is like because it's all available for you, too. Imagine your freedom, and you'll see nothing tastes better than the whole and free you in Christ.

When Did This Start?

One of the best things my mother did for me was encourage me to get baptized at six years old. I remember talks with the Lord as a child throughout my tumultuous home life. There were moments I could touch His presence, although I didn't know how to use my faith to withstand the turmoil in my heart or home.

One night, my dad came home in a substance-induced rage. In a fit, he aggressively destroyed dishes, furniture, and whatever was in his path downstairs, while we slept upstairs. Scared, my mom snuck out their bedroom window onto the carport to get help.

Determined to end her struggle with domestic abuse with her troubled young husband once and for all, my mother rallied a few college kids to help her get us out. In the wee hours of the morning, we — my two brothers, and I — escaped through a broken window on the second floor through their master bedroom. We arrived at her parent's house a short drive away.

She was clear they'd be divorced as soon as possible. And they were.

My sensitive, six-year-old heart was overwhelmed with uncertainty. My earliest memories were filled with fear and anxiety in this chaotic place I called home. I witnessed my mother being disrespected, yelled at, or outright physically abused.

My dad was a good man. He was positive, inspiring, and encouraging. But he was also tormented by adultery, alcohol, and a gripping cocaine addiction that brought out a violent side.

My parents' unresolved past hindered us all. Their explosive relationship caused consuming angst for me.

We left everything behind and lived with my grandparents. One night, my grandmother served sauerkraut and hot dogs for dinner. I hadn't experienced sauerkraut before, what a taste explosion! I stuffed it into my little mouth as fast as I could.

Three servings later, I didn't feel so good. And upchucked it all. Right there. At the table. It was gross, but my brain had found a way for me to cope with my emotional sensitivity. I had a solution for the depth of emotional pain I experienced in my chaotic young life: stuff the pain down with food! This was the beginning of a lifelong struggle with my new bestie: food.

We later moved to another suburb of New Jersey, across the street from a shopping center. Whenever I got money, I headed to the drug store to get a candy bar. Funny enough, the candy bar was my drug.

Bring on the paper route, because when I had some real money, you know ten bucks, I'd get mozzarella sticks from the local Friday's restaurant. Due to my habit of running to food since I was six years old, I didn't develop the tools to actually deal with my emotions.

Humans of all ages are meant to be seen, heard, and loved. If not, we usually deal with our need in unhealthy ways.

To make matters worse, six years later when I was twelve years old, we received headline news that struck like a tsunami.

The Root of the Cookie Craving

My two brothers and I sat at the kitchen table as we wondered, why did Aunt Lori sound so insistent for mom to call her back?

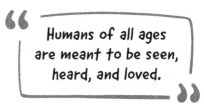

Humans of all ages are meant to be seen, heard, and loved.

My older brother took my Aunt's call after my mom left in a frenzy to calm down that October day in our Marlton, New Jersey townhouse.

We were grateful our mom did come back. At times, with a stressed-out single mom, you just never knew.

She called Aunt Lori back.

"What is it?" my mom asked my dad's sister on the other line. Seconds later, she dropped the white corded phone and hunched over in shock.

A loud wail followed, "Aaagh!" and a dam of tears broke. Her mouth grasped for air between deep sobs. Time froze as tears kindled in all of us. My stomach queasy.

My father was found dead behind the back of a Camden, New Jersey, liquor store at the ripe age of thirty-four years old. He was murdered—shot right in the face. A black cloud descended as a gang of emotional hoodlums beat down my heart.

My wounds were already raw, yet a knife seemed to cut them deeper. The bleeding didn't stop. It was the worst day of my life.

Still is.

As the cloudy months followed, I baked. My chocolate-chip cookie cakes soothed my wounds. Distracted from grief, I baked cookie cakes for everyone.

I loved my daddy. But now, my beloved daddy was gone. I'd run, jump, and hug him every time I saw him as he greeted us in the driveway with his huge smile. I'd let out girlish giggles as he'd catch me and hold me close, even when I was big.

These special daddy-daughter moments happened every time we visited the six years between the scary night we left and the worst day of my life. I ate cookies for that hug. I chewed for that sense of safety.

Every sweet memory of the first man I ever loved was drowned with morsels of America's old-time favorite. I lost my daddy, but food was faithful. I never worried about it dying or rejecting me. Food was reliable. It didn't neglect me. It was there.

Over twenty years of my life were dedicated to solving my soul holes through eating and obsessing over food and weight. I plugged these holes with food so I could stay in denial about my pain. I attempted to diet it away countless times, but truth is persistent.

Weight gain was my absent father's protection. Overeating was my working, single mother's nurturance and comfort when I was home alone or fighting with my brothers for being knuckleheads over Nintendo. At first, my eating issues were a sound strategy, but by my teenage years, weight gain and hormones turned my obsession into torment.

> **Food obsession was an attempt to control and manipulate my out of control identity crisis.**

The conflicting desires to eat whatever I wanted and look good hijacked my mind. My overeating left me unsatisfied, unfulfilled, and unhappy because self-harm always comes with a side portion of weight gain, shame, guilt, anxiety, and body dissatisfaction.

When my parents divorced, I desperately needed a loving hug, but it was food that would snuggle me. My eating measured the level of emotional pain I felt on the inside. My weight gain reflected the depth of insecurity and deep pain in my soul.

My addiction to the food obsession was an attempt to control and manipulate my out of control identity crisis, like a child seeking love and protection from a hamburger mistaken as mom and dad.

As I gained momentum to serve Christ, I wanted to live and be better, healed, whole, grounded, and disciplined. Faith helped me believe it was possible, even though I wasn't really sure it was possible.

My automatic emotional reaction to life was food. When life was difficult or joyous or boring, I found my comfort through food. What's your story?

Why We Use Food

Self-sabotaging habits with food help us to cope with life. We use food to manage strong feelings we've not had the tools to manage, such as loneliness, disappointment, anger, stress, ambiguity, and neglect.

Tough feelings can drive a person with eating issues right up to the drive through window. Our eating issues are a strategy that our psychology uses to help our soul's emotions. It starts having negative effects in our lives and in our relationships because it's a false form of love.

When we're dysfunctional with food, we're trying to gain love. The biochemical power of the brain and body that's tied to our emotions is strong.

We use food to self-medicate as an anodyne. We use it to stuff down, avoid, hide, numb, celebrate, and comfort.

Where's My Miracle?

If you want to be a whole and free, authentic believer, you must take back your power to respond and own your full self. To own our emotions, mindset, health, and eating habits is tough.

It's easier to be a victim of the cookies than to say no to them. It's easier to blame than it is to own our part. It's more comfortable to stay stuck than it is to grow up. I dieted and never actually made changes. I was interested in

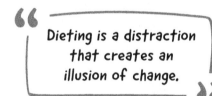

Dieting is a distraction that creates an illusion of change.

a healthy, slim body, but I wasn't committed to healthier habits—nor a healthier me.

Dieting is a distraction that creates an illusion of change, but when you look at the fruit of it, there's no supporting actions to create lasting change.

I, too, wanted to be zapped with deliverance from my weight and eating issue. Lord knows I cried out, "Deliver me, Lord!" believing it

33

was possible to be instantaneously delivered by some weight loss miracle. *Where is a Benny Hinn Healing Crusade when you need one?*

I remember calling my mentor and asking her, "Why won't God just deliver me from this?!"

My painful inner turmoil got the best of me. I felt frustrated, angry, confused, and hopeless around the whole matter. I felt trapped in a cement chair. At times I'd rather die than deal with my tormenting hell. I felt stupid talking about it to anyone. And when I did, they didn't get it. "Eat right and exercise," they said. I felt like I was the only one with this craziness going on inside of me. It felt so shameful to wear extra poundage that I hardly wanted to go anywhere.

My mentor replied, "Jendayi, sometimes we have to walk out our deliverance."

With her words, I realized our wonderful Savior has compassion on those who suffer in their self-induced bondage.

Receiving His love would heal the torment. "There is no fear in love; but perfect love casts out fear, because fear involves torment" (1 John 4:18).

He has compassion for the struggle. His strength is made stronger in our weakness. He knows our psychology—after all He created it. He knows what we can handle and what we can't. He loves us in spite of it all.

His grace and mercy are truly sufficient. "And we know that all things work together for good to those who love God, to those who are called according to *His* purpose" (Romans 8:28).

Our weight and eating issue is our measurement of our growth in receiving God's love for who He's made us to be. It's about your heart. It's not even about your weight or food, but we'll address both because both are a part of this multifarious condition.

Ultimately, this food and weight issue is the Lord's way of helping us draw closer to Him. It's a call to heal. It's our call into the greater freedom of the kingdom of God. We're in bondage in body, soul, and spirit until we fully commit to freedom—wholeness—holiness.

REFLECTION QUESTIONS ❓

1. What was difficult for you growing up that you may still binge over?

   _____

   _____

2. When did your story with food struggles begin? When did you first notice it?

   _____

   _____

3. What new freedoms are you looking forward to as you conquer this battle?

   _____

   _____

PRAYER

Father,

I cry out for help today. Please locate the root of my weight and eating bondage. Help me to walk out this deliverance with boldness. Help me relate Jendayi's story to my own story. Let my story also bring you glory.

Help me to connect the dots of why I struggle so much. Help me to allow for change and transformation from the principles outlined in this book and your truth. Help me heal. Help me grow. Help me transform. Help me to be holy as you are holy. Make me whole and free to impact your kingdom for good!

In Jesus' name,
Amen!

CHAPTER 4

DO YOU WANT FREEDOM WITH THAT?

Freedom in Body, Soul, and Spirit

"Now may the God of peace Himself sanctify you completely; and may your whole spirit, soul, and body be preserved blameless at the coming of our Lord Jesus Christ"

−1 THESSALONIANS 5:23

When we don't like the fruit, we must look at the roots.

The Bible says, "Wisdom is the principal thing; Therefore, get wisdom, and in all your getting, get understanding" (Proverbs 4:7). Get your highlighter out, I'm going into teacher mode. Before we get into actions in the next chapter, I want to build on a foundation of body, soul, and spirit so we're on the same page.

Integration of Body, Soul, and Spirit

To understand the body, soul, and spirit's integration, I'd like you to imagine a glass.

The glass is your body, and in it is:

Red juice, your soul.

Water, your spirit.
Oil, the Holy Spirit.

What would happen if the glass broke? Right, we couldn't drink the liquid. What about if the glass cracked? The liquid would then leak out. In other words, an effect on one inevitably affects the other.

This research and insight comes from Watchman Nee's 600 page, three volume work *The Spiritual Man.*[1] The Bible speaks of a spiritual man as one whose soul is governed by the Spirit. Our goal is just that, our soul working through God's Spirit. We're the driver, but God's our GPS. A spiritual man or woman follows His directions. The carnal man or woman doesn't, hasn't downloaded the app, or has a bad connection.

> **We're the driver, but God's our GPS.**

The Scriptures call the process of transformation from a carnal to a spiritual christian sanctification. The word sanctify is to "set apart for particular use in a special purpose or work and to make holy or sacred."[2]

We know God's heart is to sanctify us in body, soul, and spirit. "Now may the God of peace Himself sanctify you completely; and may your whole spirit, soul, and body be preserved blameless at the coming of our Lord Jesus Christ" (1 Thessalonians 5:23).

In previous attempts to take back your health, did you take your soul into account? The sanctification process? Your identity? Your beliefs? Or your past?

Or have you only approached it from a physical body perspective? Chances are you have overlooked the soul and spirit aspects in health.

We need to have a holistic approach to solve the weight and eating dilemma. Let's review the functions of each.

Body – Instrument, Sensory, Sacred

Imagine the complexity of this miraculous collection of more than 37 trillion cells that are all multiplying, regenerating, and interacting twenty four hours a day.[3] Only God could create this amazing vessel for us to dwell in.

God wants us to care for this precious gift He gave us to live in. How we take care of our body indicates how much we honor Him and His irreplaceable gift. And for the record, this doesn't necessarily mean no flab, wrinkles, or on the flip-side looking like Hercules. And according to body mass index calculations, Hercules is obese!

I'm saying, the most high-end Tesla can't touch the power and engineering of your physical body. It's precious, sacred, and supernatural machinery.

> **The most high-end Tesla can't touch the power and engineering of your physical body.**

You're fearfully and wonderfully made, and you house His Spirit along with your soul (Psalm 139:14).

It allows us to engage with the material environment. We do this with our five senses. We love to look at beautiful flowers, smell perfume, taste delicious food, hug our loved ones, or hear the ocean waves. Life is the greatest gift we have. And we experience it through our body.

As a conduit of God's Spirit, your body is a temple of the living God and is to be used to glorify Him (1 Corinthians 3:19–20). We're to keep our bodies holy and honoring toward His word (1 Peter 1:15–16). We need to exercise body stewardship to protect our sacredness.

Think of it like this, if you lent your computer to someone and they messed it up with coffee spills, marker stains, and missing keys, you'd be furious. When I understood how much damage I did to this divinely created machine, I repented. A lot.

Our body is more valuable than any computer, car, home, or possession we'll ever own. It's the only home we live in our entire lives, it's our permanent earthly address.

As a vehicle or instrument it carries out good or evil. It can do what we want only, or it can do what God is leading us to do. Paul says we must discipline the body and bring it into subjection, or it can rule us with temptations and lusts (1 Corinthians 9:27). Well isn't that the truth. We've been there, done that.

As a result of it being a vehicle, we need to fuel it properly. Like a cell phone charger charges your cell phone, your body recharges with food, water, sleep, movement, affection, sunshine, and air.

If we don't breathe for three minutes, we die; if we don't drink water for a week, we die; and if we don't eat for a month (this is where body fat really comes in handy!), we die.

Signs of Bondage in Body

- Can't say no to temptations that titillate your senses. My cookie story in the last chapter had its physiological aspects of bondage, because the brain was addicted to sugar, caffeine in the chocolate chips, and flour. I simply couldn't say no.

- Obsessed with how you look, extremely self-conscious, or negative about your face, body, or features.

For freedom, we'll **Habitize Body Stewardship** in upcoming chapters. And in Book 2, we'll consider your personal white-stuff threshold—the sugar, flour, dairy, rice, refined corn, and potato-type foods we eat that spike blood sugar and cause us to crave and overeat. I call this the *white foods matter movement*. We'll also discuss food addiction and body shame.

Soul – Emotions, Intellect, Volition (Will)

The soul is unique and so special our Lord Jesus Christ died to save it for Himself, yourself, and others. Oftentimes ministers neglect teaching about the soul or taking the soul into account when looking at a person's issues.

We either over-spiritualize it, such as, "Just pray about it," or "God will handle it," or we neglect it all together, pretending psychological factors don't or shouldn't exist.

The word soul is mentioned in Genesis 2:7 where God breathed life into Adam's body and it became a soul or speaking spirit. We can't see the soul like we can the body, but our voice is evidence we exist.

Soul also means psyche, self, personality, or psychology.[4]

The Scriptures say that the voice of Abel's blood cried out from the earth to God when Cain murdered him (Genesis 4:10). The blood, the red juice, carries the life of a person (Leviticus 17:11) as in the DNA of the personality, interests, strengths, desires, weaknesses, character traits, and values that make a person fundamentally who he or she is—your identity.

> **Health ailments may manifest in the body, but they've got soul roots.**

Your soul has heart. To feel is difficult for most Chubby Church members. But we need to get good at it. Because, health ailments may manifest in the body, but they've got soul roots. Psychologists call this somatization when a health issue manifests from emotional anxiety or an unresolved trauma.[5]

Henry W. Wright, author of *A More Excellent Way*, studied physical ailments from a spiritual and psychological perspective. He said, "The key roots behind disease are bitterness, accusation, occultism (witchcraft/satanism), envy, jealousy, rejection, unloving spirits, addictions, and fear."[6]

When negative emotions aren't resolved, we'll see dysfunctional patterns, such as addictions, broken relationships, and lack of professional and personal progress.

Our soul can be bound in emotional states, especially those that run through generations in our family, such as anger or grief.

Traumas, like verbal, physical, sexual, emotional abuse, or neglect, we experience as children can injure our soul. Injuries create soul wounds also called emotional wounds. And much of the time we emotionally eat because a soul wound was pushed.

What's interesting is, no matter what you do you can't stop your baby boy from growing up into a man. But the emotional body can have its growth stunted at the time of the trauma, and it can stay stuck as a child in an adult body. It's called arrested development.

And now you've got your answer for why fifty-year-old people act fifteen and why people sit in a congregation every Sunday for thirty years but still act the fool during the week. Amen.

Emotional wounds of the past pull on our present. And our soul's past affects our present weight and eating condition. When a binge happens, it's a signal that we've triggered an unresolved soul wound. We'll focus on this when we **Enact an Emotional Strength Training Plan** in Chapter 18.

Also note that the psychological needs of the soul are just as strong as the physiological needs of the body. These psychological needs are what holds in place our validation of our self-worth, for good or for harm. Bad habits reinforce a strong psychological need, despite the irrationality. We'll walk through these psychological factors in **Grubbology** (why we eat excess) and **Chubbology** (how excess weight keeps our soul safe).

42

Our intellect consists of mindsets, mentalities, value systems, and thought patterns. Your soul and mind are scientifically integrated with the body and brain.

Thoughts are words, and words carry the power of life and death (Proverbs 18:21). A healthy mind supports a healthy body. The mind is bound in the form of the dieter's mindset because it's a mindset that entraps us in poor health. We'll explore this in **Adopt the Freedom Mindset** in Chapter 17.

Volition is our soul's right to use our mind and emotions for our decisions. We get to choose. We can choose life or death (Deuteronomy 30:19). In reflection, I wondered why humility wasn't a fruit of the Spirit as listed in Galatians 5:22. I sensed that humility is an *act* of the soul's will.

We get to choose to grow, learn, change, heal, and transform with God as we submit our soul to the Holy Spirit. When we humble our soul (mind, will, emotions, and behaviors) to God's will, He gives us grace. Therefore, He says: "God resists the proud, But gives grace to the humble." (James 4:6) We need all the grace we can get to walk this out!

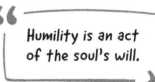

Humility is an act of the soul's will.

Signs of Bondage in Soul

- Emotions are difficult to identify or express
- Difficulty controlling emotions, emotionally reactive or driven
- Thinking distortions – all or nothing, negativity, unrealistic
- Past traumas, abuse, or neglect
- Easily triggered or offended
- Feeling followed by a dark cloud
- Self-sabotaging behaviors and choices
- Confession of Christ doesn't match conduct of daily life

Soul Encouragement

God is the master chef. In His kitchen He makes souls with special sacred ingredients. He sprinkles in talents, strengths, and special experiences to shape you to find them. He bakes in His purpose for each soul. He puts heavenly spices in and infuses us with His love. What's amazing about His recipe is that no two are alike.

Each soul recipe is made once and only once. It cannot be duplicated. It's an expression of His Glory and of His master creativity. He makes each soul with joy to enjoy. You are special and loved.

Therefore, He wants you free. When we're in bondage to the soul, we're unable to love others because we can barely love who He's made us to be. And by the way, your body—your physical looks—are a part of that unique beauty.

He knows you and created you the way you are for many reasons. I like to remind people that the Lord did not die for free. His blood in His opinion was worth your soul.

The blood of Jesus is priceless. Your soul was worth that price. Those who say "yes" to Him are called worthy. You've got to believe that you're a child of the most high God and He calls those who answer His call worthy.

I do understand we're, in truth, undeserving of this grace and mercy, but it's harmful for the body of Christ to believe that they're worthless. Worthless people are prideful people who refuse to humble themselves to God, according to Proverbs 6:12–15. Prideful people look for worth in things that please their flesh.

Essentially low soul-worth, as evidenced by how we mis-care for our bodies, health, and souls, is in opposition to the growth of the kingdom because insecurity and false humility creates self-focus, self-consciousness, and all-about-me attitudes, looking for validation and love in all the wrong places.

To be free, we choose to heal. The establishment of the kingdom of God depends on our willingness to grow with God. Your desire to make a commitment to freedom from poor body stewardship is a giant step in the right direction. There's amazing fruit from a restored soul.

Spirit – Conscience, Intuition, Communion

The Spirit is the breath of God and gives every living thing life (John 6:63). Think of Spirit as what causes animation. A cat or dog has life, as does a plant.

Every living thing has the breath of our almighty God. If it's born, lives, and dies, it has the spirit of life (Genesis 7:22; Job 33:4). The human spirit, however, is comprised of conscience, intuition (innate wisdom), and communion with the supernatural. It's the water.

Genesis 2:7 says, "And the Lord God formed man of the dust of the ground and breathed into his nostrils the breath of life; and man became a living being [soul]." In other words, the soul is created when the body meets the spirit.

Therefore, every person alive has a spirit that connects us with the supernatural. The difference in Christ lovers is Jesus imparts to us the Holy Spirit, the oil. The human spirit is life whereas the Holy Spirit can bring us the truth of Jesus and His wisdom. He is the Way, the Truth and the Life (John 14:6).

Our conscience helps us to discern between right or wrong. As children we tend to know when something feels right or wrong, this is our conscience at work. Conscience supports deeply embedded emotions, such as love, fear, shame, or guilt. It helps us to discern general human moral behavior—good from evil.

Intuition is our gut sense that helps us discern beyond the five senses of the body. Did you ever want to call a friend, but then suddenly she's calling you? This is your intuitive sense at work. Intuition is a sense of going the right direction. Let's allow listening to our intuition to guide positive choices. Another word for intuition is wisdom.

Your Spirit connects with the *spiritual realm*. Ideally, we commune with the Holy Spirit. However, a person can deal with spirits other than God. Jesus mentions the Holy Spirit and also spirits, such as fear, strife, or rebellion. Saul was plagued with a spirit of jealousy of David. Or just look at the news. Have you seen it lately? Enough said. Some of our headlines are the working of a wrong spiritual connection.

Signs of Bondage in Spirit

- Strange creepy presence
- Legalistic or controlling
- Lack of fruit of the Spirit
- Carnally minded, worldly
- Perversity
- Sense of heaviness

Every human has a spiritual side to cultivate. Some Christians aren't yet in touch with their spiritual side. I know this because some Christians aren't yet Christ followers, as they come across as prideful, horribly judgmental, unkind, ungrateful, and shaming toward their own self and others. This self-righteous attitude comes from a soul insecurity like the need to be better than someone else because of low self-worth, not out of God's love for each person.

When we don't like the fruit, we must look at the roots. Weight struggles are a symptom. They're a manifestation or fruit of our body, soul, and spirit. We're always able to connect to spirit and cultivate the fruit of the Spirit because, like a healthy body, the fruit of the Spirit is already inside of us.

"But the fruit of the Spirit is love, joy, peace, longsuffering, kindness, goodness, faithfulness, gentleness, self-control [temperance]. Against such there is no law. And those who belong to Christ have crucified the flesh with its passions and desires. If we live in the [Holy] Spirit, let us also walk in the [Holy] Spirit" (Galatians 5:22–25).

> When we don't like the fruit, we must look at the roots. Weight struggles are a symptom. They're a manifestation or fruit of our body, soul, and spirit.

As our soul heals, we manifest more fruit of the spirit. Being in spiritual bondage means being in ways contrary to God's ways. To heal spiritual bondage, Jesus must be both our Lord and our Savior.

We're to crucify our flesh daily to follow the Lord's Spirit (Galatians 5:24; Mark 8:34). "Now this I say, brethren, that flesh and blood cannot inherit the kingdom of God; nor does corruption [carnality/flesh] inherit incorruption [eternal life]" (1 Corinthians 15:50).

The way to freedom in body, soul, and spirit is to be led of the Spirit. The Holy Spirit is our divine connector and help.

Let's learn to walk by the Spirit and not the flesh. You've got a foundation, it's time to get to work. Next up, we'll put together an action plan to finish through to Book 2 and beyond.

REFLECTION QUESTIONS

1. Can you sense the differences between your soul, body, and spirit?

   _____

   _____

2. In what areas of your life are you walking by the Spirit?

   _____

   _____

3. In what areas of your life are you walking by the flesh?

   _____

   _____

PRAYER

Dear Heavenly Father,

Thank you that I am fearfully and wonderfully made. Thank you for this revelation on body, soul, and spirit. Please, help me to love and appreciate the sacred temple of my body. I choose to love it exactly as it is and pray that it may heal and reveal itself even greater out of the spirit of love. I pray for the fruit of the Spirit to manifest in my life. Help me to walk by the Spirit and not the flesh.

Make me a spiritual Christian and not a carnal one. Reveal every unconscious emotion and thought causing me to make unhealthy choices. Help me to mature emotionally and spiritually. Heal every dysfunctional way within me. Search me and test me. Heal me and cleanse me. Sanctify me fully in body, soul and spirit for your glory!

In Jesus' name, amen.

CHAPTER 5

THE CALL TO WEIGHT & EATING FREEDOM ACTION PLAN

"For a dream comes through much activity, and a fool's voice is known by his many words"

—ECCLESIASTES 5:3 NKJV

Commitment is like a balloon. Apply a little pressure ...POP!

The path to weight and eating freedom starts with our commitment to freedom. Freedom is the ability to exercise options, to choose, to be in control. But we often don't feel in control in weight or eating behaviors.

The way we gain freedom is to commit to freedom itself, not diets, crazy workouts, starvation, or temporary fixes—but freedom. Christ is our liberator. He's the One who sets us free, but we still need to work out our freedom by actions (John 8:36; Philippians 2:22) because faith without works is dead (James 2:17). God's desire isn't for us to live in torment, temptation, or intemperance. It's to live transformed.

> God's desire isn't for us to live in torment, temptation, or intemperance. It's to live transformed.

The Call to Weight & Eating Freedom Action Plan boosts your commitment to get through the hard conversations we'll need to have, and the real habit change you'll want to make, to enjoy a whole and free life in Christ. The journey isn't easy ahead. These six actions help build your commitment to freedom on days you'd prefer to retreat into a bag of denial. So, let's roll up our sleeves and get to work, shall we?

Action 1: Commit to Freedom

Let's acknowledge our truth: we don't want to change. A part of us likes to eat whatever greasy, fatty, crunchy, salty, or sugary food we can get our hands on. The nature of our human flesh is self-pleasing because it simply wants what it wants. The path to permanent weight release is God pleasing.

I dream often, and one dream was telling. I was in a jail cell. A wide-open door stared back at me, but I remained on top of the plush bed, just looking at the door. Our lives in Christ are like this dream. We've been set free. Salvation has come. The door is open. But because we're so comfortable in our plush beds, we stay there, unwilling to pick up our beds and walk.

> We don't know what to expect in our freedom.

Just like the children of Israel longed for what they had in bondage, their cucumbers, melons, and garlic, we know what to expect in our bondage, too (Numbers 11:5).

We don't know what to expect in our freedom.

To get out of bed, walk across the room, and out the door into the unknown is far scarier than lying in the comfort of what we know.

Jesus healed a man who had the same unconscious desire to stay stuck in the all too familiar bed. "Jesus said to him, 'Rise, take up your bed and walk'" (John 5:8). The man's obedience led him to freedom. It's not Jesus' desire for us to stay in bed—otherwise known as what's comfortable. We are to move and walk. Walk in love, walk by faith, walk in joy, walk in peace, walk on water. All of it requires action and a commitment to being free instead of bound.

Even though dieters make at least four attempts to lose weight each year, 90 to 95 percent of dieters regain weight.[1] This means the first, second, and third attempts weren't successful. Consider, all the times you've stopped and started a diet. Insanity is doing the same thing over and over again and expecting a different result. What if you stopped the temporary attempts altogether and committed to freedom instead?

Good news: freedom starts today. No more commitment to procrastination. You've already waited long enough for a weight loss miracle. It's not coming. Isn't that a relief? The miracle is your commitment to freedom.

To overcome one day at a time, we'll need to take our weight and eating front and center to God in prayer every day for help. Your freedom starts with your next bite—not when you're ready, not when you want to, but right now.

If you don't feel "ready," that's okay. Are you willing? Willingness and readiness are two different things. If you're willing, you'll soon be ready, but we're rarely ready without first being willing. Let's be bold and speak our commitment out loud.

Take Action: Speak Freedom Declarations

Take a few minutes to declare your willingness to **commit to freedom.** It's not willpower, but your will surrendered to God's Spirit that helps you to win the weight and eating battle for good. Words have the power of life and death, so use them to declare your personal freedom (Proverbs 18:21).

Freedom Declarations: Say the following declarations out loud like you're rooting for your favorite sports team or seeing outlandish news reports:

I surrender my weight and eating struggles to the Lord!
I commit to becoming my best in body, soul, and spirit!
I allow God's Spirit to lead my food choices!

I live healthfully one day at a time!
I am healthy and fit!
I am whole and free!
I am enough!

These seven declarations set the stage to complete this material. What other declarations do you need to say aloud? Declare them often, especially when you feel temptation.

Action 2: Cultivate Desire

"Delight yourself in the Lord, And He shall give you the desires of your heart" (Psalm 37:4).

Why do you want to be free? It's a simple but oh-so-important question. Is it for yourself? Your kids? Favorite pants? We need to know why we want our freedom. As Lisa TerKeurst says in her book, *Made to Crave*, "we've got to *want to*" end the weight and eating battle for good.[2]

Lasting weight release is a side effect of a strong commitment to freedom in body, soul, and spirit. What other side effects do you believe God has for you? Desire is a fertile farmland. We cultivate it with the seeds of faith. Each seed is a pumpkin patch of possibility of true fulfillment in Christ. Think long and deep about all you hope to gain from your commitment to your best life in Christ.

One way to strengthen your list of why you want to be free is to tap into your anger about what weight and eating torment has cost you over the years. John 10:10a says, "The thief does not come except to steal, kill, and destroy."

> **How much has weight and eating bondage killed your joy, stolen your mind, and destroyed your health?**

How much has weight and eating bondage killed your joy, stolen your mind, and destroyed your health? How many hours have you wasted thinking about this? How has this issue limited your career? How many events have you canceled because you felt too ashamed about your body size? How many times has low body esteem affected photo taking with your spouse or loved ones? We know we don't want the double chin, heart disease, diabetes, self-consciousness, or difficulty breathing, but what do you want?

Take Action: Create Your List of Reasons

Create a list of specific reasons you want to be healthy and free for life and win the weight and eating battle for good. Be unfiltered. List whatever your heart whispers. If animal print speedos pop up in your heart, don't judge or try to make it wrong or right, just jot it down.

You'll need to be real with yourself to stay motivated throughout the journey to weight and eating freedom. By the way, this won't be a list you set and forget.

This list will actively grow. Add to your list any reasons that come up as they pop up. And post your list somewhere you can be reminded of your reasons, like the refrigerator, car dashboard, or your desk. Be creative.

There're thousands of reasons to make a change in your health. List as many as you can. My list has more than 200 reasons. Reasons such as: I want to honor God in all things, be around for my children and their children, complete my divine assignments well, and easily bend down to pick something up.

Create your list by answering the following questions:

1. Why do I want to be free from weight and eating bondage? List as many reasons as possible.

2. What's my biggest reason to make a change? Put a star next to your biggest reason.

3. What do I want to gain from letting go of weight and eating struggles? Add to your list of reasons.

4. What don't I want any longer? Flip your answers from what you don't want to what you do want.

Action 3: See Your Vision

"Then the Lord answered me and said: 'Write the vision and make *it* plain on tablets, that he may run who reads it" (Habakkuk 2:2).

A vision motivates us. A good one excites us so much we run with it. As the vision of the life and health you desire sharpens, you increase your commitment and chances of success.

We see this in action with the Israelites. The very hope of the promised land gave significant encouragement to move forward. A promise holds a vision. In Exodus 3, Moses was given the hope of the promised land, a land without Pharaoh's bondage and cruelty. There was still a wilderness to wander and battles to fight, but the promise was from God that the land would be theirs. In the battles of cravings and the wilderness of soul healing, the promise is you'll get there. It won't be easy, but it will come to pass if you're willing to keep going.

> A vision motivates us. A good one excites us so much we run with it.

The most powerful example of visualization is Jesus' words on the cross. He saw glory first, and His vision supported enduring the painful agony experienced in His journey from human bondage to resurrection. He said to one of His criminal cross companions, "Today, you will be with Me in Paradise" (Luke 23:43b). Jesus saw the other side in advance, holding tight to the promise of what the Father spoke to His Spirit and the vision of joy set before Him (Hebrews 12:2b).

Hold to the promises for God's vision for your life to come to pass. Psalm 68:6 says, "… He brings out those who are bound into prosperity." And He says, "Therefore if the Son makes you free, you shall be free indeed" (John 8:36). "Being confident of this very thing, that He who has begun a good work in you will complete it until the day of Jesus Christ" (Philippians 1:6). Your freedom in weight and eating is a part of that good work to come to fruition.

To illustrate the scientific power of visualization, Guang Yue, an exercise psychologist from Cleveland Clinic Foundation in Ohio, compared "people who went to the gym with people who carried out virtual workouts in their heads."[3] While a thirty percent muscle increase was attained by those who went to the physical gym, a thirteen and a half percent increase was attained by those who did a mental workout.[4]

Don't use this as an excuse to eat donuts and imagine lifting weights in your head. Use it to complete the next action. Go ahead and design your promised land vision.

Possibility starts with imagination.

Take Action: Write Your Day in the Life Vision

Write your day in the life of your personal promised land vision. Use your list of desires to guide you. Think about an ideal day in your healthiest life. From the time you wake up to the time you retire at night, write out what you'd like to do, how you'd feel, what you'd eat, how you'd eat, and how you'd interact with the people around you. Use your creativity but write every detail out and be vivid.

As a second option, if your vision feels as fuzzy as an old-school television station before cable, don't be discouraged. Just like with a wire hanger antenna, visions can be adjusted to sharpen them. Possibility starts with imagination.

Try to look at your life as though it were a page in a magazine. See yourself doing a healthy activity and decide what you're wearing and what emotions are expressed on your face. If you can't imagine yourself whole and free, it won't come to pass.

It was William Arthur Ward who said, "If you can imagine it, you can achieve it. If you can dream it, you can become it."[5] And Solomon who said, "For as he thinks in his heart, so *is* he" (Proverbs 23:7a). Write all about what you envision.

Action 4: Take 100 Percent Responsibility

"Arise, for *this* matter is your *responsibility*. We also *are* with you. Be of good courage, and do *it*" (Ezra 10:4).

Toddlers make messes other people clean up. But as mature adults we realize our rooms are messy because we made them messy. If we want it clean, it's our job. Responsibility is just that, cleaning up our mess.

The secret to freedom is that it's not free. Freedom requires our willingness to take ownership over our full self—body, soul, spirit, thoughts, emotions, actions, and choices—past, present, and future.

We blame God for what's ultimately our own unwillingness to surrender our Spirit to His and admit, "God, I need you! I can't do this without you!" We need His supernatural power to help us because our human power has failed us. This is partly because we've given our power away with the blame game.

It didn't work for Adam, and it won't work for you. Your current condition isn't your spouse's fault, your children's fault, or God's fault. It's yours. Own it.

And as tempting as it is to blame the devil, genetics, the media, the food and drug industry, an underactive thyroid, or a demanding job, we're not going to allow anyone or anything to be responsible for our own choices but us.

We're taking our power back from all blame. This is how we gain momentum, hope, and more power to reach our goal. You need God, but you are powerful so stop giving your power away.

> We're not going to allow anyone or anything to be responsible for our own choices but us.

God gave us dominion. He wants us to use it with Him as our partner. God doesn't just puppet His children. He's an active partner holding your hand, if you allow Him to hold it. He's ready and willing to help us through by the power of the Holy Spirit as we learn to take responsibility (John 14:26).

Perhaps, the best way I found to take 100 percent responsibility was to walk through the twelve steps of recovery, although the Holy Spirit empowered me to work the steps before I knew there were twelve steps to work. When I learned about the steps, I realized this is the way we ought to be healing with God anyway.

Bill Wilson and Dr. Bob Smith discovered these steps when hopeless from alcohol. Bill, a successful broker, and Dr. Bob Smith, a physician, both damaged their lives with alcoholism.[6]

Alcoholics Anonymous is a successful tool in the journey of freedom for those with a drinking problem, as Celebrate Recovery, Overeaters Anonymous, Food Addicts Anonymous, Full of Faith, and many other groups are also tools for those who have a weight and eating problem.

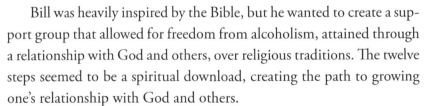

The twelve steps aren't for the weak, foolish, or struggling, they're for the strong, wise, and responsible.

Bill was heavily inspired by the Bible, but he wanted to create a support group that allowed for freedom from alcoholism, attained through a relationship with God and others, over religious traditions. The twelve steps seemed to be a spiritual download, creating the path to growing one's relationship with God and others.

The twelve steps are a powerful tool in the journey to freedom. I strongly believe we, as people of God, should be doing them as a way of life. This book covers what's not covered in a twelve-step group for holistic transformation.

The twelve steps aren't for the weak, foolish, or struggling, they're for the strong, wise, and responsible. We take full responsibility when we practice the twelve steps as a way of life, stop making excuses, and take charge of our own insanity.

Work the twelve-step process: it's one of the most responsible, respected ways to do just that.

Take Action: Work the Twelve Steps[7]

What are your answers to the following questions?

1. Do you admit you need God?
2. Do you believe God can help you fully overcome?
3. Do you give God permission to help you?
4. Do you know what your character flaws are?
5. Do you seek constant character improvement?
6. Do you admit mistakes and errors?
7. Do you pray for God's help to remove character flaws?
8. Do you ask God to remove your shortcomings as they come up?
9. Do you apologize when you mess up?
10. Do you monitor your morals daily?
11. Do you pray for God's will and lean on Him to carry it out?
12. Do you help others get free?

Did you answer *yes* to the above twelve questions? Each question above relates to the spiritual path and things we ought to be doing anyway as a way of life. These steps are principles of the word of God at work. They provide a way to take responsibility of our harmful issues.

Sit your pride in the corner and work the steps. You can review the questions above and put them into action or research a twelve-step group you'd like to attend. Most groups meet over the phone, online via webinar access, or in person locally. You'll gain connections and a safe environment to share with people who understand. To win, you must be willing to take full responsibility.

> Power of temptation in everyday life can consume the strength of conviction.

Action 5: Enroll Accountability

"Where *there* is no counsel, the people fall; But in the multitude of counselors *there is* safety" (Proverbs 11:14).

Humility to realize you don't have the power or ability to do this alone is a crucial step to freedom. God provides people for us to be accountable to—a husband to his wife, a mother to her children, or a child to his parents. Just as churches have elders and the United States President has Congress, we also need accountability to keep our delusional human egos in check.

Ultimately, we're all accountable to the Lord (Romans 14:12). And ideally, we commit to the Lord to gain conviction in our mishaps, but the power of temptation in everyday life can consume the strength of conviction. Therefore, God built in accountability checks and balances by our being in relationship with others to support our better choices.

Jesus had twelve disciples. He gave them authority over unclean spirits to drive them out and to heal every disease and sickness (Matthew 10:1). In the not-so-exact same way, an accountability partner is granted permission to call you out on any unclean thoughts or limiting behaviors to what you say you want.

To emphasize our need for others, Jesus' work couldn't have been done alone; otherwise, it would've been. The twelve disciples were critical to the success of the mission in Jesus' pursuit of our freedom. Enroll accountability for your mission to freedom as well.

> The twelve disciples were critical to the success of the mission in Jesus' pursuit of our freedom.

According to the Association for Training and Development, the probability of completing a goal is 95 percent if you have an appointment with a specific person.[8]

Get to your next level by enrolling an accountability partner. Doing it alone—well, you've been there, done that, and it's time for lasting change.

Take Action: Connect with an Accountability Partner

Get a sponsor, therapist, accountability partner, or group. Schedule consistent daily, weekly, bi-weekly, or monthly meetings with this person or group. Use one, a couple, or all four of the types of accountability partners mentioned below in your journey.

For accountability enroll:

1. **A professional you pay.** The most powerful results come from someone you pay. A secret weapon in reaching our next level is hiring a therapist or a coach who, unlike our loving but fickle friends or family members, will show up because of the high motivator of cash, checks, and any other forms of payment.

   Find a good therapist or accountability coach. Just as there are medical doctors for the heart, there are emotional doctors for the heart, too, called counselors, therapists, coaches, or psychologists. Hire a professional. But, if you're wondering, "How in the world will I pay for this and shop organic?!" No biggie. Enroll one of the freebies below. (No organic shopping required.)

2. **A sponsor from your twelve-step group.** A sponsor is a dedicated person who has been where you are. When you get into a twelve-step group, request a sponsor and someone will be willing to support your efforts to abstain from binge foods, diets, and overeating.

3. **A mentee you give advice to.** Who do you give the most advice to? Nothing puts steam under us more than the possibility of disappointing people who think we're saints. Asking a mentee

for help not only qualifies you for a humility honor award, but also creates a higher chance of success in meeting your goals. Your integrity with the appropriate mentee, adult child, younger sibling, or dysfunctional friend creates wins. If this person is mature enough to follow through, give them a try.

4. **A support group of friends.** Birds of a feather flock together. A group of friends, colleagues, or, better yet, get the book course *Whole & Free Health* activated at your church. Chances are you aren't the only one in your circle who struggles with weight and eating.

   Round up two or more people and meet for an hour once a week via phone conference, at the park, or in your home. Be sure you don't meet around food. We don't want to be counter-productive by meeting at Chubby's Grill or Fat Burger, for example.

   Keep in mind, most people don't set goals to be free. They set goals to lose weight fast. Whatever you do, stay focused on freedom, not diets, agreed?

To request your accountability of choice, do so in humility. Say something like, "Accountability Partner, I've struggled with weight and eating for a long time, and I'm ready to change. I need your support as I read through *The Chubby Church* and make small, meaningful changes over the next several months. I'm not looking for dieting advice here, but accountability. Would you support me as an accountability partner?"

With your accountability partner, set small attainable goals between appointments, such as: finish chapter 5, post on *www.WholeNFreeHealth.com*, buy pants that fit my current size, pray, find supportive Scriptures, attend a twelve-step group, don't buy the bag of popcorn, or choose to eat green vegetables. If it helps your accountability partner, support her in something she may want to achieve, too.

Action 6: Persist through the Lows

"And let us not grow weary while doing good, for in due season we shall reap if we do not lose heart" (Galatians 6:9).

The struggle with weight and eating is a weary one. We start making progress at breakfast then eat our hearts out at dinner. This up and down, back and forth pattern exhausts our motivation, and we lose faith in our own ability to win and in God's ability to help us.

The struggle at times makes us feel like God's an ant compared to the almighty French fry, making us too discouraged to persist through the hard times. But when the going gets rough—and it will—we'll keep getting back up. And we do this by standing on God's Word.

As the Scriptures say, "A righteous *man* may fall seven times and rise again" (Proverbs 24:16a).

> **Thoughts of I quit, I give up, or this is too hard aren't part of a winning mindset.**

Thoughts of *I quit, I give up,* or *this is too hard* aren't part of a winning mindset. Our motivation is to be authentic believers who do whatever it takes to serve the King of kings, refusing to live in torment, temptation, and intemperance.

It's not a straight line from point A to point B. This journey in weight and otherwise will look a lot like the stock market. It's a daily process of working out our salvation with many peaks and valleys to find out why we've been hiding in excess weight.

Unlike that cabbage diet, in this journey failure doesn't exist. To give up is an operation of the flesh, not of the Spirit. If you feel like giving up, then you're normal, but your motivation still needs purification.

The heart of your motivation must be freedom. Freedom is created in Christ's full-loving, Lordship over our lives. With a pure motive, we can't fail.

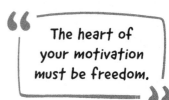

> **The heart of your motivation must be freedom.**

The road to freedom is also lifelong.

When the weight releases, you'll need to strengthen your commitment to freedom even more because your mind will trick you with suggestions like, "I'm healed, so I can eat whatever I want," and the chains of bondage can tie you down again. To get through, stand on the Word of God.

Take Action: Pick a Scripture to Stand On

Search the Scriptures and pick a Scripture to stand on. Like the inspiring movie *War Room* shows us, Minister Priscilla Shirer played the role of a wife hurting from her husband's emotional abuse.

A wise, older woman took on the role of mentor to support Priscilla's character to learn how to fight God's way. Priscilla was lackadaisical at first, but then she got serious, using her once cluttered closet as a prayer room to put Scriptures on the walls and command evil to flee her home.

Well, if you haven't seen it, I won't ruin it for you, but let's just say, it was a happy ending. Scriptures and prayer are weapons to win back freedom in your life.

What Scriptures can support you in the journey ahead? There are many that pertain to persistence so pick one, then find a meme (online picture) and post it as the backdrop for your phone or computer or write it out on an index card to get you through the lows. Examples of this Scripture can be seen below:

- "Being confident of this very thing, that He who has begun a good work in you will complete *it* until the day of Jesus Christ" (Philippians 1:6).

- "For I consider that the sufferings of this present time are not worthy *to be compared* with the glory which shall be revealed in us" (Romans 8:18).

- "But also for this very reason, giving all diligence, add to your faith virtue, to virtue knowledge, to knowledge self-control, to self-control perseverance, to perseverance godliness" (2 Peter 1:5–6).

Keep Going

Whew, we got through some serious work. But glad you did it, because spiritual and emotional resistance is real when we're going for a victory of this magnitude.

The war for your soul's freedom is fierce. You'll use your action plan to persist through the spiritual and emotional resistance and lean into the discomfort of your chubbology one page at a time, one day at a time, one bite at a time. But smile at yourself when you look in the mirror because your victory is on its way. And because you're cute.

PRAYER

Dear Lord,

I'm asking to be in complete alignment with your good and perfect will for my life. I thank you in advance for help and strength to commit to freedom, cultivate my deepest desires, create a vision, take 100 percent responsibility, enroll accountability, and persist through the lows. Purify my motivations to honor you. And please empower me to reach my goal!

In Jesus' mighty name, I pray. Amen.

CHAPTER 6

HABITIZE BODY STEWARDSHIP

Chain #1 – Body Neglect

---

*Do you not know that you are the temple of
God and that the Spirit of God dwells in you?*

—1 CORINTHIANS 3:16

I didn't mean to, it was a snaccident.

Chronic diseases in America represent 90 percent of the $3.3 trillion in health care expenditures per year.[1] Obesity is $147 billion alone.[2] Not only are chronic diseases, such as diabetes, cancer, heart disease, and obesity, on the rise, but on average 40 percent of them are preventable and many reversable with diet and exercise.[3]

Furthermore, 117 million Americans are dealing with at least one chronic disease.[4] And worse, America's youngest generation is at risk of dying before their parents if we continue these trends.[5] Physical health is one thing, yet mental-emotional health is on the same trajectory.

One in five US adults are suffering mental illness.[6] And because of a lack of affordable solutions, professional helpers, and the stigma of mental illness, over 40 percent of mental illness goes untreated.[7, 8] Hence, our spiritual condition, evidenced by our health—mentally, emotionally, and physically, is due for an overhaul.

My passion about health started in early 2000. As a fast-food junkie, I was amongst many Americans who ate what I wanted without a thought that I had responsibility for my health or any influence on it. I was at the mercy of a doctor's opinion or my taste buds as I shared earlier. However, I came to the realization that food is our fuel. If we have the wrong fuel, it will reap havoc on all of the body's organs and systems. If you feed a dog chocolate, you'll quickly see how that's not the right fuel as evidenced by its extra repugnant output.

> "
> Food is our fuel.
> "

If you're sick and tired, you're losing the health battle because fatigue is a primary sign that your body's fuel sources aren't working.

The very nature of good fuel is to produce energy. If you find it difficult to stop snacking, get out of bed, play with your children, make love to your spouse, or walk up a few stairs, then you've got to be willing to upgrade your inputs.

Our fuel source affects our soul and spirit that are housed nowhere else but inside the body. And because the body is an interconnected, miraculous instrument, when one system is off, it affects another system and so on.

The statistics and research around the current condition of American health—physical, mental, and spiritual—is painful, grieving, and sickening. But there's always hope in Christ. No matter what your condition, the resiliency of the human body is incredible.

And we mustn't forget the healing power of God is still alive and well today!

Body Stewardship

"Do you not know that you are the temple of God and *that* the Spirit of God dwells in you?" (1 Corinthians 3:16). It's a question Paul posed to help us understand that we're not just a human body walking around.

Our choices—what we eat, where we go, what we drink, what we watch, what we listen to, and what we do—matter in our body stewardship.

Do you honor your body? To properly steward the body is to honor, respect, and appreciate it. It includes operating in self-respect and the respect for others in our sexuality, environment, clothing, hygiene, and physical needs.

We value, respect, and honor our physical body's needs by applying proper self-care. You may be out of touch with your physical body. You may not know when you're hungry or thirsty for water. You may not yet realize that you're eating because your exhausted or your dessert-like breakfast meal is causing your cravings for a midday coffee run.

As we move along, we'll discuss several triggers. We'll start with the body's *physiological triggers* because what may seem like emotional eating over sad feelings may be because the body's off balance chemically, since your body is a profound chemistry lab.

A dear friend of mine is a facilities manager of a church. His job is to make sure that the church is in good condition. To get the trash out, keep the bathrooms clean, take care of repairs, make sure it's protected from vandalism, and ensure the sanctuary's prepared for worship.

We're that sanctuary. You are the church. Together, we're to build a holy temple for the Lord (Ephesians 2:21–22). God's Spirit is in you, and there's a responsibility to steward your body well. Just like a good facilities manager, we need to get and keep our temple in order.

The Chain of Body Neglect

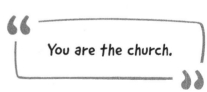

You are the church.

Body stewardship is caring for the vehicle that will fulfill our assignments in life, love our children, get to work, share the gospel, or cuddle with our pets.

We have the light of God, but it's not always glowing. We're so busy we rebel against good health by not making self-care a priority. We're overworking or overindulging on entertainment.

We neglect healthy habits and cause and create health problems. The American way of eating and drinking isn't working. And just because executives in high places are selling disease (packaged as edible deliciousness) doesn't mean we have to buy it.

You see, self-neglect screams, "I don't care about me! I'm unworthy of time and attention! I don't matter! I can't take care of myself! I can't manage my life!" Take care of yourself. It's selfish not to because, again, self-neglect leads to dependency on others and an inability to be there for others.

Body neglect is also a reflection of carnality. Carnality is being driven by the taste buds of the flesh more so than the needs of the body (organs, tissues, and systems). Most of the standard American diet isn't made by the sun and earth. It's made by machines inspired to addict carnally-minded consumers.

> "Carnality is being driven by the taste buds of the flesh more so than the needs of the body."

To be carnally minded is death (Romans 8:6). The less discretion we have over what we eat or do with our bodies, the more evidence we're in our carnal, not spiritual, nature and driven by lust (1 John 2:16, Galatians 5:17).

Our carnal nature puts a halt on God's transformative power in this area of our lives. I find I'm also not the most loving if I've overindulged or been neglectful of my body.

What about you?

BODY NEGLECT STRONGHOLD QUIZ

Put a check next to the answer that describes your body stewardship and add the total points below. The higher the score, the more body neglect is present.

1. How often do you skip breakfast?

☐ (5) ALWAYS ☐ (4) OFTEN ☐ (3) SOMETIMES ☐ (2) RARELY ☐ (1) NEVER

2. How often do you drink half your body weight in ounces of water?

☐ (1) ALWAYS ☐ (2) OFTEN ☐ (3) SOMETIMES ☐ (4) RARELY ☐ (5) NEVER

3. How often do you cleanse your colon, liver, kidneys, or other organs?

☐ (1) BI-ANNUALLY ☐ (2) ANNUALLY ☐ (3) SOMETIMES ☐ (4) RARELY ☐ (5) NEVER

4. How often do you have gastrointestinal problems?

☐ (5) ALWAYS ☐ (4) OFTEN ☐ (3) SOMETIMES ☐ (2) RARELY ☐ (1) NEVER

5. How often do you exercise?

☐ (1) ALWAYS ☐ (2) OFTEN ☐ (3) SOMETIMES ☐ (4) RARELY ☐ (5) NEVER

6. How often do you take a multivitamin or supplementation?

☐ (1) ALWAYS ☐ (2) OFTEN ☐ (3) SOMETIMES ☐ (4) RARELY ☐ (5) NEVER

7. How often do you neglect your body when you're busy?

☐ (5) ALWAYS ☐ (4) OFTEN ☐ (3) SOMETIMES ☐ (2) RARELY ☐ (1) NEVER

8. How often do you sleep 7 to 9 hours per night?

☐ (1) ALWAYS ☐ (2) OFTEN ☐ (3) SOMETIMES ☐ (4) RARELY ☐ (5) NEVER

9. How often do you complain of being tired?

☐ (5) ALWAYS ☐ (4) OFTEN ☐ (3) SOMETIMES ☐ (2) RARELY ☐ (1) NEVER

10. How often do you get sick?

☐ (5) ALWAYS ☐ (4) OFTEN ☐ (3) SOMETIMES ☐ (2) RARELY ☐ (1) NEVER

Total Score:

_____

Score Sheet
30–50 | You're in the right place!
20–30 | You've done some work and it shows!
10–20 | You're doing awesome!

Focus on Habits

In the next several chapters, we'll focus on body habits for health correction because they're the easiest to correct and prevent. In order to improve weight and eating, we'll start with understanding our physical triggers.

A *physiological trigger* is caused by neglecting a biological need of your body. When triggered physically, we're vulnerable to overeat, emotionally eat, negatively obsess on body weight, shape, or size, and make other unwanted chubby choices.

We need the right habits in place to deter these triggers. There are six physiological triggers and six habits that we'll discuss.

The physiological triggers and their corresponding body habits are:

PHYSIOLOGICAL TRIGGER	BODY HABIT
Micronutrient Deficiency	#1 Nutrient Load
Toxic Overload	#2 Cleanse
Dehydration	#3 Hydrate
Poor Sleep	#4 Sleep
Inactivity	#5 Exercise
Hormonal Imbalance	#6 Balance

With all the talk on what to do with your health—take this prescription, do keto, do paleo, eat eggs, don't eat eggs, don't eat bananas, eat lots of bananas, eat this new superfood, drink wine, no, don't drink wine—it's confusing to figure out what to do. God is not the author of confusion but of peace (1 Corinthians 14:33).

It's been said the secrets of our future are hidden in our daily routine. Let's not continue to reject our souls' knowing: we must change our daily habits. Everyone who desires health has to habitize it. It's got to become who we are and part of our lifestyle. If you focus on the right habits, over time your health is guaranteed to transform.

We avoid confusion by focusing on the basics. The body habit basics bring the blessing. So, eat up the following chapters because the principles of the body habits will begin to work in you to create change.

Do so quickly so we can get to the really juicy soul section of the book.

Let's get to it.

REFLECTION QUESTIONS

1. How have you neglected your body?

   _____

   _____

2. How long have you procrastinated on making daily health a priority?

   _____

   _____

3. Do you believe your treatment of your body influences you spiritually? How so?

   _____

   _____

4. How have diets prevented you from adopting lifelong healthy habits?

   _____

   _____

PRAYER

Father,

Thank you for helping me change how I care for this precious gift of my body. I repent for any and all damage I've done to my body. Open my mind and heart to receive the body habits into my daily life and teach others around me to model my example.

In Jesus' name, amen

Note: All references to diabetes refer to type 2 diabetes, not type 1 diabetes.

Disclosure: Remember to consider all advice with a medical doctor. And the author and any affiliation with this book is not held liable for health recommendations.

CHAPTER 7

HABIT #1 NUTRIENT LOAD AM I MALNOURISHED?

Physiological Trigger – Micronutrient Deficiency

*"And God said, 'See, I have given you every herb that yields
seed which is on the face of all the earth, and every tree
whose fruit yields seed; to you it shall be for food'"*

–GENESIS 1:29

*Processed foods have eternal life without being
saved or having ever been alive in the first place.*

Experts point to fancy terms for the cause of excess weight such as inflammation, insulin resistance, or high glucose sensitivity. Yes, there's scientific proof of these things, and they matter. But why do we have inflammation, high insulin, or high glucose issues in the first place? Because on a daily basis we're eating processed foods and beverages loaded with chemicals and refined fats, sugars, flours, and salts causing *processed food addiction.*

Processed foods, stress-induced lifestyles, and environmental toxins are wreaking havoc on *all* of our body systems, making it more difficult to correct health, release weight, and eat better.

The one thing that seems to cure just about all major chronic diseases, according to books such as *The China Study, It Starts with Food,* and *The Micronutrient Miracle,* is quality nutrition. Friends, simply put, we've disobeyed God's ideal food plan and we're paying the price.

The problem is deceptively obvious – ridiculous temptations from processed food addictions cause disobedience to how God instructed us to eat.

Micronutrient Deficiency Facts

1. Processed meats, such as bacon, hot dogs, salami, sausage, and lunch meats, can increase your risk of colon cancer by 18 percent, and raise the risk of pancreatic and prostate cancers.[1]

2. Americans buy and consume 60 percent of their dietary calories from highly processed foods.[2]

3. A minimum of 400,000 of the 600,000 annual deaths from heart disease are directly linked to poor diet.[3]

4. Deficiencies of vitamins A, D, K, B1, B3, B6, B12, folate, iodine, potassium, iron, magnesium, zinc, chromium, and manganese can contribute to mental instability and violent behavior.[4]

5. Genetic causes predict about 5 to 10 percent of cancers, whereas 90 to 95 percent of cancer is due to lifestyle, diet, and environmental factors.[5]

6. In a super study of 537,000 AARP members, those who ate red meat daily (pork, beef, lamb) had a 26 percent chance of dying from cancer, stroke, heart disease, respiratory disease, diabetes, infections, chronic kidney disease, or chronic liver disease during the sixteen-year study compared with those who ate it once per week.[6]

7. In the same AARP study, those who ate white meat daily (fish, chicken, and turkey) had a 25 percent lower risk of dying.[7]

8. Most Americans have low stomach acid levels due to a poor diet, which reduces nutrient absorption.[8]

9. Obesity and diabetes are linked to significant deficiencies in vitamin D, omega 3, chromium, magnesium, B3, B6, B7, B12, C, K, zinc, iodine, and iron.[9,10]

10. Plant-based eating heals heart disease, lung diseases, brain diseases, digestive cancers, diabetes, high blood pressure, liver diseases, blood cancers, kidney disease, breast cancer, suicidal depression, prostate cancer, and Parkinson's disease.[11]

The Great Physician, also our Master Nutritionist, said to eat all the green plant and seed-bearing vegetation (Genesis 1:29). In other words, He said to eat foods rich in micronutrients. Micronutrients are amino acids, vitamins, minerals, and fatty acids that are the building blocks of the body.

We all know we should eat more fruits and vegetables and drink more water. And we know it deep inside our souls. Yet, we ignore that still small voice, until it becomes the doctor's voice who tells us we have cancer or congestive heart failure.

Sadly, on average, medical doctors receive about seven hours of nutritional education, but most barely get three hours.[12,13] So, they're ill prepared to recommend ways to help you heal with foods, only drugs.

Let's listen to America's favorite doc, Dr. Oz, who said, "Of all the personal choices you can make about your health, nothing holds greater influence than the food you eat. It has the power to fix your body, prevent some diseases, and even reverse others. Food is the extension cord that energizes and lengthens your life."[14]

If you're a heathen and you eat well, you're going to live longer than you deserve based on this biblical eating principle.

It's a fact that those who suffer from binge eating and/or obesity are malnourished.[15,16] Founding editor of the medical journal *Obesity Surgery* and Bariatric Surgeon, Dr. Mervyn Deitel said, "The commonest form of malnutrition in the western world is obesity."[17]

Nutrients are found in abundance in just about any fruit or vegetable. But they are rather scarce in engineered options.

> If you're a heathen and you eat well, you're going to live longer than you deserve based on this biblical eating principle.

Food giants that promote denatured, engineered processed foods and beverages are like those anti-Christ evangelists the Scriptures warned about. They're wolves in sheep's clothing. They call something good that's leading us way off the path from righteous eating.

Books like *Salt, Sugar, Fat* by Michael Moss, *Think & Eat Yourself Smart* by Dr. Caroline Leaf, and *Food Politics* by Marion Nestle explain the political landscape surrounding the food industry, and it's ugly. For now, we've got to learn how to eat better given the tantalizing environment we're in.

Micronutrient Deficiency Factors

Exploited Soil

Over the centuries, due to the exploitation of various pesticides and soil usage, we've seen dramatic changes in the quality of vitamin and mineral density in vegetables and fruits.

Nutrient density changes, as reported by the USDA, show that a tomato today has significantly less vitamin A, phosphorous, calcium, and other micronutrients than it did years ago.[18]

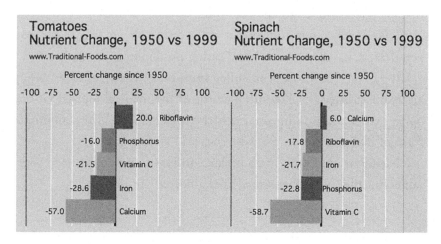

Figure 7.1 Tomatoes and spinach over a fifty-year period.

In the same timeframe researched, spinach shows a significant decrease in riboflavin, iron, and phosphorus, as well as more than a 50 percent decrease in vitamin C.[19] This means we need to eat more micronutrient rich foods to prevent diseases and heal, not less.

> **Micronutrient rich foods sustain not only physical health but physical freedom from hospitals.**

And those who are overweight or obese already have significant micronutrient deficiencies. In studies, over 55 percent struggled with iron deficiency (anemia) and more than 90 percent lacked vitamin D.[20] See fact #9 for other deficiencies researched. And the exact nutrients that are deficient in gastric bypass patients are the same nutrients it takes to digest food and the processed foods we're eating. Go figure.

A randomized Chinese study showed obese patients given a twenty-nine-ingredient multivitamin supplement over a twenty-six-week period improved their fat metabolism, reduced their body mass, and experienced better caloric absorption.[21] What are you waiting for? Take your vitamins.

Processed Foods and Meats

You, like me, may have grown up with French fries, ketchup, and over-cooked collard greens at holiday dinners as your only vegetables. The standard American diet creates micronutrient deficiencies.

Big food corporations hire talented food engineers who use lengthy formulas to create a bliss factor taste in processed foods.[22] This bliss formula calculates the exact combination of refined fat, salt, and sugar for us to become addicted to them.[23]

Therefore, when we eat processed foods, we don't get the micronutrients we need. And for our system to digest any food, we utilize nutrients. Micronutrient rich foods sustain not only physical health but physical freedom from hospitals. Deficiencies cause cravings and poor organ functioning, including brain issues like dementia.[24]

Surprisingly, when you get more micronutrient foods you can correct ailments to the tune of several prescriptions. In the documentary *What the Health*, an excellent watch exposing our morally twisted environment, two women experimented with a micronutrient rich eating plan.

Amy was burdened with her blood work, as she should've been because it revealed she could die of a heart attack any second. Amy's meds included heart pills, chronic pain pills, stress pills, muscle relaxer pills, and asthma pills. She had no energy, trouble walking, and couldn't breathe well. After two weeks of micronutrient rich foods, no meat, and no processed food, she eliminated all those pills.[25]

The same thing happened to Jane who had chronic arthritis in her hips. She used a walker to get around in her early sixties. She took six asthma medications, antidepressants, and more medications to manage their side effects.

After two weeks of nutrient dense plant foods, she walked normally, felt vibrant, and stopped her medications. Amy and Jane reversed disease through God's first instructions for what to eat most.[26] And weight and eating freedom was a side effect of their renewed health. God's foods give without sorrow.

> "Any way you slice it, we're not meant to eat human-engineered foods in the amounts we do."

Not only does micronutrient deficiency drive up prescription bills, as a physiological trigger it causes cravings. Specific links to micronutrient deficiencies are found with various cravings.[27] For example, someone who lacks magnesium or iron may crave chocolate or coffee.

Due to deficiencies, cells become stubborn, toyless toddlers in a toy store, like *Bebes Kids* or *Children of the Corn*. When cells are in need, they'll take from other organs. Over time deficiencies create reduced capacity from our organs and systems. Seriously, it's scary to the neighboring organs to consistently lack nutrients, especially for the bones.

Any way you slice it, we're not meant to eat human-engineered foods in the amounts we do. Nutrient dense foods are plant-based foods with one word that describes their content, such as kale, spinach, apple, or onion. Remember, God fed the Israelites for forty years with only manna from heaven. Besides one horrible, no good, rotten day of quail, manna was it.

Toxic foods have toxic ingredients you can't pronounce. A simple (yet complex) remedy is to commit to increase your ratio of real to processed foods. Think about it: how much of your daily intake is processed? Reduce that number and increase real foods.

Poor Digestion

Due to poor diet, evidenced by digestive issues such as diverticulitis, irritable bowel syndrome, gas, belching, stomach aches, or constipation, processed foods cause our intestines to have less than optimal absorption.

An estimated 74 percent of Americans have digestive health problems each month.[28] After a meal if you find yourself tired, bloated, or mitigating unwanted music that insists on coming out of your rear end, chances are your digestive health is off. To extract more nutrients out of your food, we'll need to practice digestive wellness.

Chew. Digestion starts well by chewing well. It's a simple free thing we can do to increase our nutrient absorption. Salvia is enzyme rich. When we chew well, there's less work for other organs. Do you eat fast? I used to be queen of fast eating. Once I ate a grapefruit and forgot I ate it because I ate it so fast. I spent at least fifteen minutes looking for it! Slow down to thirty chews per bite.

Churn. When food hits the stomach, it churns into chyme. According to Dr. Elizabeth Lipski who wrote *Digestive Wellness*, most Americans suffer from low stomach acid and don't know it.

Many symptoms exist, but a few are indigestion, bloating, brittle nails, leaky gut, or autoimmune disease. Low stomach acid throws off the endocrine system that's needed to regulate body weight and appetite related hormones.[29]

Stomach acid naturally reduces with age. But it's decreasing sooner due to our diets. When you eat a heavy meal consider betaine hydrochloride supplements or try apple cider vinegar in water to turn up the heat.

Synthesize. The liver and pancreas secrete digestive enzymes to break down foods. Processed foods and binge eating causes digestive enzymes to deplete.[30] We may not have enough lipase (breaks down fat), protease (breaks down protein), amylase (breaks down carbohydrate), and a host of other enzymes to synthesize what we consume.

In particular, we may have a stressed gallbladder or have no gallbladder at all. This tiny organ supports fat metabolism by secreting lipase and bile to break down fats.

I wore mine out when I ate whole sticks of butter … daily. As my Inner Glutton would say, *What's matzah without a heap of butter on top?* Digestive enzyme supplementation is essential to support absorption for those of us who have, up until now, overindulged on cheese, chocolate, and chips.

Utilize. The small intestines are a tremendous factory to distribute chyme into usable or non-usable raw materials that feed organs and systems.

Hippocrates, the father of modern medicine, said, "All disease starts in the gut."[31] And the more research I do, the more I see this truth.

Your gut is a strong influence on the whole body and talks to your brain.[32] Much of the body's neurotransmitters like serotonin, dopamine, and epinephrine are made in the gut. Our gut has an incredible field of insight in its enteric nervous system (ENS), which affects mental health and, consequently, emotional eating.[33]

Gut health is vital to micronutrient absorption. A few problems in the gut that are interrelated may be:

Leaky Gut (Intestinal Permeability)

Dr. Josh Axe's research shows that leaky gut is a leading cause of many health problems.[34] Symptoms include digestive problems, thyroid issues, bloating, and fatigue.[35]

With leaky gut, the digestive lining in the intestines leak toxins, bacteria, and other particles into the blood stream that typically would go through the small intestines for elimination.[36] It's causal to malnourishment.

Candida Overgrowth

Your gut—out of balance—may be what's behind intense cravings. Candida is a naturally occurring fungal yeast in the gut. When overgrown, it causes insatiable cravings.

Candida feeds off sugar (natural and artificial) and is exacerbated by refined fats, such as safflower, canola, or hydrogenated oils.[37]

A range of symptoms exist for overgrowth that includes yeast infections, bloating, psoriasis, eczema, and fungal nails.[38] Specific probiotics (healthy gut bacteria) help kick overgrown candida out of the gut house.

Small Intestinal Bacterial Overgrowth (SIBO)

The gut has three to five pounds of bacteria, in a ratio of about 15 percent streetwalkers to 85 percent happy housewives.

Now, we need streetwalkers, they keep us prayed up. But, if the bad bacteria in the gut universe take down the good bacteria's effectiveness, it doesn't look so good for the future generation.

Due to antibiotic use, low stomach acid, processed foods, and other factors, bacteria gets imbalanced, which impairs nutrient absorption.

A doctor can check total microbes (bacterial organisms). Under 103 organisms per mL is healthy, over 105 organisms per mL is considered overgrowth. Symptoms include diabetes, obesity, bloating, gas, fibromyalgia, pancreatitis, leaky gut, and candida overgrowth.[39]

Wheat Gluten

I must mention frankenwheat—a genetically altered version of wheat that is in baked goods, pizza dough, and pasta.[40] It's a featured ingredient in many processed foods.[41]

My friends, wheat isn't what it used to be six decades ago. Food manufacturers use frankenwheat or hybridized, genetically altered versions, because it binds to opiate receptors in the brain that cause appetite to increase.[42] It's addictive. This explained my cookie addiction, and it also explains your bread addiction.

All wheat isn't bad, in fact our body is made to digest it.[43] But refined, hybridized wheat and any other refined flour (even gluten-free versions) is asking for disease.

Author of *Wheat Belly*, Dr. William Davis, found that these new strands of wheat lead to leaky gut and over 200 medical conditions in the body.[44] Bottom line is our denatured wheat supply destroys the gut, our ability to absorb nutrients, and a healthy relationship with food.

Dr. Davis said, "The amazing thing about wheat elimination is that removing this food that triggers appetite and addictive behavior forges a brand-new relationship with food."[45]

But whole grains, including whole wheat, such as kamut or spelt, do have significant benefits to reduce disease, namely diabetes.[46] Do your best to reduce refined flours, find whole sprouted grain alternatives, or eliminate refined wheat flour altogether to reduce micronutrient deficiencies. We'll discuss this more in Book 2.

The best defense will always be a combination of micronutrient rich vegetables and fruits, as God intended. They're loaded with fiber and probiotics to strengthen the body's ability to heal. Specifically, fermented foods, like miso soup, kimchee, or sauerkraut, support gut repair.

Heal with Food

Let Daniel be our guide. Many churches do a Daniel fast each year. What they don't consider is that Daniel ate healthfully. Most of the time it wasn't a fast, it was how he ate. He chose not to eat rich delicacies of wine, meats, and desserts often. Instead he chose God's primary dietary instruction—vegetables. His strength—physically, emotionally, and spiritually—reflected that (Daniel 1:3–17).

Just like Daniel, we need more living foods—foods that seed, grow, die, and decompose—to get our micronutrient health back on track. Living food brings life as opposed to dead foods like meats that putrefy, processed foods that seem to have eternal life without being saved, and vegetables once bright green turned black from overcooking.

> " A balanced approach with substitutions works best. "

A long shelf life isn't life. Most processed foods aren't beneficial at all—let alone in large amounts. They're tasty takers, not givers. As believers we're to choose life in all areas of our lives (Deuteronomy 30:19).

A balanced approach with substitutions works best. Switch from soda to club soda, from fried wings to baked wings, from candy bars to whole foods nutrition bars, and from packaged items with ingredients you can't pronounce to packaged items you can pronounce.

Good nutrition mitigates cravings. In a healthy state, we want real nutrient dense foods, not junk food. While it's encouraged to research eating plans to increase your nutrition, don't obsess over diet fads. Keep it simple. Habitize body stewardship. On days you make eating mistakes or feel you've messed up, still nutrient load.

Everything is okay. There are no rules.

Create a (your name goes here) Eating Plan. A bio-individual eating plan is one that you create based on what works for your total wellness as far as foods, ingredients, and beverages. With a bio-individual approach, you honor your uniqueness and allow yourself to be more in tune with what your body, soul, and spirit need to thrive. Tap into your soul's quiet yet persistent desire to eat foods that nurture, restore, and heal.

Observe how what you consume impacts you. An ideal eating plan

> " An ideal eating plan is one that decreases cravings, reduces negative emotions, and nourishes you at all levels. "

is one that decreases cravings, reduces negative emotions, and nourishes you at all levels. Eat the highest quality your budget can afford. Most of all, be led by the Spirit to reduce processed foods intake causing Christians and people everywhere to die before their time or to be really unhappy with their bodies while living.

Nutrient load in your meals. Add green vegetables to most dishes. I suppose a lettuce wrapped Snickers® bar may be too much of a leap, but eat mixed greens with meals or order spinach instead of the mac and cheese.

It's better to skip dinner than breakfast.[47] A quality breakfast is a habit that reduces chances of obesity and diabetes by 35 to 50 percent.[48] When someone tells me they're not hungry at breakfast, it's usually because they've binged the night before.

I think a nutritional start predicts a nutritional finish. In the morning, train yourself to nutrient load with a whole foods multivitamin (liquid, capsule, or gummy), omega 3 fat, fruits, and vegetables.

I mix things up with organic eggs (no yolks due to my butter damage) and kale, millet with fresh pineapple chunks and a green drink, juice a few bunches of celery, or blend a head of lettuce with kiwis, blueberries, and a scoop of plant protein. Mix it up. Food can be fun.

Tips to Habitize Nutrient Load

- Consider supplementation, such as B-complex, vitamin D, omega 3, whole foods multivitamin, digestive enzymes, pre and probiotics, and possibly betaine stomach acid for when you eat rich meals. I believe supplements now will reduce prescription pills later. For specific ways to heal your body, consider the reference guide: *Prescription for Nutritional Healing* for various supplementation protocols by Phyllis Balch, a certified nutritional consultant.

- Set small goals to increase green foods, such as eat three cups of green vegetables per day—the amount proven to ward off cancer.[49] A green smoothie in the morning makes it easy. Spinach, kale, collard greens, chard, romaine, celery, cilantro—the list is endless! Any of these options mixes wonderfully with fruit or a protein scoop. Green smoothie recipes are all over the internet, but JJ Smith leads the pack with her *Green Smoothies for Life* recipe book.

- Find ways to put living foods into each meal. Making spaghetti? Serve it on top of swiss chard. Like my green drink, there's plenty of twenty-first century ways to get your nutrition from companies that care about your health. Research a few.

- Keep learning. Learn about foods, organic living, or healthy cooking to support motivation and recipe knowledge. Attend nutrition related seminars or listen to podcasts. Definitely check out *What the Health* and *What's with Wheat* documentaries.

- Reduce inflammatory foods, such as cooking oils, sugar, flour, refined grains, processed foods, and cured meats. It helps to prepare your food at home and dine out less.

- Reduce television, it's correlated with obesity and diabetes.[50]

- Work one-on-one with a health coach or registered dietitian.

- Use a nutrition-focused food tracker. Chronometer, developed by physician and health researcher Dr. Joseph Mercola, is a wonderful way to track your nutrition intake to see what you need.

- Soak your grains and beans prior to cooking to reduce harmful digestive pectin on the outer shell for better digestion.

- Join me at *www.WholeNFreeHealth.com*.

REFLECTION QUESTIONS ❓

1. How much processed foods did you consume in the last twenty four hours?

   _____

   _____

2. How many real foods did you consume in the last twenty four hours?

   _____

   _____

3. What tip can you implement right away to improve your real to processed food ratio?

   _____

   _____

PRAYER

Heavenly Father,

Fill me. You are my bread. Thank you for the changes I can make now for better digestion. Help me to eat more of the foods you created to heal my body, soul, and spirit. Help me to take this one day at a time with you.

In Jesus' name, amen.

CHAPTER 8

HABIT #2 CLEANSE AM I TOXIC?

Physiological Trigger – Toxic Overload

---

*"First cleanse the inside of the cup and dish, that
the outside of them may be clean also"*

—MATTHEW 23:26

The hardest workers you're in charge of are your organs.

S everal weeks after I detoxed fast food out of my system, I tried
Chinese food again. I played it safe with steamed chicken and
vegetables with brown rice. It came with a sauce, and I figured a
little couldn't hurt.

After my lunch, I ran the Cooper River in New Jersey. About a mile
in, my lungs tightened, and I started to wheeze. I got halfway around
the 3.8-mile bridged track and couldn't go any further.

Desperate for help, I tapped on the door of a highly suspect dude
chilling in the middle of the day looking at the river in a tinted low
rider. Got to love Jersey. Because I was in a medical emergency, I begged
him to take me to my car.

I'll never forget when he dropped me off. With fear in his eyes he
zoomed away like he just stole something. I got in my car, looked in the

driver's side rearview mirror, and "Aaah! Sweet Jesus!" I retrieved my cell phone from the glove box to call my mother who lived closest to the scene.

Between strained breaths I said, "Call 911. I'm having an allergic reaction. I'll be right there."

My skin drooped, my lips enlarged by the second, and I turned various shades of red. Suddenly, my young twenty something fully detoxed hot self was now an eighty-year-old looking hot mess from the *Twilight Zone*.

I drove the five minutes to my mom's house, got out of the car, and crawled my way to the front lawn. The ambulance showed up right on time and the rest of the day was spent in the hospital with IVs of commercial grade Benadryl®.

The doctor insisted it was Monosodium Glutamate (MSG), a toxic ingredient in many Chinese foods, as well as processed and fast foods. In the past, I could tolerate chemical foods. I'd eaten them all the time. But after cleansing my body, I saw exactly which ingredients carried out a deathly attack against my system.

We need to detox on every level.

I don't recommend being extreme like I was in my early twenties, but peek at the ingredients on any box you have lying around the house. From cleaning products, hair products, skin products, the office building, car exhausts, and electronic devices, toxins are everywhere. We're consuming things that are far from nature.

And our toxic environment is also toxic for us mentally, emotionally, and spiritually with so many violent and immoral acts on television. We need to detox on every level.

Toxic Overload Facts

1. Genetically Modified Organisms (GMOs) are in 95 percent of soy beans, 88 percent of corn, 95 percent of sugar beets, 90 percent of canola oil, and about 90 percent of all wheat grown in the U.S.[1]

2. In nine people tested, more than 249 toxins were found in each of them. Of those chemicals found, 147 are toxic and 76 are known cancer causers.[2]

3. There are over 3,000 chemicals in the processed foods arsenal.[3]

4. BPA (Bisphenol A) is a proven endocrine disrupter found in receipts, plastic materials, lined canned goods, and more. Those with higher BPA in urine were five pounds heavier than those with lower BPA in urine.[4]

5. Toxoplasma parasite infects 40 to 60 million Americans and is found in lamb, venison, and cat feces.[5,6]

6. Environmental Protection Agency (EPA) tests show more than 2,100 contaminants, including pesticides, heavy metals, radon, radioactive participles, and parasites in the tap water we drink.[7]

7. Children with the highest amount of pesticides in their blood stream are diagnosed twice as frequently with Attention Deficit Hyperactivity Disorder (ADHD).[8]

8. Glyphosate, an herbicide used in pesticide, is applied to all non-organic soil each year in the U.S., and it inhibits enzymes critical for body detoxification, healthy gut bacteria, and digestion.[9]

9. Wi-Fi, cell phones, and microwave ovens emit RF/MW electromagnetic radiation and studies not paid for by manufacturers found it can result in traumatic brain injury.[10]

10. Parabens, synthetic preservatives found in makeup, cough medicine, antidepressants, body lotion, and beverages, have been found in 99 percent of breast cancer tissues. Testing in 2,500 people found parabens in their urine samples.[11]

King Hezekiah pleased the Lord most when he cleansed God's temple. He didn't delay. Within the first month of rulership he said, "Hear me, Levites! Now sanctify yourselves, sanctify the house of the Lord God of your fathers, and carry out the rubbish from the holy place" (2 Chronicles 29:5).

The facts speak to our need to get the rubbish out. Per Habit 1, we reduce toxins first in our system with nutrition. Nutrition heals best. Then, we cleanse our organs. And we'll eventually need to cleanse the environment and products we use—but that's someone else's book.

I know you thought your kids would be good workers for a family business, but the hardest workers you're in charge of are your organs! Our hardworking organs experience reduced capacity as we age. Most of this is due to the toxicity of the chemicals in foods we eat and drink, along with our environments.

> **" In this environment, our organs are working overtime to handle the toxic overload. "**

Organs such as the liver, colon, lungs, and kidneys, as well as the spleen, have the task of filtering thousands of chemicals day in and day out. And to filter that many toxins is way beyond their daily job description in this millennium.

For most of us Chubby Church members, they've barely been able to clean up one job before another load hits the scene. In this environment, our organs are working overtime to handle the toxic overload.

Like our homes have functional operations and appliances so do our bodies. Imagine your toilet not being cleaned for a year. What about for several years? Your organs need to be cleansed, too.

When was the last time you cleaned your liver or colon?

In his book *Toxic Relief*, Dr. Don Colbert strongly urges us to cleanse our bodies from the myriad toxins we face every day. If our blood is toxic, we'll have all kinds of issues, like food cravings, edema, brain fog, and a host of illnesses.[12]

Three Areas to Clean Up

The Colon

First, we want to clean out the colon. Colon cancer is the second leading cancer in the United States and affects men and women almost equally.[13]

The five foot long colon also has five segments and toxin-cleaning lymph nodes.

This thing has to work well.

If it doesn't, toxins clog our lymph system and recycle back into the bloodstream. Some toxins collect in the colon for decades. Most colon cancer patients are diagnosed after the age of fifty.[14] Emotionally, the colon is linked to bottled up hate.[15] And research shows about 42 million Americans are suffering from constipation.[16]

> "The less fiber in our diet, the filthier the colon is."

Are you one of them?

To cleanse the colon regularly, eat more high fiber plant foods. The less fiber in our diet, the filthier the colon is. God designed us to need fiber and food to provide it.

High fiber consumption results in healthier body mass index, a healthy heart, and reduced cancer risks.[17] The recommended amount in America is 38 grams for men and 25 grams for women.[18] Most Americans eat 16 grams.[19] And years ago we ate 50 to 100 grams per day.[20]

If you don't have at least two bowel movements per day, your colon could be working harder for you. After all, how many meals do you eat per day?

Try black beans with 29 grams per cup, kale with 2.6 grams per cup, mangos with 6 grams per cup, and raspberries with 8 grams per cup, but not all together—that would be gross.

Healthy elimination is between twelve to twenty four hours after consumption.[21] You can check digestion speed by taking charcoal tablets. Track the time you take them until the time you see black stool.[22]

Besides adding more fiber into your daily diet, also consider a colon cleanser product. A good one takes a week for proper colon clean up. Don't be scared. You may imagine running to the restroom in khakis as you hold tight to your seat cheeks, but it'll be okay. Do a colon clean up on a stay-cation or work from home week to avoid loose stool fear. But hey, a little excitement in the office may spice up the work day.

Another thing I like to do, but it's not for everybody, is a colonic. I gave my seventy-something-year-old grandmother a gift of a colonic, and soon after she was zipping up and down the stairs. I was shocked. She leaped up those stairs like an African hyena. Prior to that she took f-o-r-e-v-e-r.

A colonic, also called colon hydrotherapy, is an enema process where several gallons of water are used to gently clean the rectum (the last part of the colon) which helps empty toxins.

You go to a colonic center, sit on a specialized toilet, and they fill your colon entrance up with warm water. They may sell you on more, but one or two should clean things up. Too much can stress the large intestinal lining, so it's not recommended.

Preparation for a colonoscopy is also a good cleanser, but it doesn't cleanse the colon adequately. The point here is to cleanse the colon on a regular basis, ideally with high fiber foods and a periodic cleansing program (quarterly to twice a year). Do whatever it takes to clean it up.

Harmful Organisms

Our blood carries all kinds of toxins, critters from fungus, molds, bacteria, genetically modified organisms (GMOs), viruses, and parasites. I'm going to emphasize parasites because they stimulate massive problems in health.

Most parasites get into our systems if we eat meat, drink tap water, eat sushi, have pets, or travel abroad. Dr. Hulda Clark, physiologist, has researched proof that "all illness comes from two causes, parasites and pollutants."[23] In her insightful book *The Cure for all Diseases*, she proves that parasites are a source of disease, including cancer, insomnia, asthma, diabetes, infertility, and HIV.

For example, diabetics are affected by pancreatic fluke worms in raw beef or cow's milk, called eurytrema.[24] Eurytrema can only live and multiply if wood alcohol is present in the pancreas.

Are you a cola drinker? Well, wood alcohol is found in most soda cans, water bottles, and packaged products. When the amount of wood alcohol elevates enough in your system and eurytrema is present, adult onset diabetes is birthed. This goes beyond what we learn around glucose-insulin levels, yet both need to be addressed.[25] However, medical doctors aren't as knowledgeable about the pollutant parasite factor.

I've had asthma since I was a child, but because I practice body habits, I haven't had to use my inhaler in years. Well, I noticed my breathing was rather troubled while writing this book. Of course, I started praying against spiritual warfare, rebuking the devil, and took my inhaler, but it got worse.

> " Dr. Hulda Clark, physiologist, has researched proof that "all illness comes from two causes, parasites and pollutants. "

I ordered a parasite cleanse. After the first day of taking the cleanse, my lungs cleared up. Dr. Clark found ascaris parasites in her asthma cases, and Chinese researchers found the same.[26] Any parasite, but especially ascaris, can decrease nutritional absorption as well. As nasty as it is, parasite fluke worms get lodged in our organs.

Janelle, a participant in Whole & Free Health course, saw a nasty pool of parasites in the toilet after her parasite cleanse. This isn't something you'd tell your spouse about or anyone else for that matter. But no one was there to stop her excited surprise parasite party, so she told her husband. And against sexier spousal perceptions, she showed him. He admitted that he had passed the same. They were both parasite free. Anyone under your roof, including pets, could use a parasite cleanse.

To get rid of harmful organisms, certain herbs work miracles. Herbs like wormwood, cloves, and black walnut hull extra strength do an effective job killing them.

Dr. Clark has a great website that provides cleansing protocols and products. My miracle working parasite cleanse was from Global Healing Center. Whatever brand you choose, it should last six weeks to be most effective, which is the length of the parasite lifecycle. And like Janelle did, be sure to get your spouse on board with your detox adventures.

The Liver

The liver is a *Fortune* 50 company executive administrator (EA) to the CEO. It's where the blood is filtered for use. Like an EA would protect the CEO by filtering calls, meeting invites, vendors, and more, the liver's primary job is to filter toxins in the blood. Blood carries the lifeforce. And the liver transacts cellular metabolism with it that allows us to live our best life. Is it clean?

It's both a production factory and storage site for enzymes, hormones, vitamins, and minerals. It has approximately 2,000 chemical functions.[27] And amazingly, it can grow back up to two-thirds of its mass. We process about ten thousand pounds of toxins through the liver in a lifetime.

Like that toilet I mentioned, the liver uncleansed can get really congested. We know it's congested when we're fatigued or can't release weight despite efforts. It gets this way because we feed it drinks like soda and alcohol, and processed foods, which all create toxic by-products and slow functioning.

Other symptoms of liver congestion include low stomach acid, small intestinal bacterial overgrowth (SIBO), acne, gallstones, bloating, eczema, gout, psoriasis, diabetes, and autoimmune disease.[28]

The liver also gets congested with high fat consumption. You want to eat good quality fats. Find the best balance for fat intake for your body. The US government recommends 20 to 35 percent.[29]

The problem is most Chubby Church members eat fast food or indulge in a five-layer chocolate cake for dessert, which is three days' worth of fat intake in just one sitting—food porn is real. And don't be deceived, deep fried anything, including French fries, are fat, not potatoes.

> **Medications are like getting a safety pin to close the frontside of your pants, while a split happens in the back.**

Fatty liver diagnosis began in 1980.[30] It's caused by a high fat diet. If we often indulge on chocolate, cheeses, meat, or high fructose corn syrup (which converts quickly to fat), we cause fat storage in the liver to overflow into the rest of the liver where it shouldn't be.

The liver must clean up the by-products of drugs, too—whether prescribed, over-the-counter, or otherwise. Medications are like getting a safety pin to close the frontside of your pants, while a split happens in the back. You take a pill to solve a problem, but you get other problems as a result.

It's reported that 70 percent of Americans take two medications and half of Americans are on at least two.[31] Medication, while beneficial in some way does have chemicals that cause toxicity and, hence, comes with a two paragraph list of possible side effects.

Anthony William is called the Medical Medium because of his spiritual gift into medical conditions since he was a child. In his book, *Liver Rescue*, he says, "Weight gain is really about the liver since there's no such thing as a fast or slow metabolism." He says that the two typical factors in weight gain—the thyroid and adrenals, which we'll cover in Habit 6—still relate to a sluggish liver.[32] It's about how fast or slow your liver functions, not metabolism.

This is good because Valerie in the Whole & Free Health course got her energy back and was able to release weight easier after her first liver cleanse. She used a liver cleanse program and did a liver flush.

A liver flush cleanses bile ducts in the liver. Typically, gallstones also get released in the process. Dr. Clark says, "Cleaning the liver bile ducts is the most powerful procedure that you can do to improve your body's health."[33]

A liver flush protocol involves taking a liver cleanse supplement, then using Epsom salts and olive oil to flush out stones. Ideally this is done twice a year. Before deciding on a liver flush think about your medical condition. You can use vegetables high in fiber to cleanse your liver instead. Focus on foods that heal the liver, such as dark green leafy vegetables, celery, apples, or squash. Emotionally the liver is the anger center. It harbors emotions of unresolved anger, resentment, and regret.[34]

Cleansing Protocol from Dr. Hulda Clark[35]

Dr. Hulda Clark recommends we start with a colon cleanse, then do a digestive candida cleanse per Habit 1, then the kidneys, liver, and heavy metals.[36] Heavy metals are a major source of toxic overload from old tooth filling mercury amalgams (from all that sugar), the environment, and mercury in fish.[37] Cadmium, used to make dentures, is five times as toxic as lead and correlated with high blood pressure.[37]

Look into a variety of cleansing systems and find one that resonates with you. It takes work, but it's worth it. A full system cleanse helps you to attain and manifest your weight and eating freedom.

Cleanse Flowchart
The following is a suggested sequence for those completing the full Dr. Clark cleanse protocol.

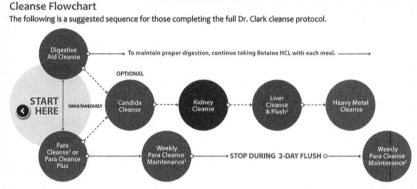

1 Stay on the weekly Para Cleanse Maintenance Program until the 2-day Liver Flush. Do not take during the 2-day Flush. Continue after the Liver Flush is complete. A minimum of 4 weeks of the Maintenance Program is recommended.

2 Repeat the 2-day Liver Flush 5 times. Wait 2 weeks between each Liver Flush.

Cleanse the Inside

Jesus gave a stern warning to the Pharisees about looking good on the outside but not minding their character. He said, "Blind Pharisee, first cleanse the inside of the cup and dish, that the outside of them may be clean also" (Matthew 23:26).

While cleaning your body internally isn't the same as character, consider its principles. Some of us spend more money on clothes, makeup, shoes, suits, houses, or fancy cars to look good on the outside while our organs die inside. They're crying out for water, nutrients, and cleansing. And like Jesus's words to them, if we clean up the inside, it manifests on the outside. Be like Hezekiah—quick to clean it up.

Tips to Habitize Cleanse

- Schedule one to three full body cleanses per year. Scheduling your cleanse on the calendar will help you get it done.

- Get the junk out of your house. Remember it's not loving your children or your spouse to allow processed foods for daily consumption in your home. Despite what commercials portray, real love doesn't promote disease.

- Research cleansing products to support completing a cleanse in the near future.

- Consider Epsom salt baths, infrared or dry sauna visits, or exercise to assist in healthy detoxification.

- Use a loofah bar in the shower to stimulate your lymph glands to move toxics out. Brush under arms and behind knees.

- Fasting periodically is a great solution to cleanse for physical and spiritual reasons. We'll discuss this more in Habit 6, as well as in Book 2.

- Drink from a BPA free water bottle and decline receipts made with BPA.

- Try natural, one-ingredient oils to moisture your skin instead of chemical-laden lotions. Coconut, olive, or grapeseed oils work great for hair, skin, and nails.

- Deep breathe to pull the lymph system into activation and calm the nervous system.

- Join *www.WholeNFreeHealth.com* to support your process. You'll also get ideas for products that have worked for others. And you can share any cleansing surprises without judgment.

REFLECTION QUESTIONS

1. How do you think an internal cleanse will support your weight and eating freedom?

   _____

   _____

2. What do you need to research in order to start a cleanse?

   _____

   _____

3. When will you commit to your next cleanse?

   _____

   _____

PRAYER

Father,

   Thank you for this insight to cleanse my temple. Remove all fear of cleansing my organs. I want to get the rubbish out. I ask you to help me find the right products and protocols to get my health back on track. And reveal to me what else I may need to cleanse in my life and character.

In Jesus's name, amen.

CHAPTER 9

HABIT #3 HYDRATE AM I THIRSTY?

Physiological Trigger – Dehydration

"Whoever drinks of this water will thirst again, but whoever drinks of the water that I shall give him will never thirst"

–JOHN 4:13–14A

It's better to have a pee dance than no pee dance at all.

Something most people don't know about me is that I'm a pee dancer. When I have to pee, I have to pee—now. Otherwise, I may dance in my pants.

As a professional speaker, I'm on my feet all day. I remember one time I needed to pee, and the class kept asking questions as I did my awkward pee dance. I darted to the rest room at the first break opportunity. When I came back in the room, embarrassed, I wanted to shout, "I'm okay! I didn't pee my pants!"

A friend, also a pee dancer, had me beat. At a campfire as stars glistened and the fire crackled, what started as an, "I'm laughing so hard that I'm crying," turned into, "I'm laughing so hard I just peed my pants!" In front of everyone, she shouted, "I'm peeing! Oh, my goodness, I'm peeing my pants!"

She quickly hovered to hold her privates, squirming every which way. Unable to stand upright, her face turned red and her smile transformed into a horrified O-like shape as she looked at the group. "It's running down my leg!" Someone ran over to give her a blanket to help her out. I wish I could say it was me.

No, I was with the other forty witnesses, hysterically laughing on the cold, dark, dirty benches stomping our feet in utter elation. But she was hydrated. Yes, ladies and gentlemen, she was hydrated.

Water drinkers are often inconvenienced by bathrooms. Yes, the inconvenience of relieving your body from its hard-working self to take two minutes to go to the rest room. What a pity.

Often, I pray, *God, please send me a restroom, quick.* Or, *thank you so much, Lord, for providing this toilet.* Truly, I'm super grateful when I'm in a room that has a bathroom nearby. It lets me drink my water in peace, knowing I'll have a place to pee. *Aaah, the little things.*

It's better to have a pee dance than no pee dance at all.

Your pee dance may not be fun in the moment. But, by golly, it's better to have a pee dance than no pee dance at all.

Dehydration Facts

1. We're made of 60 to 75 percent water. Our brains need 85 percent water to function, along with every other organ and function in the body from bones to eyes need water.[1]

2. Soda, energy drinks, and the like deplete your body of water causing dehydration because of high sugar and caffeine contents.[2]

3. Cancer cells survive in low-oxygen environments that are acidic. Water is the best, most cost effective way to increase oxygen to the blood flow.[3]

4. You get 20 percent of your daily hydration needs from fruits and vegetables that contain the highest quality water available.[4]

5. Light yellow urine and six to eight pee stops per day indicate we flush our systems well.[5]

6. In an eleven-year study of more than 190,000 people, one liter or less of water per day increased the risk of kidney stones by 75 to 86 percent.[6]

7. Water also hydrates the colon and supports healthy bowel function and elimination.[7]

8. Dehydration prevents sex hormone production, which is a primary cause of impotence and loss of libido.[8]

9. While not causal to stroke or dementia, one study showed that people who drank one diet drink per day were three times more likely to have a stroke or dementia.[9]

10. Dehydration causes toxic sediments to store in tissue space, fat, joints, kidneys, liver, brain, and skin. Water clears toxins.[10]

To survive we don't need as much water, but to thrive in health we do. I agree that it's not always fun finding a restroom when you're on the road, on a plane, or at the store. But body neglectors won't hydrate at the cost of inconvenience. That cost may be higher than you want to pay.

Cells are like sand—too many to measure. Each one needs H2O. In, *Your Body's Many Cries for Water*, Dr. F. Batmanghelidj—we'll call him Dr. B—shares incredible research on the impact of dehydration on health.

He attributes a lack of water to several physical concerns which include obesity, asthma, cancer, high cholesterol, insomnia, ADD, overeating, hormonal imbalance, anxiety, pain, allergies, Alzheimer's disease, depression, high blood pressure, and arthritis.[11]

That's a mouthful.

He believed physicians should first recommend hydration therapy to their ailing patients. In his research proved by thousands of testimonials, it's evident most diseases stem from a chronic case of dehydration at the genesis.

Are you dehydrated? Besides the issues mentioned, other signs of dehydration are thirst, constipation, dry eyes, dizziness, poor concentration, joint pain, dry scalp, confusion, down mood, unexplained hunger, headaches, excess saliva, dry skin, or dry mouth.

We know we're hydrated when we show no symptoms and urinate about 800 to 2000 mL a day (3.38 to 8.4 cups) or have six to eight pee stops of urine that's light yellow in color.

Blood plasma is the part of the red blood cell that carries raw material for use. About 90 percent of it is water.[12]

For example, that plasma water goes to places such as the brain to make sleep hormone melatonin or the good mood neurotransmitter serotonin. Melatonin and serotonin, as well as many other hormones and neurotransmitters, are dependent on hydrogen and oxygen molecules of H_2O atoms for their chemical composition.

Dr. B in his book *Obesity, Cancer, Depression: Their Common Cause & Natural Cure* said, "The brain's need for water is constant and urgent."[13]

Per Habit 2, every day of inadequate hydration is toxin multiplication. The less hydration the more toxins get lodged in various places in the body. As babies, our bodies were about 75 percent water, and by old age it's about 50 percent.[14] Health declines mid to late life when we're severely dehydrated. Most cancers are diagnosed after age fifty.[15] Coincidence? I think not.

Dr. B calls high blood pressure a "gross body water deficiency."[16] Because groups of capillaries in the vascular system begin to go out of business until they get the water funds they need to reopen, blood pressure increases.[17]

> " The less hydration the more toxins get lodged in various places in the body. "

One in three Americans have high blood pressure.[18] Dr. B is also adamant about the brain going from a grape to a raisin in diseases like Alzheimer's as a result of hydration deficit.

Orthopedic Surgeon, Dr. Lorraine Day, had a breast cancer tumor that grew at lightning speed. She saw death taking over her chest. No matter what she did, it grew as big as a cantaloupe.

Days before she thought she'd die, she found Dr. B's book *Your Body's Many Cries for Water*. Hydration shrank the tumor in weeks. She blamed her excessive coffee drinking for her malignant tumor.[19]

Russell had "chronic unintentional dehydration" like many others.[20] He did the recommended water cure from Dr. B's suggestions, along with a home water filtration system. In two weeks flat he cured both anxiety and depression. How's that for an inexpensive prescription bill?[21]

Why We're So Thirsty

Everyday Water Demand

Our bodies are like a Big Gulp®. And each one of our trillions of cells has to take a sip.[22] This makes water the most in-demand substance in our bodies. We lose water every time we sleep (perspiration and breathing vapor), eat (water is used in the digestive process), or move (perspiration). Water needs also increase if you exercise, live in high altitude like me (Colorado), or live in a hot climate where you sweat more.

We need to replenish water on a daily basis, but once the day is gone, you can't get it back. Like sleep, each new day is an opportunity to make sure to fill your body's cup.

Too Many Options

Another problem is we're drinking soda, sugar-sweetened beverages (SSBs), coffee, and alcohol. Each has a diuretic effect, especially caffeinated drinks and alcohol. It's a good practice to drink a cup of water for every cup of caffeinated beverage.

Alcohol is also a diuretic, for every 2 ounces of alcohol consumption (the size of a shot glass) diuretic hormones activate and excrete 200 mL of urine.[23]

If you don't drink alcohol, do you drink soda? Americans drink roughly twelve cans of soda per week or about 38 gallons of soda each year.[24] Sugary drink consumption, especially sodas, increase one's chance of obesity by 27 percent.[25] And one can per day increases diabetes risk by 18 percent.[26]

Furthermore, 4-Mel is a known chemical ingredient in darker sodas that helps to caramelize their texture and is a proven cancer catalyst.[27] Like cigarettes, I believe these drinks should come with a warning label.

On the flipside, one can release twenty-five pounds a year just from replacing sugary drinks with water.[28] Given that diabetes is the seventh leading cause of death in the United States and cancer the second, it may be a good idea to pass on the cola or sweet tea.[29]

We're super blessed to have drinkable water available to us. Water drinking is a habit that must be a daily focus, and we're blessed because there's little cost to do so.

> These signals can be confusing to an overeater because he or she will eat solid food when water was what was needed.

Medications

It's no secret medication causes the most chronic dehydration symptom, dry mouth. Medications require more water intake than average. It's sad to see how many prescriptions are filled that cause dehydration for diseases and ailments that may have been a by-product of dehydration masked in other names. If not treated properly with adequate water intake you'll be hooked on high cost prescriptions for life because the first issue wasn't properly treated.

Mixed Signals

The physiological trigger of dehydration is one because the brain gets energy from either hydroelectricity (energy by cellular water) or glucose.[30] This is a major problem leading to weight and eating bondage because the executive pre-frontal cortex in the brain sends signals for water or sugar based on its needs.

These signals can be confusing to an overeater because he or she will eat solid food when water was what was needed.[31] If you drink water before eating food, you'll be able to better discern when you need food or water. And if you just ate within an hour or so, chances are you need water, not food.

Several testimonials from Dr. B's water cure involve men and women releasing over thirty pounds or more from drinking the recommended amount of water with a tiny bit of high-quality salt on the tongue every few liters.[32]

Water was the beverage of choice for humans prior to hundred million-dollar marketing campaigns for soft drinks. If you want to win the weight and eating battle for good, you'll want to trade your sweet cancer-causing sodas, warm cup of joe, good times alcohol, and energy drinks for good old fashioned H_2O.[33]

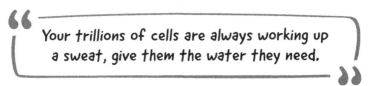

> " Your trillions of cells are always working up a sweat, give them the water they need. "

Solve Dehydration

Water is the primary source of energy. When fatigued or foggy headed, a tall glass of water is the first line of defense. Sources that dehydrate like an energy drink, should be the last. Your trillions of cells are always working up a sweat, give them the water they need.

The optimal amount of water to drink is not eight cups but much higher. The National Academies of Sciences, Engineering, and Medicine recommend 15.5 cups (3.7 liters) for men and 11.5 cups (2.7 liters) for women.[34] Dr. B recommends a half an ounce of water per pound of body weight.[35] But depending on your lifestyle, drink the amount that seems to work best for you.

Grab a Calculator to Figure Out Your Ideal Amount of Water Consumption
Total ounces = Your weight x .5
[Divide by 8 ounces to figure out how many cups you need per day]

Start today, drink your body's specific needs.[36] Also replace table salt with Himalayan pink salt or another high-quality unrefined sea salt of choice to get a greater spectrum of nutrients, which is vital in the body's water regulation process. Not much, but a little salt in your intake has many positive functions including opening up blood flow according to Dr. B.[37]

The best thing you can do as far as water quality is to get an in-home filtration system. A filter of some sort is necessary for tap water. Don't be a water snob, but just do what you can and follow all the habits to maximize effectiveness.

Whatever temperature water you drink is fine. Cold water is perfect for people who exercise or get a lot of activity. Hot water is great before, during, or after a meal to support digestion. Room temperature works well before a meal to increase fullness.

Dr. B recommends that we drink two cups about thirty minutes before meals and two cups every couple of hours after meals, but don't be legalistic about it. I sit a jug at my desk, pop lemon and straw in a glass, and pour and chug all day. It's better to drink up as much as you remember during the day so that you're not up at night interrupting sleep doing a horizontal pee dance.

Our True Water

With the woman at the well, Jesus said, "Whoever drinks of this water will thirst again, but whoever drinks of the water that I shall give him will never thirst. But the water that I shall give him will become in him a fountain of water springing up into everlasting life" (John 4:13–14).

Ladies and gentlemen drink your water. He said that we will thirst again for natural water. Jesus knew our human body was dependent on it. Second, He made it clear that the Word is our water and to be filled on spiritual water of His Word would bring us health in our bodies and everlasting life. Praise the Lord.

All this to say, carry your water bottle around like you do your cell phone. Water will help you to curb cravings. And you'll get used to hourly or bi-hourly bathroom visits.

Carry your water bottle around like you do your cell phone.

If the worst that can happen to you is a couple moments of the pee dance from time to time as you wait for the bathroom at a gas station, so what? At least you won't pee your pants in front of forty onlookers, right?

Tips to Habitize Hydration

- Carry your water bottle around like you do your cell phone. Keep water by your bed and at your desk.

- Drink as little as you can from plastic bottles but instead get a large, BPA/toxin-free plastic water bottle with a built-in straw. Replace all soft drinks with water. Reserve soft drinks for rare special occasions.

- Drink at least sixteen ounces first thing in the morning. Add lemon for more cleansing effects.

- To find out what your cellular hydration looks like, some fitness or natural health centers offer a body composition analysis. Try one.

- Eliminate caffeine and alcohol from your beverage options.

- Add flavor aids like fresh lemons, oranges, cucumbers or mint leaves, or flavor packets with no or low sugar.

- Set an alarm on your cell phone for every ninety minutes that reminds you to drink water.

- Take ten sips every time you do sip water. (Tip from a Whole & Free Health course participant.)

- Consider a reverse osmosis home filtration system to block up to 99 percent of toxins in the water supply.

- Read *Your Body's Many Cries for Water or Obesity, Cancer, Depression: Their Common Cause & Natural Cure* by Dr. F. Batmanghelidj, MD.

REFLECTION QUESTIONS ?

1. Which tip will you try to support your water intake?

    _____

    _____

2. What beverages have you consumed in the past twenty four hours?

    _____

    _____

3. How can you replace your current beverages with water to support
    your health?

    _____

    _____

PRAYER

Father,

I love how you've created my body and you know its needs. I'm not always the best at drinking the amount of water my body needs to thrive. Will you show me how to change this? Reveal to me any blocks I have to drinking more water. And help me to solve them. May I fulfill my thirst first with you, the water of my life, and with clean, filtered water for my body.

In Jesus's name, amen.

CHAPTER 10

HABIT #4 SLEEP
AM I TIRED?

Physiological Trigger – Poor Sleep

"It is vain for you to rise up early, To sit up late, To eat the bread of sorrows; For so He gives His beloved sleep"

−PSALM 127:2

We seek out junk food when tired as though taken over by the sugar demon.

L ack of sleep is the root of all evil—evil attitudes that is. We don't realize how much we take a lack of sleep out on our waistlines or loved ones. We've all nodded off a time or ten at church. But maybe your pastor isn't all that boring. Perhaps your nodding off was just a sign that you're sleep deprived—along with other symptoms, such as road rage, snappiness, and overeating.

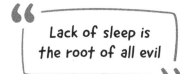

" Lack of sleep is the root of all evil "

In Psalm 127:2 King David said that all the getting up early and going to bed late to toil is in vain, but God gives His beloved sleep (peace). Sleep is a gift to yourself. However, if you're not sleeping, it doesn't mean your toiling or that you're not God's beloved.

Some people have the spiritual gift of sleep, but that isn't me.

I've struggled with sleep in Colorado's dry climate. So, I've had to learn all of these ideas from my own sleep changes. And sleep is similar to weight and eating issues because there's multiple factors that contribute to the quality and quantity of it. But the body habits help the most.

If you're like me, you may just like to stay up late in what researchers call intentional sleep deprivation. Only, burning the midnight oil on a consistent basis is detrimental to our health. We'll do our part to master the habit of quality sleep, which is seven to eight hours on a frequent basis. Note some people need up to nine hours for sleep quality.

Poor Sleep Facts

1. Less than six hours a night of sleep increases the likelihood of diabetes by 30 percent.[1]

2. Short sleepers are three times more likely to get a cold than eight hour sleepers.[2]

3. The gut produces 95 percent of serotonin and hormones that affect sleep. When gut balance is off, it can create chronic insomnia.[3]

4. Inadequate sleep causes hormonal changes that lead to overeating, slow metabolism, higher insulin resistance, and larger BMI (Body Mass Index).[4]

5. Blue light from cell phones, laptops, televisions, and other devices influence lesser quality and sleep duration if not shut off at least two to three hours before bed time.[5]

6. Partial sleep deprivation led to eating 385 extra calories per day.[6]

7. The largest body mass index is associated with less than five hours of sleep on average. Obese persons are likely to sleep less than seven hours per night.[7]

8. About 47.5 percent of obese short sleepers suffered sleep complaints compared with 25.5 percent of non-obese individuals in a study of 1,300 people.[8]

9. Psychological disturbances of hypochondriasis, depression, and hysteria are associated with obese short sleepers at higher rates than non-obese short sleepers.[9]

10. Alcohol may cause some women to fall asleep faster, but research shows they don't sleep as deeply through the night and have depressive moods.[10]

Wouldn't it be strange not to know you got to work until you were leaving? Sleep is one of those mysteries in life. You don't even know you've had it until you wake up from it. Sleep has two major functions. One is to clean up the brain and the other is to process the day's memories.

Your brain is a computer, sleep is the charge.

Adequate sleep happens in two main phases. Non-Rapid Eye Movement (NREM), which surveils the world around us so we're safe and Rapid Eye Movement (REM), the deep sleep, which puts us in a state of paralysis to not act out our dreams.

> **Your brain is a computer, sleep is the charge.**

These phases ebb and flow in their five stages over about four to five cycles per night. Ideally, our brains move through the cycles over seven to eight hours. If it does, we wake up beating our chest with enthusiasm to take on the world. Isn't God miraculous to build in a process to do all of these things?

The Case for Sleep

Poor sleepers don't fall or stay asleep smoothly, nor do they get enough sleep. Sleep apnea, snoring, insomnia, and short sleep are signs of an underlying health condition. Research confirms poor sleep or insomnia causes cognitive decline, difficultly learning, poor memory, bigger waistlines, accidents, and errors.[11]

On the note of accidents, drowsy drivers are the cause of 17 percent of fatal car accidents.[12] Not only is sleep deprivation while driving a horrible idea, poor sleep while we attempt to improve health is tragic.

Eve Van Cauter, Professor of Medicine at the University of Chicago called poor sleep the "royal route to obesity."[13]

> "Poor sleep while we attempt to improve health is tragic."

We're setting a new route.

Americans slept more in the past year or two.[14] But about 30 percent of us get less than five hours of sleep per night.[15] Most sleep less than six hours a night, which is 20 percent less than twenty years ago.[16] Research shows that being awake for eighteen hours affects the brain like a blood alcohol level of .08 to 1. Folks, that's DUI worthy.[17]

Shawn Stevenson, host of the podcast *The Model Health Show* suggests several tips for healthy sleep in his fantastic book *Sleep Smarter*. He said, "If you're focused on cutting calories to lose weight, then you might as well go ahead and buy yourself bigger clothes right now."[18]

Sleep is the bigger picture for weight and eating freedom. In particular, obesity and weight gain are attributed to less than seven hours of sleep per night.[19] Short sleep (less than seven hours within a twenty four hour period) can happen easily in what researchers call work week sleep debt. Those who slept an average of less than seven hours a night each week due to work had a 72 percent likelihood of obesity.[20]

And an even higher body mass index is correlated with less than five hours of sleep per night.[21] Research showed that people who got less than five hours were 29 percent more likely to gain about thirty pounds over the next decade and a half than those who slept at least seven hours.[22]

When tired, we eat more. When we lack sleep, the hunger satiation hormone leptin, which tells you not to eat, decreases by about 15.5 percent while the appetite hunger hormone ghrelin, which tells you to eat, increases by 14.9 percent.[23]

This explains poor sleep as a physiological trigger. We seek out junk food when we're tired as though taken over by the sugar demon. We eat 300 to 550 more calories following a night of inadequate sleep quantity or quality.[24]

> **We seek out junk food when we're tired as though taken over by the sugar demon.**

I've heard it called *tungry* (tired and hungry), which can make one *hangry* (hungry and angry). Studies also show our executive brain function that helps us with impulse control is compromised by poor sleep.[25]

Poor sleep equates to poor choices.

Let me emphasize this point a bit. We need sleep to rejuvenate our energy. When we don't sleep well, we're vulnerable to eating for energy. When we eat for energy, we choose energy dense foods—what's energy? Calories. Carrots are nutrient dense but not as energy dense (caloric) as candy.

And while the crackers, coffee, or candy bar seem like a quick fix, it's like duct tape on a car door: you'll need to keep taping it up to stay shut. Sleep quality and quantity patterns mimic poor eating choices.

Oftentimes we see exercise as the hallmark to better health, but sleep is just as important. In one study of two groups who ate well but one group exercised and the other group slept, both groups lost fifteen pounds.[26] So, if you eat well and sleep well, you're in for great benefits, including weight release, just as much as if you ate well and exercised. This is probably the best news you've heard all day if you're a couch potato. Soak it in, you actually don't have to exercise for health benefits.

But be careful not to oversleep either. Under sleepers increase cardiovascular risk by 11 percent, but over sleepers (more than nine hours consistently) are at a 33 percent increased risk of heart disease.[27]

> **Poor sleep equates to poor choices.**

Sleep is the ultimate fuel to productivity, mental clarity, and good moods. Please, don't make bedtime an option. It's non-negotiable in the pursuit of health.

A Few Reasons for Poor Sleep

Toxic Overload

Toxic overload does affect our sleep. Toxic overload makes every system stressed in your body, including the brain's ability to fall and stay asleep. Dehydration plays a part here as well because the less hydrated one is then the more toxins multiply.

Dr. Hulda Clark tested high ammonia levels in the brain of those with insomnia.[28] Ammonia is a by-product of the metabolic breakdown of foods, especially processed ones and proteins.[29] In addition, ammonia levels paired with certain parasites create disease.[30]

There are a few amino acids Dr. Hulda Clark mentions that support the body's natural detoxification of ammonia. Namely, arginine, ornithine, and tryptophan.

Another piece to the toxic overload puzzle is high levels of histamine that affect sleep. We eat many allergenic foods, such as wheat gluten, dairy, soy, and peanuts, that processed food companies know are allergens.[31] Allergens can create addictions to the foods that raise histamine, a neurotransmitter.[32]

High histamine levels affect sleep. This is why antihistamines like Benadryl® typically put us to sleep. Per Habit 1, gut health is related to good sleep. A healthy gut will support healthy histamine metabolism to keep levels at bay.

With all the toxin overloads from daily life pollutants, processed foods, and such as discussed in previous habits, the sleep hormone melatonin gets depleted.[33] Besides sleep, one of melatonin's other functions is to rid the body of free radicals, making it an effective anti-cancer agent.[34]

In Chinese medicine, the circadian rhythm is also in sync with organs. Type something like "Chinese circadian organ clock" in a search engine for images of organs that are associated with specific times your sleep is interrupted. It may be a specific organ is congested.

For example, if you wake up between one o'clock and two o'clock in the morning, your liver is probably congested and overactive. Chinese medicine usually heals whereas western medicine, although I appreciate it, chops off or prescribes.

High Cortisol Levels

Cortisol, a stress hormone produced in the adrenal glands, is a strong determinant for rejuvenating sleep. Cortisol works in cycles, and it's supposed to be high in the morning for get-up-and-go and lower at night to relax into sleep. It works in the natural body cycle called the circadian rhythm.[35]

High cortisol happens whenever we feel anxious, are stressed, or eat sugary foods. Dr. Pauline Harding, MD says, "A single late meal, skipped meal, or high glycemic snack will raise cortisol at night and disrupt sleep."[36]

The body's ability to handle sugary, starchy flour products like pizza, potatoes, rice, bread, cupcakes, or pasta gets worse as the day progresses.[37]

> " A single night of missed sleep can raise cortisol by 100 percent. "

High sugar, low fiber food choices increase cortisol for five hours following consumption.[38] Insulin increases are higher after eating for those who are overweight and obese, and so is cortisol.[39] A single night of missed sleep can raise cortisol by 100 percent.[40] Elevated midnight cortisol increases the risk for breast cancer.[41]

In Habit 1, I touched on grains and the gut, but non-sprouted grains are difficult on the gut because of the grain's shell. These grains secrete excess cortisol into your intestinal tract.[42] To support balanced cortisol levels, use sprouted grains (grains that are soaked prior to cooking).

Eat earlier and adopt more low sugar, high fiber foods to better relax into sleep. For us food addicts this is easier said than done, but promise you'll work on it.

There are many things you can do to balance your cortisol. The adrenal glands, the home of cortisol production, are one of the highest utilizers of vitamin C.[43] To balance cortisol, consider increasing vitamin C with broccoli, cabbage, spinach, or kale.

Magnesium also helps us metabolize food and sleep better.[44,45] Foods rich in magnesium are spinach, halibut, black beans, and pumpkin seeds. High stress cortisol depresses the immune system making us prone to infection".[46] This is why poor sleep makes us susceptible to colds and sickness.[47]

Caffeine is a deterrent to restorative sleep as well as to hormonal balance. A tiny amount increases cortisol, insulin, and other stress hormones.[48] It's best not to drink any at all, but you can drink decaf, drink black (no sugar which makes things worse), have seldom, or drink early in your day to reduce sleep problems.

Coffee has benefits but quality sleep, lasting energy, or hormonal balance are not one of them. Alcohol is also problematic for cortisol reduction and deep sleep. Refrain from alcohol on most nights or enjoy only on special occasions.

Poor Sleep Hygiene

Dr. Vyga Kaufmann, a psychologist in my neck of the woods (Colorado), has had success in her Cognitive Behavioral Therapy practice in treating insomniac clients with behavioral adjustments, such as using the bedroom only for sleep, making love, or reading a hardcopy book. She says, "Healthy sleep is shaped by the things we do all day."[49]

For example, if we work in the bedroom, where we should be sleeping, it will affect our ability to relax. I admit, I'm guilty of this at least twice a month, so I'm with you in efforts to reduce bad bedroom habits like spooning with the laptop.

Sleep hygiene describes protocols to set your bedroom up for successful sleep. It encompasses blackout curtains and removing screens, which include television, cell phones, electronic note pads, or computers from your bedroom.

" Reduce bad bedroom habits like spooning with the laptop. "

Other bedroom oasis recommendations experts suggest are skin tone or neutral colored walls, high quality cotton sheets, a humidifier, *Fung Shui*, and green plants. Shawn Stevenson has the best sleep power tips in his *Sleep Smarter* book.

Artificial Lighting

Humans used moonlight, lanterns, and candles to enjoy the evening for centuries—none of

> " For better sleep, it's best to shut off all screens at least two hours prior to bed. "

which reduced sleep quality. But now with artificial lighting, we can stay up all night. Ever been to New York City's Time Square? Screens embedded into buildings makes it daylight all the time there. And bedrooms are like this, with constant exposure to screens through devices.

We don't get enough natural light, which deters great health. Sunlight exposure during the day helps with restful sleep at night. Research shows that vitamin D is a missing component to quality sleep. Weight problems are also linked to vitamin D deficiency. Studies show that supplementation of 4,000 to 10,000 uL's of vitamin D can support more sleep.[50] Enough sunlight per day would be closer to 10,000 uL's of vitamin D.[51]

Screens pose another major threat to sleep. While there are benefits to blue light from screens, such as focus, there's tremendous research that proves blue light reduces the quality of sleep, quantity of sleep, and melatonin secretion.[52] For better sleep, it's best to shut off all screens at least two hours prior to bed.

Sleep Tight

In addition to the suggestions in this chapter, my best sleep advice is to practice body, soul, and spirit stewardship. The body habits, as well as emotional fitness and spiritual disciplines, support healthy sleep.

Also, place boundaries around your bedtime. Figure out that perfect evening regimen that helps you to snooze blissfully through the night.

Don't let sleep rule you either. Not getting my sleep used to stress me out. At times I felt led to pray in the midnight hour. I wanted to be obedient to the Holy Spirit when prompted to pray. But I was a little mad at praying for the same old people with the same issues that I needed to intercede for them about in the late hours. I had to let go of my need for sleep in service to the Holy Spirit and others. Use wisdom and have grace with yourself and others in the matter. Any body habit can become an idol.

Let nothing rule you except our King whose grace is sufficient.

Sweet Dreams

Remember, it was in deep sleep that God took a rib from Adam and made Eve (Genesis 2:21). And it was in deep sleep that Abraham was given a dream about the times to come (Genesis 15:12). Not that God will make you a spouse out of rib, but sleep is important, not only naturally but spiritually.

Dreams are noted throughout Scripture as a primary way God speaks to His people. I've had prophetic dreams since I was a child. Sometimes my sleep issues are a call to pray because insight from the Spirit needs to get to me via REM sleep.

The Lord said He'd pour out His Spirit on all people and we would have dreams (Joel 2:29). Check out fun reads like Jim Goll's *Dream Language* or Adam Thompson's *The Divinity Code to Understanding Your Dreams and Visions* to better interpret what God may be speaking to you.

> Dreams are noted throughout Scripture as a primary way God speaks to His people.

And yes, sometimes dreams are because of an ice cream and pizza binge, but you'll look forward to going to sleep when you get to see a movie in your mind.

Be mindful of the physiological trigger of poor sleep going forward. Personally, it's my hardest habit to master, but we need to keep pressing forward in the pursuit of health. Are you with me?

Tips to Habitize Sleep

- Create a bedtime routine and stick to it most nights.

- Eat three to four hours before bedtime to support lower insulin and cortisol levels.

- Take time before bed to thank God for all He did in your day and is doing in your life. Gratitude generates better sleep vibes.

- Research natural supplementation to improve sleep quality if needed. A sleep oriented herbal tea with herbs like chamomile, valerian, skullcap, kava kava, or uva ursi may help. Or try magnesium, tryptophan, ashwagandha, or melatonin supplements. Sleep medication is linked to premature death. [53] Given our goal is abundant life, sleep meds may be counterproductive.

- Try apps that stimulate REM brain waves. Brainwaves, Theta and Delta, can help to get us into deep sleep. Punch Delta or Theta sleep into YouTube for soothing sounds.

- Have a cut off time for electronic devices at least two hours before bed.

- Get the temperature right. The best temperature for sleep is 68 degrees or cooler.

- Do your best to drink water during the day and take your last pee right before you go to bed. Peeing in the middle of the night can be problematic to get back to sleep.

- Figure out ways to support your spouse's sleep including regular sexual relations, which releases oxytocin. Oxytocin reduces cortisol and stress. [54]

- If you didn't get the spiritual gift of sleep either, listen to Shawn Stevenson's enjoyable book *Sleep Smarter* on Audible for more tips.

REFLECTION QUESTIONS

1. How would you rate the quality of your sleep?

   _____

   _____

2. What time do you need to get to bed to ensure seven to eight hours of sleep?

   _____

   _____

3. What types of bedtime boundaries do you need to put in place?

   _____

   _____

PRAYER

Father,

Thank you for insight into better sleep. Help me to prioritize sleep for my health. Please reveal anything hindering my sleep quality. I appreciate that you can speak to me through my sleep. Please give me dreams to make going to sleep more exciting.

Thank you for all you're doing in my life.

In Jesus's name, amen.

CHAPTER 11

HABIT #5 EXERCISE AM I INACTIVE?

Physiological Trigger – Inactivity

---

*"He who says he abides in Him ought himself
to walk just as He walked"*

−1 JOHN 2:6

Get fit and stay fit, not zero percent
body fat but enough to outrun a street cat.

The first time I ran a 10k race I was about twelve years old. It went something like this.

"You want to come run a 10k for cancer with me in Philadelphia?" Aunt Lori asked over the phone.

"Yes, Aunt Lori, I can't wait!" I replied.

"Great, I'll pick you up Sunday at six o'clock in the morning. Be ready," she said and hung up.

Eager to hang out with my cool Aunt Lori, I didn't know what a 10k cancer run was, but it sounded good and noble, so why not? With no training and tight sneakers, it took me hours to run the 10k. I'll never forget the energy drain of the last mile. How I must've looked like such a goober, running with wild, large leg and arm movements in desperation, pleading for the finish line, rapidly panting until I got there.

I couldn't go to school the next day because the alarm went off and my arms, legs, and back refused to move. *Oh no, I'm paralyzed!* I thought. Panic set in. A scary moment as to be expected from a young person who piddled around from time to time with Mom's Jane Fonda workouts but never ran a 10k or a 1k anywhere.

I was so grateful when I realized I wasn't paralyzed. Nope, just young and dumb. My poor feet were smuggled into tight, new, black Nike sneakers in an attempt to make my big feet look smaller to peers. Blisters, black toe nails, and an aching body chased me for the rest of the week.

As a kid you don't think about weight or calories burned. I'd dance for hours in my bedroom because I loved to dance. It was easy to get lost in the joy of movement. Somewhere inside my head my desire to dance changed into a desire to lose weight. This switch made exercise a chore. It's like reading a book for homework. No one wants to do homework, but everyone wants to read what they want to read.

Children have boundless energy. As children we danced, jumped, swam, and annoyed adults to no end because adults can't keep up. Where did this energy go? What did you do as a kid for play? How can your kid play work for you in adulthood?

Inactivity Facts

1. A 2016 study of more than 1.44 million men and women showed that regular exercise decreased the risk of thirteen types of cancers, including liver, lung, breast, and colon cancers.[1]

2. Ages forty and up make up 50 percent of marathon finishers in the U.S. these days. In 1980, this figure was only 26 percent.[2]

3. Exercising for any amount of time reduces the premature death risk by 20 percent. Exercising thirty minutes most days reduces death by 31 percent. And exercising for ninety minutes most days reduces early death risk by 39 percent.[3,4]

4. Roughly 80 million Americans live a sedentary lifestyle.[5]

5. Any amount of strength training resulted in a lower body mass index and better eating, a 30 percent decrease in the risk of diabetes, and a 17 percent lower cardiovascular disease risk.[6]

6. People who do strength and cardio/aerobics at least 120 minutes per week lower their chance of diabetes by 65 percent.[7]

7. Ninety percent of people who have kept off thirty pounds or more do an hour of exercise most days.[8]

8. A study of women who walked each week had a 42 percent drop in breast cancer mortality risk.[9]

9. Disability risk is cut by 50 percent by walking.[10]

10. A high intensity interval workout for one minute can improve endurance and lower blood pressure.[11]

Do you wonder why someone hasn't invented the exercise-for-you robot yet in this technically advanced millennium? The odds of that happening are pretty low. If you want the benefits of exercise, you'll be the one who has to *do* the exercise.

And once you start, don't stop.

The National Weight Control Registry showed that one hour of exercise most days was a causal factor to permanent weight release. [12]

If you've mastered this habit, well done! If not, we've got to get this habit down, albeit not at the expense of other body habits.

God's Natural Remedy

> Once you start, don't stop.

Exercise is a miracle drug. And it's free. Like water, sleep, cleansing, and nutrition, activity is another natural remedy to a whole host of problems. With modern vehicles, we forget we have miracle wheels of our own, legs. One study of 80,000 females reduced their risks of cancer by 45 percent just by walking.[13]

> We forget we have miracle wheels of our own, legs.

The case for exercise is overwhelming. Exercise reduces the risk of more than thirteen types of cancer.[14] Exercise boosts mood and productivity and reduces anxiety and depression.[15] It reduces the effects and appearance of aging and extends life on average by four and a half years.[16,17] And exercise is so potent a medicine, it both prevents and reverses high blood pressure and diabetes.[18,19,20]

The best combo of exercise is a mix of cardio and strength training a couple times per week, which decreases the risk of diabetes by as much as 65 percent.[21] And any amount of strength training resulted in lower body mass index and better eating, a 30 percent decrease in diabetes risk, and a 17 percent lower cardiovascular disease risk.[22]

One study of mice that were near death divided the sick mice into two groups. One group exercised while sick and the other stayed sedentary. The mice who exercised three times per week regained strength and vitality. And they looked no different than the healthy mice despite their terminal illness.[23]

> Unless you're LeBron James, you have no business spending all day exercising when there's not millions attached.

Get Started

If you're an exerciser already, focus on other habits. But if it's arduous to think about moving off the couch in the evenings, don't worry about it. Studies show that diet alone can create powerful health outcomes. But those who exercise and don't change their diet won't get all the benefits.

When your energy shifts from mastering the body habits, you'll be compelled to move. It seems hard to get started, but most marathon runners start over the age of forty. Be the exception. Bryan Reese, at age forty-seven, broke his thirty-year sedentary lifestyle to complete three

Ironmans, which involve a 2.4 mile swim, a 112 mile bicycle ride, and 26.2 mile marathon run.[24] Be inspired. It's better late than never.

The World Health Organization recommends we get 150 to 300 minutes of exercise per week or 30 to 60 minutes five days per week.[25] The key here is not to associate weight loss with workouts. I know, it's counterintuitive. But therein lies a big problem.

Shows, like the *Biggest Loser,* make us think exercise is the only way to lose weight. But the biggest losers worked out six to seven hours every day![26] Um, yeah. That's ridiculous. Unless you're LeBron James, you have no business spending all day exercising when there's not millions attached.

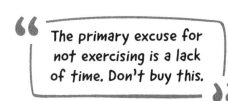

The primary excuse for not exercising is a lack of time. Don't buy this.

Ideally, we can dedicate one hour a day and combine it with some worship music or Bible study via an app because we know that exercise is mega-profitable, but not at the expense of godliness (1 Timothy 4:8). But all of the super fit people I know work out for two hours a day or do long workouts a couple times a week. And half of these people are in the fitness business—again a payment is attached.

Other research showed up to 450 minutes per week, or up to ninety minutes five days per week, was more beneficial.[27] I agree that some days I need more exercise and thrive on it. But this isn't always realistic or recommended in modern life, nor is it sustainable if you consider walking from the car to the front door a workout at the moment.

The primary excuse for not exercising is a lack of time.[28] Don't buy this. Chris walked every time he made a phone call. You can trade all the television time for sneakers, and you'll burn 120 calories more per day.[29]

Studies show a simple five-minute brisk walk once an hour can do the trick of reducing cravings and elevating mood.[30] One minute of ultra-intense exercise, like running upstairs a few times per week, delivered positive health improvements.[31]

For me, friends, sometimes I work out five minutes, and my mantra is something is better than nothing. On some days five minutes may be all you have. Just do your best and create the quantity that's realistic for you.

I also suggest finding activities you enjoy doing with loved ones. When you enjoy an activity, like basketball, tennis, or running, you're more likely to be consistent. This is especially true for female exercisers.[32] Workouts like pickleball are gaining traction for women because it's a sporty kind of fun.

Make it your mission to find something you love to do, such as dance, kickbox, or CrossFit. Try things until something jazzes you and do it often.

Move Motivation

Going forward, associate exercise with more short-term benefits to motivate yourself to do it. Short-term results are more motivating than longer term possible outcomes like weight loss.

First, mood. An immediate benefit is a happier mood for up to twenty four hours.[33] You may grunt the first ten minutes, but within twenty minutes of cardio exercise, significant physiological benefits occur and endorphins increase to buoy the worst of moods.[34] Depressed adults who did forty-five minutes of cardio three times per week improved their mood more than Zoloft (an antidepressant).[35] Exercise combined with water and nutrition will make you feel like your younger self in no time.

Second, productivity. When you need to get things done, exercise is one way to do it. Exercise improves blood flow to the brain, so people feel more productive because they learn faster and have a better memory.[36] Studies show that people who strength train had a better ability to plan and organize.[37] It also wards off Alzheimer's. Exercise also helps you accomplish more tasks in a day. Those who exercise think better and have better memory retrieval.[38]

Third, reduced appetite for junk foods. Studies show that people eat better when they exercise because they don't crave as much junk food.[39] I find all these benefits for myself.

Besides reducing other negative health risks, exercise is one thing you can do to improve your body image, body mass index, self-esteem, and overall happiness.[40]

We're made to move.

When healthier, you'll want to move, walk, run, skip—okay skip is a stretch, but you get my point. It's normal to want to move. It's abnormal not to. I'll share with you why it's been difficult to want to exercise in Habit 6.

> **We're made to move.**

Keep energy at the forefront. Focus on fitness itself. I mean, if you were chased right now, how far could you run? Get fit and stay fit, not zero percent body fat, but enough to outrun a street cat.

To get motivated, attach money to it. One study took money away from one group of participants (individually) each day they missed exercising. Money loss proved to be the best form of motivation compared with money gained.[41]

Put it into action, give your accountability partner 100 bucks for the month, and every time you miss working out, you lose three bucks while they keep it. That'll motivate you to hightail it outside. You can also try entering a competition. Nowadays there are apps that provide fitness challenges, or you can check out your workplace health incentive programs.

If you've failed at exercise attempts in the past, it's easy to think of excuses not to do it. You may think thoughts like I'm too busy, too big, too lazy, too scared, or too tired. You've probably taken a defibrillator to your dead exercise goal to revive it every January 1st, only to stop January 3rd. You're tired of making promises to yourself that you can't keep.

I get it.

But you know what, you're worth the try, try, try, try until you succeed strategy that's available by the grace of God. Start small but start.

"
You're worth the try, try, try, try until you succeed strategy that's available by the grace of God.
"

Go for consistency. Calendar activity five to six days per week. God said we're to do all of our work in six days (Exodus 20:9–11). Work used to be physical; therefore, we had activity built into our daily lives. But if you're not a farmer working sun up to sun down physically, you've got to get moving.

Start slow. It doesn't make sense to start off too strong because it's unsustainable.

A man, about sixty years old, came into the gym. From his attire, it looked like he hadn't worked out since the '80s. He sported tube socks up to his knees, canary yellow short shorts, a sweat band around his head, and wristbands. Since the fashion police weren't around, he started the treadmill at about six miles per hour, and shortly after, he turned red, was fighting to breathe, and sweating bullets, not to the oldies.

Meanwhile, I was on the treadmill next to him, praying to God he wouldn't have a heart attack, *Oh God, please, please, please don't let him die right here!* Suddenly, he stopped running, grabbed his gym bag, and left. I saw him months later, which provided relief, but don't be like that guy scaring innocent bystanders into heart palpitations. Start slow. Walk before you run, because slow and steady wins the race.

Next is a list of creative ways to get moving. As you review the list, check for excitement in your heart. When you decide what you like, be consistent using the sticker strategy.

Fun Checklist

What types of activities below seem to generate natural interest? Check all that apply.

☐ Complete a 5k	☐ Get a dog and walk it three times a day	☐ Learn to rollerblade
☐ Adult night at the skating rink	☐ Row at your local row club	☐ Jog around a lake or park
☐ Walk whenever you talk on the phone in evenings	☐ Tennis with people from *meetup.com*	☐ Plan a paintball visit
☐ Hit balls at the driving range	☐ Try Zumba	☐ Play volleyball with a church group
☐ Join a church league basketball team	☐ Join a men's or women's soccer group	☐ Worship dance in your house
☐ Flag football	☐ Hike the closest trails	☐ Hit homeruns at the batting cage
☐ Mountain bike in the woods	☐ Indoor rock climbing	☐ Salsa dance lessons
☐ Attend a ballroom dance event	☐ Line or country dancing	☐ Join a running group
☐ Walk around the city with friends	☐ Ride a bike-a-thon	☐ Test out a kickboxing workout

The Sticker Strategy

In 2009, I finally got fed up with my yo-yo exercising. That's when you exercise for a day and then you're off the next year. I decided to do what Jerry Seinfeld did with writing. He focused on his writing consistency. Each day he wrote, he gave himself an X on a wall calendar where he could see it.[42]

I did the same thing, but with stickers. Positive reinforcement when I did exercise and indifference (not self-condemnation) when I didn't paved the way for more grace, healing, wholeness, and exercise consistency in my life.

Despite popular belief, you and I both know it takes a lot longer than twenty-one days to form the exercise habit. So, I used the sticker strategy for two years. And this year I'm celebrating ten years of working out three to six days per week for fifty weeks per year. Thank you, Jesus! He can and will help you do it too!

I also recommend you track for at least one full year and post in the *WholeNFreeHealth.com* group when you've celebrated your first year.

Devices or apps for tracking are fine too, but old school, visible stickers are amazing. Yes, the smiley face ones, emoji's, heck, even stickers of ice cream or burgers. Get it done and post a sticker. Positive reinforcement works in pre-school through the lifespan to geriatric day care. Enjoy tracking, however you do it.

Be consistent. Whether you start with once a week or five days a week, be consistent. The sooner you start, the sooner the habit forms.

Also stay focused on body habits, especially nutrition, because you can't outrun a poor diet. And be mindful of not over-exercising because this could be a possible sign of an eating disorder called bulimia.

> Positive reinforcement works in pre-school through the lifespan to geriatric day care.

Bulimics may work out for many hours per day to burn off yesterday's binge eating episode. They do so to keep a normal weight. If you're prone to this, set a limit of ninety minutes on your exercise. I'll equip you with insight on compensatory eating behaviors in Book 2.

Jesus Walked

Walking is a hidden spiritual discipline that Christ demonstrated throughout the Scriptures. Jesus and the disciples didn't have the luxury of a car to ride around in or a desk job. They walked for miles per day. I know their movement strengthened them spiritually. Test it for yourself to see if exercise strengthens you spiritually.

The Scriptures say, "He who says he abides in Him ought himself also to walk just as He walked (1 John 2:6). See, we're to walk by the Spirit, but we also need to actually walk—and we know Jesus walked. A lot.

Exercise is a spiritual discipline. It brings too much body, soul, and spirit health not to be.

People, like my friend Chris Natzke, leadership coach and author of *Black Belt Leadership*, did the *Camino de Santiago*. Also called *The Way of Saint James* because the path leads to a cathedral built in his honor. The Camino de Santiago is an early Christian pilgrimage in which Saint James traveled to preach the gospel in Spain.[43]

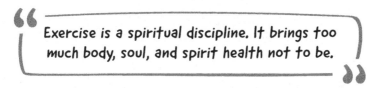

> Exercise is a spiritual discipline. It brings too much body, soul, and spirit health not to be.

Over 300,000 people still do this spiritual path annually for the enlightenment it brings.[44] Most start at the French-Spanish border and travel parts or all of the inspirational 500 mile journey. People typically walk ten to thirty miles per day and fellowship with strangers on the common path of life.

Walking is how we got the Gospel.

I don't walk, I run. But I use exercise to set my heart right for the day. A run outside with worship music on opens my heart for being more in the Spirit's flow the rest of the day. It doesn't replace quality time with the Lord, but it's a great combination. Not only is my heart in a more loving space, my prayer times are deeper. And my worship is stronger. Exercise connects us back to our healthiest identity of who we are, and we are children of God. It gives a greater sense of our Father's powerful presence.

Tips to Habitize Exercise

- Track progress using the sticker strategy, a device, or app to positively reinforce progress.

- Schedule your exercise on the calendar to increase your chance of getting it done.

- Combine prayer, worship music, and/or Scripture reading (apps) first thing in the morning.

- Join a gym with accountability. New fitness training centers are popping up everywhere, some require you to sign up for classes and pay a fee if you miss it. If there is no gym in your town, try apps like *StickK.com*.

- Start small, aim for five to ten minute walks, and each month increase that number.

- Unlink exercise from weight loss and link it to other immediate benefits, such as productivity, confidence, eating less junk, energy, or a happy mood.

- Routinize your exercise by making it a part of a daily routine. Don't think about it. Most of our delay is because we think ourselves out of doing it. Decide in the morning, jump out of bed, and get to it before you can talk yourself out of it.

- Find a fit friend to tag along with. We tend to become like the people we hang out with. You can join running groups, walking groups, or hiking clubs to meet fit people. Many faith focused fitness groups are on *meetup.com*.

- Make it competitive or join a fitness team. Research shows competition provides better results than social exercising.[45]

- Adopt the mantra "something is better than nothing" on days you don't want to do anything. Also pray. Plenty of times, I've asked the Holy Spirit to help me work out when motivation waned, and it works every time. Use exercise as a way to grow in the fruit of temperance.

- Enjoy your exercise. Stop forcing yourself to run if you hate it. It's harder to sustain exercise you don't enjoy. Be active. You don't have to burn a thousand calories. Just move. Hey, you can work out first then sit as your reward, fair?

REFLECTION QUESTIONS

1. Which tip to habitize exercise do you want to try next?

   _____

   _____

2. How long have you desired to make exercise a part of your daily routine?

   _____

   _____

3. How can you increase your activity within your lifestyle?

   _____

   _____

PRAYER

Holy Spirit,

Please reveal to me what I need to do to increase my physical activity. Heal any blocks and fears I may not even know I have about exercising. Help me to make exercise a part of my daily regime to do my part to ward off disease.

In Jesus' name, amen.

CHAPTER 12

HABIT #6 BALANCE
AM I HORMONAL?

Physiological Trigger – Hormonal Imbalance

---

*"But put on the Lord Jesus Christ, and make no
provision for the flesh, to fulfill its lusts"*

−ROMANS 13:14

Insulin conserves our energy. It says, "I've sat and I can't get up."

entlemen, please don't skip this habit assuming it doesn't
pertain to you. Insulin, estrogen, cortisol, thyroid, testosterone—hormones affect us all. The fifty odd hormones that
make up our endocrine system are major predictors of our vitality.

As we age these potent regulatory messengers send signals that
change our energy, weight, and mood. Think about it, too much estrogen and a man will grow breasts. Too much testosterone and a woman
will grow a beard.

Hormones are powerful.

Like a hurricane when out of balance they swoop in and wipe out
our efforts for better health. Hormonal imbalances are the strongest
physiological triggers that directly impact emotional health, eating decisions, and weight.

Hormonal imbalance is in the Scriptures. The woman with the issue of blood had a hormonal problem that Jesus healed (Mark 5:25). The mothers of Isaac, Esau and Jacob, Samuel, and Samson suffered from infertility (Genesis 16:1–2, Genesis 25:21, 1 Samuel 1:8, Judges 13:2–3).

I don't think Samson took steroids, but boy I can imagine he had more testosterone than a whole football team—way high on the testosterone spectrum. Sarah's drama with Hagar, hormonal (Genesis 16:3–6). Hormones make provisions for the flesh in spite of instructions not to (Romans 13:14). We need God to help us with hormones. And we can keep our flesh in check by balancing them.

Hormonal imbalances are the strongest physiological triggers that directly impact emotional health, eating decisions, and weight.

Hormonal Imbalance Facts

1. Caffeine increases epinephrine, norepinephrine, and hormones that affect weight, cortisol, and insulin.[1]

2. In men, unforgiveness raised cortisol and aged them.[2]

3. Men experience 20 percent declines in testosterone each decade after the age of thirty-five.[3]

4. An estimated 52 percent of Americans have an underactive thyroid function.[4]

5. Women with hormonal imbalance consume 275 percent more refined sugar than women who are hormonally balanced.[5]

6. Cortisol, insulin, estrogen, testosterone, and the thyroid all affect body mass.[6]

7. Exercise increases testosterone for up to three hours after a workout.[7]

8. Alcohol has a direct negative impact on the liver, brain, hormones, and blood sugar. Eliminate or reduce alcohol consumption to balance cortisol, estrogen levels, and your risk of cancers.[8]

9. Sperm counts dropped in half between 1973 and 2011 in North America, Europe, Australia, and New Zealand.[9]

10. Experts estimate that 47 million Americans have metabolic syndrome, a symptom of hormonal imbalances.[10]

Endurance to exercise, energy to meal plan, or enthusiasm to take back our health from snaccidents is difficult with hormonal imbalance. Hormones decline as we age, but with the Standard American Diet, endocrine disruptor chemicals, and hormones in conventional animal foods, our hormones decline sooner.[11,12,13] Body fat needs vary for men and women, which tells us that sex hormones go into the process of storing body fat.[14]

More than 50 percent of women who reduced caloric intake and exercised over a two-month period couldn't reduce body fat due to hormonal imbalances.[15] Hormonal imbalance symptoms take many forms like unexplained weight gain or loss, excessive water retention, hair coarseness, dryness, or loss, sleep problems, fertility challenges, and more. Endocrine system problems coexist with most chronic diseases.

Hormones get out of balance for several reasons we've already discussed like consuming highly refined processed foods and beverages, dehydration, inadequate activity, micronutrient deficiency, poor sleep, endocrine disruptors, and environmental toxins.

Another contributor is the meat supply.

The Meat Supply

All animal foods have some level of hormones by nature. However, since 1950 the FDA has approved hormonal steroids in both natural and synthetic forms.[16] In 1993, Recombinant Bovine Growth Hormone (rBGH also labeled rBST) was introduced to get meat to market faster. It's reported that it's injected in about 80 percent of cattle.[17] I would suspect this percentage from any fast food joint, but in the grocery version the USDA reports less than 17 percent of cows are treated.[18]

The problem is these meat hormones affect our hormones. Conventional meat and dairy versus organic grass fed is one of the biggest disruptors in hormonal management. Vegans I've interviewed report that they feel hormonally balanced as a direct outcome of not eating animal foods.[19]

The milk from cows given rBGH are a risk factor for cancer tumor growth because these hormones increase Insulin-like Growth Factor (IGF-1), which is proven to increase the risks of prostate, breast, and colon cancers.[20,21]

Concerns, like sperm quality reduction, higher rates of prostate and breast cancer, and early onset puberty seem to be consequences of hormonally charged meat and dairy.[22,23,24] Our meat is also pumped with antibiotics, which goes back to Habit 1's gut issues, because they live in concentrated animal feeding operations that have abominable, inhumane practices.

Don't get me wrong. I love a good, well-done steak. God did, too! (Leviticus 1:1–17). But consider organic, grass fed. Grass fed has more nutrients and doesn't use hormones to beef it up.[25]

Let's do basic education on what hormonal imbalances cause problems.

Hormones to Balance

Insulin

> " Insulin's primary function is to get glucose into cells and store fat. "

Dr. Jason Fung, in his book *The Obesity Code: Unlocking the Secrets of Weight Loss,* called out insulin resistance as the reason for obesity. Fung says, "Obesity is a hormonal dysregulation of fat accumulation."[26]

He refers to a weight set point like a thermostat stuck on a temperature. Our weight set point is very difficult to turn down because of insulin resistance. Insulin's primary function is to get glucose into cells and store fat.

Insulin is often described as a key to unlock cells so that glucose (blood sugar) can get into the cell. When insulin resistance occurs, insulin is unable to unlock cells for the group of glucose molecules to go inside. Insulin may be able to let one or two of them in the cell door, but the rest hang out on the front lawn.

And if glucose can't get into liver or muscle cells to be utilized for fuel, insulin sends the rowdy glucose molecules into neighboring fat cells. Kind of like if you couldn't get into your house because you were locked out, you'd go to your neighbor's house. Glucose that can't get in, goes to fat cells to hang out there instead.

The pancreas pumps insulin to handle the excess glucose in the system, becoming impaired. Insulin signals the body to eat more to support its glucose fat storage efforts. This translates into body mass growth and energy conservation.

It's an explanation for those worn butt prints on the sofa. Insulin conserves our energy. It's says, "I've sat, and I can't get up."[27] Hence, when insulin resistance occurs, it's very difficult to want to do much. A spiritual word for this is laziness. Insulin resistance promotes weight gain and lethargy. We want insulin sensitivity, not resistance. Insulin sensitivity is when cells welcome insulin to unlock their door so more glucose can get in.

High blood sugar is one indicator of insulin resistance. In a fasting blood glucose test, pre-diabetic levels that range between 100 mg/dl and 125 mg/dl are usually insulin resistant. Diabetics' blood fasting glucose is 126 mg/dl or higher.[28]

When insulin levels are high, it's almost impossible to release weight. We can gather this from research that shows insulin treatment for diabetes causes weight gain.[29] One study showed as much as nineteen pounds gained within six months.[30] And if you take insulin, you've probably seen this for yourself. Insulin as a correction may not be the best solution, especially since obesity and weight is a precursor to diabetes.

You're aware that processed foods, snacks, candies, and soda are rough for blood sugar, but they also alter hormones, all hormones. Dr. Fung says, "Refined carbohydrates, such as white sugar and white flour, cause the greatest increase in insulin levels."[31] When one hormone is out of balance it ricochets on the others too.

Some people are carbophobes (deathly afraid of carbohydrates in any form), but the type of carbohydrate makes a radical difference in fat storage. You can eat as many green beans as you want and as long as they're not smothered in gooey cheese you won't gain weight, but you'll likely release weight and certainly improve your health.

But those sugary corn muffins, expect weight gain a few hours after consumption. Let me tell you, I'm a huge fan of corn bread so I know this from personal experience. Furthermore, every time we eat, we increase insulin levels. But, those of us overweight or obese increase insulin twice as much when we eat compared with healthy weight eaters.[32]

Said another way, one of Fung's forerunners, Gary Taubes, author of *Why We Get Fat: And What To Do about It,* likens fat tissue growth to growing height. Like growth hormones are programmed to help us reach a certain height, insulin and other hormones drive us to store fat.[33]

> Those of us overweight or obese increase insulin twice as much when we eat compared with healthy weight eaters.

Overeating (gaining caloric energy) and lethargy (conserving caloric energy) is caused by our hormonal drive to store fat. A long-distance runner is driven to burn the energy of stored fat, whereas others through diet are driven to create fat instead. Taubes proves that it's the fat processing mechanisms from the dietary intake of chemicals and refined edible delights, especially high fructose corn syrup (HFCS), that throws our fat storage processing into overdrive.[34]

All fructose must be converted into glucose in the liver. Excess is converted to fat.[35] HFCS is considered the easiest to convert into fat as well because unlike fruit fructose, it has no binding agent to slow down metabolism.

When you drink soda with HFCS you speed up the metabolic process of fructose to fat, a major culprit of fatty liver disease.[36,37] Fructose consumption used to be half a pound per year in our diets from fruit,

> " HFCS consumption has a direct correlation
> with insulin resistance and obesity. "

which is positive, but in recent years we're eating over sixty pounds of fructose per person from processed foods and drinks, which is negative.[38]

HFCS consumption has a direct correlation with insulin resistance and obesity.[39] Unless we're in an end times apocalypse and food is scarce (which in that case grab a box of Twinkies® and run for the hills), please don't eat or drink it.

Besides increasing fiber intake (see Habit 2), Dr. Fung recommends intermittent fasting—the practice of giving your blood fasting insulin and glucose levels time to heal.[40]

To balance her hormones at sixty, Ann started intermittent fasting in July. By February of the next year, she had released eighteen pounds. Two nights a week, she stopped eating at seven o'clock and wouldn't eat again until eleven o'clock in the morning. This gave her hormones sixteen hours to get their balancing act together. She also overcame her processed food and sugar addiction to reduce hormonal effects.

Intermittent fasting is a fancy term for what used to be normal. In 1977, we ate three meals a day. Then meals were four and a half hours apart. Now we eat five to six times per day, with three and a half hours between meals or less.[41] Because we eat all day and night, insulin is always elevated. This makes our weight set point stay set on high.

Similar to a restaurant that gives patrons the opportunity to eat during operating hours, intermittent fasting has open feeding hours. When the feeding hours are over, the kitchen's closed.

This long period of fourteen to eighteen hours without food at night helps to heal elevated insulin levels. Although tasty, snacks aren't necessary. They're usually highly processed snaccidents waiting to happen anyway. Perhaps we balance by eating enough of the right stuff at meals to sustain not eating processed snacks between meals.

> " Although tasty, snacks aren't necessary. They're usually highly processed snaccidents waiting to happen anyway. "

In the chart below ketones represent fat burn, and glucose represents sugar burn. The arrows represent meal times.

M.P. Mattson et al. / Ageing Research Reviews 39 (2017) 46–58

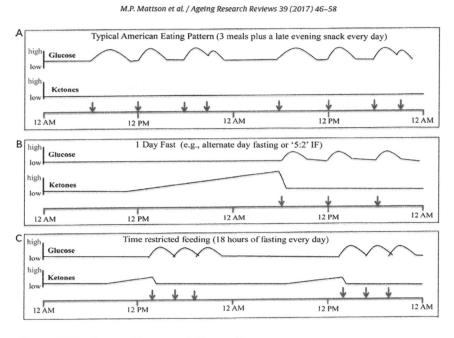

Figure 12.1 Fasting Glucose and Ketones[42]

In Chapter 17 we'll address the dieter's mindset so ideas like intermittent fasting don't become another fad diet. If you feel Spirit led to adopt this practice, try it once a week to start. An extreme approach usually causes weight gain recidivism. We'll cover more on fasting and food addiction in Book 2.

Insulin and cortisol are a dynamic duo when it comes to hormonal balance. When insulin's up, cortisol is also.

Cortisol

High cortisol increases insulin because it governs blood sugar.[43] It's also responsible for immune function and blood pressure.[44] We covered cortisol in Habit 4, but along with insomnia, other symptoms of high cortisol include a racing mind, strong task orientation, cravings for sugar after meals, the inability to go without food for four to six hours, over thirty-five inches around belly, edema, puffy face, bone loss, high blood sugar, high blood pressure, irregular cycles, or memory lapses.[45]

If you've wondered about belly fat, elevated cortisol is the culprit for missing buttons on pants. There's four times more cortisol receptors in the belly than elsewhere in the body.[46] Cortisol studies prove body mass index increases with higher levels of cortisol.[47] Those with high cortisol usually have high blood pressure and high glucose, since cortisol's job is to increase glucose and blood pressure.

To balance cortisol, practices of sleep and stress reduction work best. Remember from Habit 4, cortisol increases as much as 100 percent after one night of poor sleep.[48] So keep boundaries on bedtime.

Stress can be any sense of threat we feel. Gary Taubes said, "[Cortisol] may explain why some people get fatter when they get stressed, anxious, or depressed and eat more, and some people do the opposite."[49]

I call stressful event weight gain a *circumstantial trigger*. When we're going through a stressful event like divorce, a loved one dying, or a large financial expense, we experience weight gain for a period of time. Once the stressful circumstance is over, weight goes back to normal. This is the case with cortisol levels and stress.

In regard to stress hormones, Dr. Fung said, "Stress contains neither calories nor carbohydrates but can still lead to obesity." Do what you've got to do. Reduce commitments, manage a budget, work your life more

If you've wondered about belly fat, elevated cortisol is the culprit for missing buttons on pants.

through a calendar, and relieve stress. After all, that bumper sticker said, "You're too blessed to be stressed."

One outcome of elevated cortisol over time is adrenal fatigue. Adrenal fatigue speaks to chronically high cortisol and other stress hormones in the adrenals like adrenaline that make you feel exhausted, depressed, and anxious.[50]

It's a sign that the stores of stress hormones are depleted. Adrenal fatigue thwarts health efforts. One physical sign of adrenal fatigue is a darker indent around your eye sockets that seem to be sinking in. Reduce your stress to protect them from burn out or rebuild them if they already are.[51]

Thyroid

> " Take your temperature each day for a week, and if it's under 97.8 degrees most days, you likely have low thyroid function. "

The thyroid is in the throat area near the larynx. Thyroid hormone is produced at the direction of the hypothalamus (the hormone divisional leader under the brain's leadership) and made by the pituitary gland, but also converted to active use in the gut, liver, and tissues.[52]

The thyroid is responsible for utilizing caloric energy in all cells and heartbeat regulation, affecting metabolism, weight, and mood.[53] Symptoms of a low thyroid are thinning outer eyebrows, hoarse voice, puffy face, fatigue, dry skin, weakness, often feeling cold, sleep problems, impaired memory, or slow speech.[54]

Nutritional deficiencies of iodine, tyrosine, zinc, selenium, vitamins A, C, D, B2, B3, B12, and healthy fats contribute to a slow thyroid because they aid in its function.[55,56] Take your temperature each day for a week, if it's under 97.8 degrees most days, you likely have low thyroid function.[57]

Have your doctor check for TSH, thyroid stimulating hormone. The higher the TSH the slower the thyroid function. A TSH level toward the middle or lower end of the range may alleviate symptoms.[58] The standard TSH normal in medical practice is below what current research shows is most effective for thyroid function, which is why many go undiagnosed.[59,60] You can also check T3 (active thyroid hormone) and T4 (thyroid hormone in storage which converts to T3 when needed).

Studies show that a higher TSH is associated with obesity, but researchers haven't found a causal reason why.[61] Some who take medication for thyroid don't see much of an effect on weight—probably because it wasn't causal to their weight symptom.[62]

Low thyroid influences weight, but the American Thyroid Association states that weight release is only effective for about 10 percent of weight gained pre-treatment.[63] This is why managing overall hormonal balance is a more effective strategy for weight and eating freedom. If weight releases with thyroid support medications, then the thyroid was likely the causal problem. If not, it's probably another condition.

Anthony William, author of *Thyroid Healing*, attributes thyroid symptoms to a low-grade Epstein Barr Virus (EBV) in the liver not being properly treated.[64] He suggests that the sixty variations of EPV that affect an estimated 225 million Americans are causal to mystery illnesses like fibromyalgia, chronic fatigue syndrome, and hypothyroidism.[65]

> " Thyroid health affects a gang of reproductive health complications in women, such as miscarriages, infertility, and still births. "

He attests that an autoimmune response in the thyroid, called Hashimoto's disease, may be your immune system fighting off an undiagnosed variation of EBV.[66] Ask your doctor to check thyroid antibodies and consider Anthony William's recommendations on healing naturally.

Another worthy mention is my shero, Dana Trentini. Dana's an award-winning, hypothyroid health activist who miscarried her baby because of what doctors didn't know about thyroid health.

She found in her research that the American Thyroid Association warns about pregnancy complications because of low thyroid.[67] She also found thyroid health affects a gang of reproductive health complications in women, such as miscarriages, infertility, and still births.[68]

She wrote, "Research reveals hypothyroidism is linked to heart disease, diabetes, Alzheimer's, cancer, issues with the liver, kidneys, gall bladder, mental health, pregnancy complications, and more."[69]

Thyroid medication shouldn't be looked at as a weight loss miracle solution. But thyroid support may be necessary in your pursuit of health. There are natural ways to increase thyroid function and hormone—like kelp granules sprinkled on food which provides iodine or iodine supplementation.

Iodine is necessary for optimal thyroid function and works to increase T4 which converts to T3. Fluoride interferes with thyroid hormone, and it's in our toothpaste and tap water. Use a non-fluoridated toothpaste and filtered water to support these efforts.[70]

Testosterone

> If you feel like nothing excites or interests you, talk to your doctor about low-T.

Testosterone has many functions in the body including libido, muscle development, strength, stamina, and energy.[71] Low testosterone (low-T) symptoms are less motivation, low energy, low libido, anxiety, irritability, low stamina, weak muscles, and poor muscle growth.[72]

I figured out I had low-T when I felt blah. I traveled a great deal for work at the time, which taxed my body. If you feel like nothing excites or interests you, talk to your doctor about low-T because low-T levels may increase the risk for diabetes as well.

In one study of 300 men, 40 percent had diabetes and low-T.[73] Of those men, 25 percent weren't obese. Low-T is a factor of sub-optimal health. Low-T is also associated with a high body mass index, diabetes and insulin resistance.[74]

Check your testosterone with blood work. For women, Dr. Sara Gottfried recommends optimal blood testosterone levels to be between

75–130 uL.[75] When I had the case of the blahs, mine was at 4 uL. For men, Dr. Anna Cabeca, recommends testosterone ranges between 300–1000 uL, with optimal levels between 600–800 uL.[76]

Andropause, the male version of menopause, is when testosterone levels decline in males. It starts at age thirty-five and causes testosterone levels to drop approximately 20 percent in each of the following decades.[77] Menopause starts on average at age fifty-one. Women may see drops in all sex hormone levels.[78]

After you get your blood work, don't be surprised if yours is low. Dr. Andre Harris, OBGYN, talked about his intimacy issues with his wife as a result of testosterone imbalance in his humorous TED talk. Low-T affected their marital happiness and libido, especially for his wife. For him, it affected his weight. He felt "fat, flabby, and fatigued."[79]

> **God loves when couples connect passionately.
> Don't let low-T ruin your marital joy.**

He decided to utilize testosterone pellets, rice-sized bio-identical hormones implanted under the skin to boost levels. It worked. He and his wife eliminated marital unhappiness and poor libido. In his words, "It was on and 'poppin'" in the bedroom. God loves when couples connect passionately. Don't let low-T ruin your marital joy.

Dr. Harris also had energy to exercise before or after the work day, which affected his weight. Synthetic testosterone hormones have negative effects. But bio-identical hormone treatments are a natural way to go if other (less pricey) solutions don't work.

Overall, if you find yourself weepy or watching the soap operas, you probably could use a bit more testosterone support. However, some older men I've talked to like their new found sensitive side and really enjoy *The Young and the Restless,* which brings me to our last hormonal review.

Estrogen

Estrogen supports healthy bones, joints, and overall "juiciness" in the body as Dr. Sara Gottfried puts it in her comprehensive fabulous book, *The Hormone Cure*, geared toward women. Estrogen has a role in libido, body mass, and energy.[80] It's estimated that half of women over thirty-five are estrogen dominant, as well as anyone with a stubborn midsection.[81]

We want the optimal ranges of estrogen to be not too high and not too low. Estrogen has a direct effect on insulin resistance; therefore, it's a leading factor in body fat regulation.[82,83] Estrogen dominance can create health risk factors, including cancer, stroke, and thyroid dysfunction.[84]

By nature, fat cells produce estrogen. Obese men and women are typically estrogen dominant.[85] Dr. Anna Cabeca said, "The average sixty-year-old man has more circulating estrogen in his blood than the average sixty-year-old woman."[86] See, I wasn't kidding about the interest in soap operas in older men.

Estrogen dominance symptoms in women range from bloating, low libido, anxiety attacks, weight gain, insomnia, and memory lapses, to fuller breasts.[87] For men, signs are infertility, erectile dysfunction, and gynecomastia—the technical term for man boobs.[88] Estrogen can block thyroid function.[89]

> **Low estrogen is also pretty tough on couples in the love department.**

Low estrogen symptoms, such as irritability, joint aches, dryness, and low libido, affect men and women.[90,91] Men may have erectile dysfunction.[92] And women may have vaginal dryness. Low estrogen is also pretty tough on couples in the love department.

Another problem with low estrogen is that it stimulates binge eating.[93] Estrogen balance keeps leptin (appetite control) in check, whereas estrogen deficiency pokes leptin to request food.[94]

> **Low estrogen stimulates binge eating.**

In a study of rats who had their ovaries removed, the rats gained weight and only moved to get food, despite controls to stop overeating.[95] Ovaries are where estrogen is made in women. Although fed a normal amount of food, they gained weight. Once they were given estrogen all returned to normal, including their appetites and desire to move.

Similar to insulin, estrogen has a powerful effect on weight and eating behaviors. As Taubes quotes the researcher, "An animal doesn't get fat because it overeats, it overeats because it's getting fat."[96]

This is the power of our hormones.

And my lady friends, this explains why hormonal weeks are rough for binge eating desires because estrogen levels drop. See, overeating isn't because we're gluttons per say (we'll save the gluttony conversation for Book 2), but it's mostly a biological response.

You'll want to get your levels checked. Mayo Clinic suggests normal estrogen (as estradiol serum) ranges in women to be 13–350 pg/mL (postmenopausal about 40 pg/mL) and men between 10–40 pg/mL.[97] Dr. Sara Gottfried suggests women be in the top half of the range and postmenopausal women at 50 pg/mL for bone health.[98]

> " Overeating isn't because we're gluttons per say but it's mostly a biological response. "

Estrogenic foods may need to be eliminated. Nuances to estrogen balance are dairy and meat products. Dr. Josh Axe said, "The average U.S. citizen consumed 647 pounds of dairy. And anywhere from 60 to 80 percent of estrogens in the typical Western diet comes from milk and other dairy products. This is linked to a higher rate of testicular and prostate cancers."[99]

Soy can be a problem for estrogen and thyroid hormones, but the research is varied. Habit 2 facts note U.S. soy has genetically modified organisms (GMOs). Corn and wheat are also grown with GMOs.

Animal studies confirm that GMOs create tumors, cancers, and a host of other issues.[100,101] It's best to choose fermented non-GMO soy and organic non-GMO corn and wheat.

Keep Habit 2 in mind as BPA, dioxides, pesticides, phthalates, nonstick cookware, flame resistant chemicals, and so many more environmental chemicals mimic estrogen and attach to estrogen receptors creating toxic, bad girl strands of estrogen hormones called xenoestrogens.[102] These strands prevent real estrogen from working properly. Estrogen is especially sensitive to BPA.[103,104] Fiber intake helps keep your system clean from these toxins.

Supplements like Diindolylmethane (DIM), a phytonutrient derived from cruciferous vegetables, like cabbage and broccoli, are supportive in helping estrogens convert to testosterone and metabolize estrogen.[105]

Maca powder, put into smoothies, is effective for estrogen, thyroid, and testosterone imbalance symptom alleviation. It's also in the same vegetable family of cruciferous vegetables, like DIM, but it is grown in South America. Maca has proven results in reducing hormonal challenges like erectile dysfunction, infertility, muscle endurance, balancing estrogen, increasing muscle strength, and boosting libido.[106,107]

Consider natural remedies for the hormonal symptoms you have first. Powerful hormonal balancers, like DIM, maca powder, black cohosh, red ginseng, ashwagandha, holy basil, and rhodiola have proven results.

After you get blood work, research natural solutions to figure out which may work best for you. Synthetic hormone medications are extremely risky for sex hormones like estrogen and testosterone, do your homework first if they're prescribed.

Habitize Body Stewardship to Balance

Good news, you've learned the habits that best support hormonal balance, which is why I saved this habit for last. Keep things simple. Habitize Body Stewardship. Let's recap.

- Habit 1: **Nutrient Loading** supports hormonal balance because you get the building blocks hormones need. Vitamins, minerals, amino acids, and fatty acids all support hormonal function. Gut health is extremely important to proper nutrient absorption and hormone manufacturing.

- Habit 2: **Cleanse.** Hormones are converted in the liver. A clogged liver will affect hormone metabolism. A clean system helps to reduce xenoestrogens that create estrogen problems in men, women, and children.

- Habit 3: **Hydrate.** Hormones are messengers. To get the message to where it needs to go, they're transported. This happens through blood plasma, which is 90 percent water. Also, hormone molecules have a lifecycle. Water is vital to flush impaired molecules out of the system.

- Habit 4: **Sleep** is powerful to balance hormones, and you'll feel the effects the same day.

- Habit 5: **Exercise** is extra potent for all hormones, but specific types of exercise may benefit specific hormones. For example, walking, tai chi, and stretching help thyroid function and reduce cortisol.[108] To unleash more testosterone, reduce insulin, and balance estrogen, consider tough workouts like high intensity interval training (HIIT) and weight training.[109] A mix may be best because cortisol increases with exercise. Per Habit 5, frequency produces the most balanced results.

- Habit 6: **Balance.** Habitize body habits 1, 2, 3, 4, and 5, and the following tips.

The discussed hormones aren't the only ones to balance, but they're a great start. Focus on the fundamentals and allow your health to transform.

Tips to Habitize Hormonal Balance

- Habitize Body Stewardship. Each of the body habits are vital to hormonal balance. Eat green vegetables daily, cleanse your organs, drink plenty of water, prioritize sleep, and exercise for your hormones to naturally balance.

- Honor the Sabbath (Exodus 20:8,10–11). Enter into God's rest once a week to restore your spirit and soul by focusing on Him. A Sabbath has healing blessings (Isaiah 58:8,13).

- Get your hormonal blood work done. Ask for free and blood testosterone, full thyroid panel, estrogen, and a full metabolic panel. It's best to use a bio-identical hormone specialist or functional medicine physician.

- Take at least five minutes a day to destress. Read your Bible, pray, walk, unplug, stretch, or share your heart with someone.

- Monitor your hormonal cycles by tracking moods on the calendar.

- Try alternative therapies. Alternative therapies such as acupuncture, massage, and contemplative prayer meditation are effective at balancing hormones.

- Reduce or eliminate caffeine consumption.

- Increase protein consumption (plant-based ideal) to 20 to 30 grams per meal.[110]

- Ladies check out *The Hormone Cure* by Dr. Sara Gottfried to keep learning. Gentlemen, consider sites like Dr. Jade Teta's Metabolic effect at *metaboliceffect.com* or Dr. Anna Cabeca at *drannacabeca.com.*

- *Bonus Tip:* To the ladies that suffer with premenstrual syndrome (PMS), Lorraine Pintus, co-author of *Intimate Issues*, has an excellent, Christ-centered book around cultivating healthy attitudes around hormones, appropriately called *Jump off the Hormone Swing.* An estimated 90 percent of women experience PMS and 5 percent suffer debilitating symptoms.[111] Please consider if you want deeper healing on the matter.

REFLECTION QUESTIONS

1. How well do you manage your hormones?

   _____

   _____

2. Do you notice when your hormonal balance is off?

   _____

   _____

3. What tip(s) can you try to balance?

   _____

   _____

PRAYER

Father,

   Please reveal to me which hormones are causing stress for me. Lead me to the right doctor who understands hormonal balance. Protect me from wrong choices and support me to continue to learn about hormonal health.

In Jesus' name, amen.

CHAPTER 13

PRIORITIZE BODY STEWARDSHIP

"For as the body is one and has many members, but all the members of that one body, being many, are one body, so also is Christ"

−1 CORINTHIANS 12:12

The best caregivers honor their body, soul, and spirit.

Just like you'd prioritize an appointment with your senior pastor, do the same with your body stewardship. We underestimate how much the enemy works to distract us from great health. Satan knows if we don't prioritize health, we'll be less active in living and promoting the benefits of the Lord.

Like my dear family friend, who died on the way to church, our mission can be cut short because we don't prioritize body stewardship. Our health is a priority. Otherwise we'll prioritize it for the wrong reasons.

I'll repeat again, if we don't make self-care a priority, we'll be in a position where someone will need to care for us. Someone like a nurse, spouse, or an adult child. Crisis lurks at the door for body neglectors.

You'll find it's true, that when you honor your body, it will honor you in return. You'll have more energy to serve others well. To love others as yourself (Matthew 22:39).

> **Crisis lurks at the door for body neglectors.**

Nadine Roberts-Cornish, author of *Tears in My Gumbo: The Caregiver's Recipe for Resilience* said, "Love is the secret sauce in all the recipes of caregiving and is the healing source for our lives, for our world."[1]

Nadine understands how important it is for the caregiver to take care of others by making sure that we put our masks on first, as a flight attendant instructs. There are others in your life that you care for, give them your best. We're all caregivers to some degree, even if you only care for a plant.

The best caregivers honor their body, soul, and spirit.

Jesus took time to nurture Himself. He retreated into the wilderness or took walks alone to refresh. He served all of mankind.

The more we serve, the more critical it is to have adequate body, soul, and spirit care. Leaders know this. Many successful people nail these body habits. Body, soul, and spirit habits are critical for great success.

Nadine said to, above all, be driven by love. The love of God compels us to honor our temple, to refresh ourselves, and to care for others from His heart of love. Body habits support those efforts.

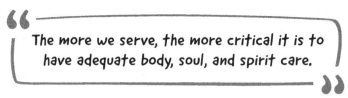

> The more we serve, the more critical it is to have adequate body, soul, and spirit care.

Chances are we'll need a caregiver at some point in our lives. Delay that point as long as you can. You have a destiny to attain. You have a purpose to fulfill. You have a calling in your life. And you have people that love you and need your love to get them through life!

I wouldn't be as soul happy and healthy as I am without the love of my grandparents. One of the benefits of my mom having me at nineteen years old was being raised with five grandparents alive most of my life. My grandparents are my heart. Their wisdom and love nurtured calm in my life of chaos.

You may be a grandparent. You may be a parent. You may lead a congregation or ministry. All of us are ministers.

The body of Christ at large has many components like the natural body (1 Corinthians 12:12–31). Each one has a function. You're needed for such a time as this.

You are important. You matter! And it's my honor to serve you with these habits.

Each body habit supports one another. Each one has a dramatic impact on your health, weight, eating, and emotions.

Consider making them easy:

- You're already eating – add green vegetables.
- You're already bathing – just clean your insides (not with soap).
- You're already drinking – make it mostly water.

> " **Seek progress, not perfection.** "

- You're already going to bed – make your bedroom an oasis.
- You're already hormonal – be intentional.

Seek progress, not perfection. Review your Call to Weight & Eating Freedom Action Plan from Chapter 5. As you declare, "I am healthy," you identify with being healthy. When these habits become who we are, body stewardship is easy.

Think of it this way, if Dwayne Johnson (The Rock), jumped inside of your body in a case of the body snatchers, do you think you'd be fit fairly quickly? Yes, indeed. He'd jump inside your body, run to the nearest gym, and start lifting weights!

After that he'd bake some fish and broccoli. Dwayne Johnson's identity drives him to be fit and eat well.[2] (But, technically, like Hercules, Dwayne Johnson is buff obese, just saying.) As you work on these habits, consider who you are. You are healthy.

It's God's will that you prosper in health (3 John 1:2). It's God's will for you to adopt these habits into your identity to prevent disease.

Fear the Lord and turn from the unhealthy desires of flesh as it brings health to do so (Proverbs 3:7–8).

To make it easier to adopt these habits, some people love an acronym for memory's sake. It wasn't authentic for me to switch the order of the chapters, because each habit builds on the next one, but it's my honest hope that you adopt these habits. So, I've changed a few words to make a good acronym. Cheers to a win-win for both of us.

THE BODY H.A.B.I.T.S.

H: Hydrate

A: Activity (Exercise)

B: Balance (Hormones)

I: NutrIent Load

T: DeTox (Cleanse)

S: Sleep

Nice, huh? Take a few moments to memorize H.A.B.I.T.S.

Congratulations for reading to this point. You're serious about taking back your health, and it shows. Every page turned is a victory.

I urge you to consider joining us in the *www.WholeNFreeHealth.com* to work on these habits with others. You'll get access to resources, as well as support to cheer on your transformation.

> **Every page turned is a victory.**

This journey takes time.

Every time you do something that honors your body, soul, and spirit, you're making progress in the right direction. Celebrate as you go, not with cake, but with worship. Praise Him for the little victories. God is with you! And so am I (in the WholeNFreeHealth.com group)!

Get great at managing your life. Prioritize body stewardship. We're not done, but you have the basics for what to focus on daily. Keep reading. Get your freedom from this book. And get your victory in Book 2 because the Lord needs you (Matthew 9:37). Yes, He used people throughout the Scriptures, and He wants you to partner with Him to establish His kingdom. May thy will be done on earth as it is in heaven (Matthew 6:10)!

He wants you to partner with Him to establish His kingdom.

REFLECTION QUESTIONS

1. How will you improve taking care of your temple?

_____

_____

2. Will you be your best for His glory? How so?

_____

_____

3. Will you break the chain of body neglect in your life once and for all? How so?

_____

_____

PRAYER

Dear Father,

I reject self-neglect. I recognize self-neglect as harmful to my spirit, soul, and body. I will no longer allow myself to operate in body neglect. Help me to appreciate the body you've created. Help me to prioritize my health in the midst of so many other responsibilities and obligations.

Show me what I need to let go of so that I can take better care of myself and enjoy my relationship with you and my loved ones more. Help me to be a vessel of love for others. Help me to give myself the time and attention I need. Show me that I am a temple of your Spirit. Use me for your kingdom. May your kingdom come and your will be done on earth as it is in heaven.

Thank you, Father.

In Jesus's name, amen.

• CHAPTER 14 •

GRUBBOLOGY

Say Hello to Your Inner Glutton

"And if a house is divided against itself, that house cannot stand"

−MARK 3:25

My Inner Glutton made me do it.

Welcome to Soul. Over the next several chapters we'll look at soul psychological aspects of the weight and eating equation. Because in regard to your relationship with food, you may have wondered, *Have I been crazy all this time and didn't know it?!* Don't worry, my friend, you're not crazy. For the purposes of this book, we'll assume you're relatively normal. But, the insanity inside of us is crazy.

Let's look at that sense of craziness this way: you have three parts within that keep the drama of weight and eating alive, and two of them are two sides of the same coin.

They are the:

Inner Glutton ⎱
Diet Nut ⎰ Both Make Up the Bound Self

Whole Self

Like a husband and wife are two people, but one unit, so is your Inner Glutton and Diet Nut. They're married—only it doesn't feel like holy matrimony, more like *Dr. Jekyll and Mr. Hyde*. They're part of the soul bound in fear, resistance, identity crisis, and the past. They operate distinctly. I'll explain both as we set up context for these psychological factors of weight and eating, Grubbology and her sister 'ology—Chubbology.

Let's start with your Inner Glutton.

Meet Your Inner Glutton

You know there's an Inner Glutton in you, but you may not have formally met. Allow me to introduce you. And, yes, I get you prefer to say goodbye, not hello, but to break free of weight and eating bondage, we'll need to get to know your Inner Glutton very intimately. Without conscious awareness, lasting change doesn't happen.

The Inner Glutton is the part of you overeating and engaging in other unwanted behaviors to sabotage health and weight. Most humans have one to some degree.

But our Inner Glutton may not show up as food choices for everyone. In our case, our Inner Glutton wants delicious food and finds herself in detention, written up for a case of food trouble. Without wisdom in the moment, she sabotages your healthy efforts. It's a story that goes just like my cookie story, only with your own version of cookie. The Inner Glutton is the part of us acting out of our hurting soul to meet internal unmet needs.

> **The Inner Glutton is the part of us acting out of our hurting soul to meet internal unmet needs.**

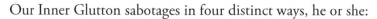

Our Inner Glutton sabotages in four distinct ways, he or she:

1. Eats too much. [An episode or binge is eating a large caloric volume within a two-hour time frame.]

2. Eats the wrong stuff. [Chooses food or drinks that cause problems mentally, physically, emotionally, spiritually, or otherwise.]

3. Avoids the right stuff. [Chooses to avoid food or drinks able to help solve problems mentally, physically, emotionally, spiritually, or otherwise.]

4. Neglects body stewardship.

Our weight and eating struggles exhaust our strength of will from this war within. Almost without any effort, we end up in a place of hopeless despair.

We resolve in our hearts:

"I'll always be this way."

"I must be made to be overweight."

"I'll never win so why try?"

"My whole family is like this, I don't stand a chance."

We then proceed to eat whatever, whenever.

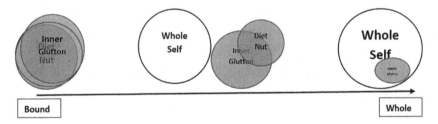

Figure 14.1 Process of Bound to Whole Self

In these cases, you and your Inner Glutton haven't begun the process of separation to integration. For some of us, the Inner Glutton is our identity. Like a Siamese twin, the lines are blurred between who our Inner Glutton is and who our whole self is.

We *are* the weight and eating struggle.

We really don't know who we are without excess fat, food crazies, binges, or dieting distractions. Consequently, we're unable to affect lasting change if our whole self isn't identifiable. Part of the vision work in The Call to Weight & Eating Freedom Action Plan was to align our hearts with our whole self.

> We really don't know who we are without excess fat, food crazies, binges, or dieting distractions.

It's also possible for the Inner Glutton to completely change faces and turn into a Diet Nut to attempt to control the out-of-control Inner Glutton side. All this mischievousness drives your whole self bonkers. You then doubt your ability to get healthy, stay healthy, and be healthy for life. And guys bear with me as I use the she pronoun to emphasize these distinctions.

Diet Nut – The Inner Glutton's Alter Ego

Meet Diet Nut. Your Inner Glutton does the sabotaging, and your Diet Nut devises diet plans to clean up the damage. Your Inner Glutton will eat all she wants on the weekends. Then Sunday night, Diet Nut gets fed up and kicks Inner Glutton back into shape on Monday, of course, with a strict, diet fix.

> Your Inner Glutton is childlike in nature, a rebel type, whereas your Diet Nut is a strict parent, a Pharisee type.

Your Inner Glutton is childlike in nature, a rebel type, whereas your Diet Nut is a strict parent, a Pharisee type. Your Inner Glutton engages in her antics and like a child says, "I'll eat whatever I want, when I want, and however much I want!" Then heads to the kitchen to bake brownies.

Diet Nut gets frustrated and says, "Why did you eat all those brownies? I can't stand you! It's all chicken and broccoli for you after this, missy!" As Diet Nut proceeds to research the latest get-skinny-quick plan.

Hence, the war within continues.

Understand this flipside of the coin because it's an all or nothing game—black or white, either all out-of-control [Inner Glutton] or all in-control [Diet Nut]. No grace. No balance. No love.

Our Diet Nut is the part of us that:

1. Devises diet plans. [Restricts eating, eats perfectly, and works out to death.]

2. Criticizes body parts, body shape, and size.

3. Distracts us from dealing with soul wounds.

4. Controls an out-of-control identity crisis.

Your Whole Self – A Health Warrior

Your whole self supersedes your Inner Glutton and Diet Nut. It's the part of you seeking freedom for lasting change, permanent weight release, and energy to do good for the kingdom's sake.

It's the part reading this book or committed to the Whole & Free Health course. It's the part that operates out of God's love and is highly connected with God's Spirit. It's your authentic identity. The real you. Whole Self emerges when your sense of identity of feeling broken or bound is cleared up. Because the truth of your identity in Christ is you're not broken or bound.

And my, oh my, is it tough to hear your true voice. When she's screaming her truth, we order a big ol' burrito to tune her out. We miss her heart's need and live in this unrelenting cycle of shame and guilt.

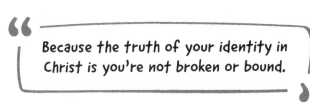

> Because the truth of your identity in Christ is you're not broken or bound.

Grubbology
(noun) Grub-ba-lo-gy
the made up psychological study of why we overeat

At this point, you're probably wondering how to get away from your Inner Glutton. But before you chase her down the street with a machete, screaming, "Stop sabotaging me, you demon child!" – know your Inner Glutton isn't to be shamed.

She's to be observed.

After all, you've shamed her enough all these years, and it doesn't create a healthier body or a happier you. She wants you to pay attention. She wants you to see her asking for your help to fulfill a need.

Your Inner Glutton is a wise teacher.

She's teaching you about your need be it spiritual, relational, emotional, physical, mental, and even financial and material. It's been said, "When the student is ready, the teacher appears." And the teacher, your own Inner Glutton, has been with you this whole time to lead you to health and back to your whole self.

This time is different because we're not going to treat this part of us in the same critical way. We're not going to fight her, shame her, or force her. There's no condemnation in Christ Jesus, but there's been plenty of condemnation within our own self (Romans 8:1).

This behavior pattern must end for true health to emerge. Rather than the constant inner brutality, partner with your Inner Glutton to understand what she's trying to tell you.

> **There's no condemnation in Christ Jesus, but there's been plenty of condemnation within our own self.**

All this to say, she has been your companion for many reasons. When she acts out, it's not because she wants to sabotage you, but it's because she's trying to help, to offer love by stuffing you with food. And like that ugly Christmas gift, you're thinking, *Thanks, but no really, you shouldn't have.*

Might I ask, how is your relationship with you? How do you treat yourself when you feel you've sabotaged your efforts? Do you offer compassion to yourself? Do you treat yourself harshly by restricting? Do you make excuses and stay circling the mountain? Or can we mistake you for a UFC boxing champ?

Over time, as you learn how to do relationships with yourself, God, food, and people better, Inner Glutton transforms, and she heals from feeling shamed and unsafe. She no longer uses food to fill unmet needs. She's a loving partner with you on the journey to a whole, free, abundant life in Christ.

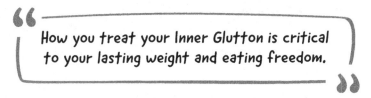

> " How you treat your Inner Glutton is critical to your lasting weight and eating freedom. "

And you may think you're great at relationships, but if we look closer, are you really sharing your true vulnerabilities? Or is food helping you to cope with all that mushy stuff?

As you gain greater consciousness, throughout this delightful reading experience (I hope), you'll learn patterns, behaviors, and self-talk from the Inner Glutton to prevent food fights. How you treat your Inner Glutton is critical to your lasting weight and eating freedom.

Let's learn how to love *all* of you—mistakes, love handles, warts, and all. Your Inner Glutton wants to help you learn how to love yourself. She seeks food because she's soul hungry, eating for comfort, fun, connection, and healing. She's using food to help get these needs met.

1. **Inner Glutton wants comfort.** Eating comforts. Life can be challenging, and we all need comfort, which is why we're given a Comforter, the Holy Spirit (John 14:16). The act of eating itself with the sensations of taste, touch, sight, and smell stimulated, gives us comfort we need in life's happenstances. From the time we're babies, sucking and chewing soothes.

Every human needs food, but when Inner Glutton is eating too much or choosing the wrong stuff, she's attempting to be comforted from a host of non-physiological needs by food. Food is and always will be a type of comfort.

And even if you don't live in the south, we know comfort foods are good for the soul but really rough on the hips. We, however, eat for comfort too frequently. And comfort isn't only at a funeral repast but in daily life. This requires intervention of the supernatural kind. How can you lean into Holy Spirit to provide comfort?

2. **Inner Glutton wants fun.** Eating is a form of fun. The average American works forty-seven hours a week according to Gallup data.[1] We wake up early to get to work and stay up late to get work done. Leisure isn't a nice-to-have part of life, it's a need. Church folk are guilty of not enough enjoyment. Some churches have so many services all throughout the week, who has time to see the world or enjoy nature?

    I know people who grew up so traumatized from the number of hours they spent in church with their grandmother as a child that now they don't ever go, and Lord knows they need Jesus. Jokes aside, perhaps fun is underrated.

    Food has been the only acceptable thing some church folks have fun with. We've given up worldly ideas of fun, but we still need fun. Hectic parts of life are managed better when balanced with pleasure.

> Leisure isn't a nice-to-have part of life, it's a need.

Enjoy family, friends, God's earth, and new adventures. To squeeze less pleasure out of food, we need to squeeze more pleasure out of life. The Inner Glutton is a girl (or guy) who just wants to have fun, but fun ends up in a brawl with mug shots. Her search to feel better, for stimulation, starts with a slice and quickly leads to a whole pizza.

Sadly, she gets amnesia the next day. Is your life too much work and not enough play? Where else can you gather pleasure instead of from food? What leisure activities can you enjoy without living around food? What hobbies can you develop?

3. **Inner Glutton wants connection.** Inner Glutton perceives food as love. According to Maslow's hierarchy of needs, every human has a need for family love, relationships, and belonging. But, what if it's unsafe or difficult to connect with others?

> **We just feel safer with food than siblings, parents, spouses, or colleagues.**

What if she feels lonely and has no one to talk to? Eating may be more reliable than people. We need others to listen and understand us. We just feel safer with food than siblings, parents, spouses, or colleagues. We try to love ourselves—only eating love is short lived because it's followed quickly by guilt. Guilt is an alarm that says the love we're trying to offer isn't real love at all.

Inner Glutton wants your love, your friendship. But you've been so frustrated with her activities you may not realize how much you condemn, judge, hurt, or criticize her. You hold a part of yourself in contempt.

Our constant attack toward unfavorable food behaviors causes more unfavorable food behaviors. It sparks a rebellion from your Inner Glutton 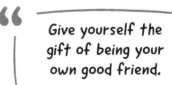 because you're not listening. Give yourself the gift of being your own good friend. Be kind, loving, encouraging, and forgive yourself, especially when you fail. How can you be a better friend to you? What real Christ-centered friendships can you develop?

> **Give yourself the gift of being your own good friend.**

4. **Your Inner Glutton wants your healing**. We eat and distract ourselves from the emotions we need to feel and identity we need to heal. Every time Inner Glutton acts up, there's a chance to learn who you are and what's eating you.

Your Inner Glutton has insight to help you to grow beyond any part of your identity that's confused, broken, hurt, or damaged from an upbringing where you were not emotionally heard, validated, approved, encouraged, or honored for the unique, fearfully and wonderfully made, marvelous soul that God made you to be (Psalm 139:14).

A shame based identity is a false identity because it lives in lies about who you are. Your real self is hidden and wants to come out of hiding. Your Inner Glutton can help you discover your truth by bringing out your identity into a restored, whole, authentic you. Your authentic you doesn't have this struggle or excess soul, body, or spiritual weight.

Let's work with our Inner Glutton to see beyond the tactics into our true heart to heal every empty place we try to fill. When Inner Glutton emerges, seek healing and ask yourself, "Am I being the real me?" or "What's on my heart?"

> A shame based identity is a false identity because it's living in lies about who you are.

We'll discuss Diet Nut in subsequent chapters. For now, can you see how much your Inner Glutton wants to help you gain comfort, fun, connection, and healing?

The Unmet Needs of Inner Glutton

Unmet needs drive our sabotaging behaviors. Essentially, unmet needs trigger Inner Glutton. At the core of our destructive behavior is an unmet need we're trying to fill. But the hole in our soul cannot be filled with the wrong filler. It's like filling a car up with water in the tank. It won't move right, and no amount you pour into the tank will make it go.

An unmet need must be acknowledged or met. A need is not, and probably won't ever be, a bag of M&M's®. This may satisfy an addicted, physiological need for sugar, chocolate, or fat but not a sincere heart need.

Common scenarios that trigger Inner Glutton:

- Your spouse yells at you when you need to feel heard. Inner Glutton is there for you with gummy bears.

- Your boss cuts you off in a work meeting when you need validation. Inner Glutton soothes your upset with ice cream.

- Your money isn't covering bills when you need financial security. Inner Glutton provides chocolate to cope with the stress of lack of resources.

In these examples, a need had to be acknowledged. When Inner Glutton is on the verge of sabotage, ask yourself, "What do I need?" Then, acknowledge that. Simply say, "I need connection." Give this need to the Holy Spirit, and He will comfort you and provide ideas to get that need met, such as "Call Cindy" or "Pray." This process is almost so simple it's silly. But it works.

> A need is not, and probably won't ever be, a bag of M&M's.

All your need *needs* is to be acknowledged. If not, your heart's cry is stuffed down with chips and guac. As you learn, observe, and seek what's underneath your Inner Glutton's episodes, you'll get to know yourself and your needs.

Human needs are God given. And life is a process of helping us gain fulfillment of Christ in all of them. As Paul said, "And my God shall supply all your need(s) according to His riches in glory by Christ Jesus" (Philippians 4:19).

What Do You Need?

The Inner Glutton struggles to get needs met in a healthy way because she learned early in life that she wasn't worthy of getting her needs met. When we learn this through subtle and overt rejection from caregivers, we stop relying on other people to meet our needs.

To meet our needs, Inner Glutton resorts to what she knows best: eating too much, choosing the wrong stuff, not choosing the right stuff, and neglecting herself.

> We've become dependent on food as an extension of our false identity, centered around shaming and guilting ourselves.

Only it doesn't satisfy.

We've become dependent on food as an extension of our false identity, centered around shaming and guilting ourselves.

We have dependency needs that we've felt too ashamed or undeserving to have met. Peek at the dependency needs below and ponder how your unmet needs have triggered you to overeat.

Self-Value	Stimulation	Socially Healthy Primary Caretakers	Structure	Security	Stroking
• You feel you matter • You're taken seriously • Sense of being for oneself • Sense of self • Being different	• Pleasure/pain • Fun • Excitement • Challenge • Play	• Mirroring/echoing • Affirmation of feelings, needs, time, and drives • Interpersonal bridge • Identification • Need to nurture • Significant relationship	• Direction • Modeling • Boundaries • Predictability • Having limits set	• Medical care • Enough food • Protection • Clothing • Shelter	• Attention • Being recognized • Being held and touched • Encouragement • Praise • Warmth

Figure 14.2 Basic Dependency Needs in Adult Life [Adopted from *Healing the Shame that Binds You* by John Bradshaw] [2]

In addition to dependency needs, consider Maslow's Hierarchy of Needs. Abraham Maslow originally created the Hierarchy of Needs Theory in 1943. He classified human needs into three areas: physiological needs (body), psychological needs (soul), and self-actualization (spirit).

If the physiological needs—food, shelter, and water—aren't met, it may be difficult to aspire to the higher oriented spirituality of self-actualization (God given potential) or transcendence (helping others get free).[3]

Which of your needs do you have difficulty getting met? Place those needs before God in prayer as we continue to gain more understanding about them.

Figure 14.3 Maslow's Hierarchy of Needs[4]

The Observation Assignment

The most important action you can do right now is become conscious to your Inner Glutton's unmet needs and triggers. Observe your Inner Glutton. Note your observations. Track his episodes. Like a detective, look for clues on your unmet needs—the when, why, what, and how he is eating.

The art of observation is first becoming conscious to the part of you that sabotages. Observation leads to exploration. Exploration leads to understanding. Understanding leads to new strategies. Through observation, we can learn to mitigate causes and their effects.

Be sure to log your observations over the next several weeks so that you'll be more alert to your Inner Glutton and Diet Nut's cycles of destruction.

As a lifelong practice:

- Observe how you respond to your eating mistakes. Pay attention to how you speak to yourself. Are you loving or critical? Kind or mean?

- Observe events, feelings, and situations that led to eating mistakes. Watch what triggers an overeating episode. Notice Diet Nut's reactions when your Inner Glutton has acted out.

- Observe your food patterns in greater detail. What foods spark obsessive eating, down moods, food cravings, or feeling ashamed of your body?

You'll get aha! moments as you observe and log your findings about your Inner Glutton. As you learn over time, he'll heal.

Like Sam realized, "My Inner Glutton was really active on Friday night after work. For as long as I can remember, I tend to overeat on Friday nights. Hmm, maybe my Inner Glutton's exhausted from the week. It seems I need fun and connection to balance out work, but I find food instead. I can plan something to look forward to on Friday nights."

Or Yasmeen recognized, "My Inner Glutton is very active after conversations with my uncle. What is it about our conversation topics that makes me eat after our calls? He always talks negatively about my mother, and I want to say something, but [aha! moment] I'm eating what I want to say!"

"I can journal out what I want to say, and the next time I speak with him, I'll be honest." Yasmeen tried this and she noticed she didn't eat so much after their calls. It was difficult to be honest, but her observation helped her gather insight and correct a piece of the weight and eating puzzle.

As you become more conscious, your whole self partners with your Inner Glutton and Diet Nut. Observation is the main daily task because we're in the process of becoming more aware to who and what we're hiding under our false sense of identity. As we move along, we'll continue to build on this foundation. Because, there's an entrenched fear to overcome to heal your Inner Glutton.

The fear of the Whole Self.

REFLECTION QUESTIONS

1. Have you felt shame around your needs?

   _____

   _____

2. What need did your Inner Glutton want acknowledged last time he/she acted up?

   _____

   _____

3. How can you offer more love and support to yourself when you mess up?

   _____

   _____

PRAYER

Dear Lord,

Praise your holy name for help today with my Inner Glutton and Diet Nut. I pray for greater awareness and strength to overcome weight and eating bondage. Increase my understanding of my relationship with myself and food. Help me to love myself when it's hard.

Help me to love me like you do, not in a worldly way of conceit but in a godly way to love my neighbors as myself and honor Your name.

Thank you for security in my identity in you and you alone. Help me to observe and find revelation that I may become all I am to be. Increase my faith so that I can heal. I ask by your power that you heal every part of me that is bound.

Help me to continue to read and relate this insight to my life. I choose to believe I'm healed, I'm whole, and I'm free.

In Jesus' name, amen.

CHAPTER 15

THE FEAR OF THE WHOLE SELF

"There is no fear in love; but perfect love casts out fear, because fear involves torment. But he who fears has not been made perfect in love"

−1 JOHN 4:18

There's a certain truth why we call love handles, love handles.

Inner Glutton and Diet Nut are a part of the bound self, the part of you bound in fear. As a foundation to lasting freedom, the spirit of fear is the root of the saga of weight and eating troubles. To heal the drama within we increase in love as we decrease in fear.

How we use food is like a measuring stick to how much we stand in love. When we use food in a way that reveals the body, more love is at work. When we use food in a way that hides the body, more fear is at work.

Some of us may not hide in weight but in berating thoughts about our body image, or never feeling skinny or muscular enough. This too is fear in operation.

Our gluttony, our obsession, is a fear of not having enough food, love, or comfort. The body of your dreams is waiting to be revealed. It's already there. You're in that handsome body now. Excess weight hides our most attractive body, which means it also hides our most vibrant, fearless self.

Surprisingly, the battle isn't with bread, it's between love and fear. The whole self and the bound self. Truth and lies.

> The battle isn't with bread, it's between love and fear.

The heart of weight and eating psychology is our transition from fear to love, from sinful to a relatively sin-free lifestyle, from carnal to spiritual, and from staunch legalism evidenced by calorie counting or strict diets to balanced grace. We're in a transformation process, and God is using your food and weight struggles to do it.

> We're in a transformation process, and God is using your food and weight struggles to do it.

The Root of Weight & Eating Bondage

In all bondage is torment and fear. Paul says, "For you did not receive the spirit of bondage again to fear, but you received the Spirit of adoption by whom we cry out, 'Abba, Father'" (Romans 8:15). There's one dominant fear we all deal with in our transformation process: the fear of the whole self. Our whole self adopts the fullness of our identity in Christ.

Fear involves torment. "There is no fear in love; but perfect love casts out fear, because fear involves torment. But he who fears has not been made perfect in love" (1 John 4:18). We all know weight and eating bondage is torment—from obsessing about food to shaming our bodies. When there's torment, we know fear took up residence.

But fear of what?

Fear of our whole self in Christ. We not only deny the godly power of our Father, but we deny our own power of God in us as well. Like Paul says, in 2 Timothy 3:5a, "Having a form of godliness but denying its power." We deny our own godliness, the healthy part of us, operating in the power of the Holy Spirit.

> " Our loving God uses every and any situation possible to help you grow in this abundant resource and source of His called love. "

Our healthiest self is a part of that light and love. In health, we're shiny, vibrant, and bright. We have energy, overflow in joy, and abound in love. We're a magnet for attracting people. We feel our best because in health we are our best. We're scared of this. We know: "For God has not given us a spirit of fear, but of power, love and a sound mind" (2 Timothy 1:7).

God is love (1 John 4:8). The fruit of the spirit is love (Galatians 5:22). We want to better embody the spirit of God. We want Him to flow through us. This requires a version of you that you've been previously afraid to receive. Our loving God uses every and any situation possible to help you grow in this abundant resource and source of His called love.

Love is the prescription for fear, shame, and guilt. Love is the currency of the kingdom of God. And love matters more than anything else. As Paul put it, we can do many things, but if love isn't at the root and the source, then it's in vain because it lacks the agape, unconditional, abundant source that is God, Who is love (1 Corinthians 13:1–13; John 4:8).

The Purpose of Torment

On the other hand, "torment is a source of vexation, infliction of torture, extreme pain or anguish of body and/or mind."[1] Yet, we know God is not in torment but that "all things work together for good to those who love God and are called according to *His* purpose" (Romans 8:28).

The goal of torment is to distract us from God given purpose, relationship with Him, other people, and momentum. It's to delay your mission. To block you from finding your mission. It's to prevent you from the joy of your current sphere of influence.

Weight and eating torment is the smokescreen over our true greatness and power in the Holy Spirit. We're conquering this battle for His glory. We glorify Him when we choose to walk whole, healed, and delivered, not in our comforts of walking broken, hurt, and bound.

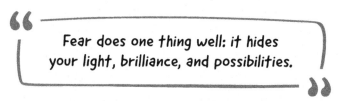

> **Fear does one thing well: it hides your light, brilliance, and possibilities.**

Fear does one thing well: it hides your light, brilliance, and possibilities. To expose ourselves in the form of reduced fat exteriors isn't safe. We're scared of who we are on the other side. In fear is every negative emotion. Shame, hate, guilt, and jealousy are all roommates in the mansion of fear.

Fear of the Whole Self

Fear of the whole self was identified by spirituality teacher Miriam Williamson in her book *A Return to Love.* She said in beautiful prose, "Our greatest fear is not that we are inadequate, but that we are powerful beyond measure. It is our light, not our darkness, that frightens us." [2]

Author and Pastor Chad Dedmon illustrated this point well. One night, while dreaming, he saw himself looking in the mirror. He looked but his reflection back was distorted, and the mirrors looked like that of a haunted house. His skin was drooped, eyes mismatched, clothes disheveled, and hands mangled. He realized this gross image in the mirror was the image of how he saw himself.

Then a light pierced the room, and the mirrors changed.

Light gathered the mirrors to show the truth to Pastor Chad of how Jesus saw him. He sensed the light was Jesus, and Pastor Chad couldn't look. The image of how Jesus saw him was too beautiful to look at fully.

Instead he raised his forearm above his elbow, staring away one second and curious the next. He was fearful of his own beauty, awe, and wonder of his God created, whole, beautiful self in Christ.

He'd rather go back to the horrifying image as that distorted image felt comfortable. But, because Christ Jesus, the Light of the World, pierced through the old man and penetrated love deep into the soul of his son, Pastor Chad was able to withstand his own greatness in Christ.

When he awoke, he cried, realizing he encountered God's love. And it would be God's love that would heal his identity.[3]

We fear our whole, vibrant, beautiful, good self, and hide under weight and poor habits to somehow reduce the greatness of the fact that we're children of God and a glowing expression of Him.

We've been confused about our identities as children of God. Instead of shining our lights fully, free of weight and eating turmoil, we stay stuck in failure with our attention on this one area of our lives that we can't seem to grasp, whereas many other strengths go uncelebrated. We are more than our weight problems.

> **To shine is to risk failure or rejection.**

These antics of trying to lose weight then sabotage with food reflects the lack of love we have within. We fear we can't get or sustain healthier bodies. We couldn't handle the success, attention, adoration, expectations, and responsibilities of being free.

We don't want to be seen. To shine is to risk failure or rejection. But it's our light God calls us to shine. "Arise, shine; For your light has come! And the glory of the Lord is risen upon you" (Isaiah 60:1).

From Bound to Free

Healing the Shame that Binds You is a celebrated book on the topic of shame by Christian psychology leader John Bradshaw. He said, "A sense of identity forms the foundation for a healthy adult love relationship." A healthy sense of identity is also the foundation for a healthy relationship with food and your body. He goes on to say, "A toxically shamed person is divided within himself and must create a false-self cover to hide (and validate) his sense of being flawed and defective." [4]

In other words, because the bound self believes, "I'm defective, broken, worthless, wrong, and inadequate," it operates accordingly and is bound in the lie of believing these things, thinking it's who she is.

The bound self keeps us stuck in the shame and guilt cycle as well as the behavioral patterns that validates feeling unworthy and guilty. The bound self rejects receiving the Father's unconditional love. Because shame says, *Who am I to be loved by a deeply loving God? Who am I to be in His presence? Who am I to be set free?*

This shame based identity crisis happens when we don't know who we are. Because of not knowing who we are, we settle for what is or has been instead of reaching for new ways to evolve and redefine ourselves in alignment with the Word of God. Because of not knowing who we are, we don't believe God can or will help us. We're stuck in unbelief.

The whole self is a healed, firm, redefined identity. It's a belief about you that aligns with God's truth about you. You're free to be joyful, happy, sincere, accepting, beautiful, and strong. The whole self is the development of the fruit of the Spirit in your life and soul. It's the spiritual Christian. It's your spiritual you.

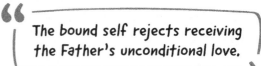

> The bound self rejects receiving the Father's unconditional love.

The key here is we're both bound and whole at the same time. And as we decrease in fear, we increase in love. The less Inner Glutton acts up, the more whole self grows.

Healing the Bound Self

Cynthia came into my therapy office frustrated about her weight.

"Jendayi, I just don't understand why I can't make progress. It's so frustrating!" Her shoulders slouched on the red fabric sofa.

"Cynthia, let's take a look at what's going on inside. How would you describe the relationship between the part of you that wants to be healthier and the part of you that doesn't?" I gently inquired, leaning in.

"One part of me keeps sabotaging myself. I hear myself saying you'll always be sick and tired, and you'll always be on medications so why bother? Just eat whatever you want!" Tears swelled in her eyes as this lie came to light.

I gave her a soft pillow to hold onto as I instructed her to close her eyes and get comfortable.

"Cynthia, ask that part of you that feels harsh, why it's there?"

A deep sob emerged, her mascara running down her cheeks.

"I don't believe in myself. I don't believe I can do it. I can't do anything right is what my mom always told me." She took the next few minutes to process, sobbing quietly. I asked her, "Will you ask this part of you to work with you going forward?

"Will you work with me and believe in me?" She inquired and then responded after she sensed her inner wisdom, "Yes!"

I asked, "How can she help you instead of criticizing?"

She asked, "Will you help me instead by encouraging me and letting me know I can do things right? Will you help me by saying you can do it Cynthia, or Cynthia, you're good enough?" As she made the request to her Inner Glutton, she unified this division of herself. Her face brightened, and a crooked smile emerged from her pink lips.

This was the start for Cynthia to create peace between her bound self that was sabotaging her and her whole self.

Paul has a similar dialogue in Romans 7:14–17 between the bound and free self.

For we know that the law is spiritual, but I am carnal, sold under sin. For what I am doing, I do not understand. For what I will to do, that I do not practice; but what I hate, that I do. If, then, I do what I will not to do, I agree with the law that it is good. But now, it is no longer I who do it, but sin that dwells in me. For I know that in me (that is, in my flesh) nothing good dwells; for to will is present with me, but how to perform what is good I do not find. For the good that I will to do, I do not do; but the evil I will not to do, that I practice. Now if I do what I will not to do, it is no longer I who do it, but sin that dwells in me.

Let me summarize in today's terms. You buy a boatload of vegetables with the intention of eating all the nutrients your body could ingest. Instead, you go the easy route throughout the week. You order from your favorite Chinese place, go out to dinner with friends, get pizza for the kids, and before you know it, those vegetables in the fridge are moldy with a stench. Why is it you intend to do such good but end up wasting pricey produce?

Paul summarizes the crux of every human being: we have a carnal nature, that is a sin nature, and it lives in us by the very law of being human.

"I find then a law, that evil is present with me, the one who wills to do good. For I delight in the law of God according to the inward man. But I see another law in my members, warring against the law of my mind, and bringing me into captivity to the law of sin which is in my members. O wretched man that I am! Who will deliver me from this body of death? I thank God—through Jesus Christ our Lord! So then, with the mind I myself serve the law of God, but with the flesh the law of sin" (Romans 7:21–25).

Paul shows us Christ's love is the answer to the inner turmoil. When we're in Christ, we operate from our whole self. We act out of unconditional love, acceptance, happiness, peace, contentment, kindness, appreciation, gratitude, and security.

The whole self believes it's worthy, capable, perfectly imperfect, and good enough. This relationship we have with self must find a place of unity, partnership, and support. In other words, the Father's love through Jesus Christ is the healing balm to your fear.

> **When we're in Christ, we operate from our whole self.**

184

Sin Is Not a Four-Letter Word

"Therefore, to him who knows to do good and does not do *it*, to him it is sin" (James 4:17).

Oftentimes people shiver at the word sin, as if they've got the cooties or just heard a pastor utter a four-letter word from the pulpit. The word sin has been used like a hammer, beating nonbelievers into hell and damnation. It causes some ministry leaders of today to neglect being upfront about sin altogether, leaving congregants struggling and unrepentant.

But, what if the word sin wasn't so emotionally charged with visions of lakes of fire and brimstone? What if sin indicated our fear of the whole self?

Sin is perceived by our Father in Heaven in the same way a parent is grieved when they see their child using street drugs or hanging out with the wrong crowd.

Jesus advocated, "Repent, [turn away from self-harm], for the kingdom of heaven is at hand" (Matthew 4:17). Jesus came to free us of the law of sin and death by His salvation and our willing obedience toward

> Sin is perceived by our Father in Heaven in the same way a parent is grieved when they see their child using street drugs or hanging out with the wrong crowd.

His ways over our own. It is by grace through faith alone that we are saved (Ephesians 2:8).

Sin is self-harm. As James says, "Therefore, to him who knows to do good and does not do *it*, to him it is sin" (James 4:17). And Proverbs 8:36a says, "He who sins against me (wisdom/Lord) wrongs His own soul." To damage the body is sin. Sin is failure or missing the mark. The mark is the Word of God or God's teaching and instruction. Living in Christ, we don't intentionally sin.

Sin is an indicator of fear. Sin is bound by shame, doubt, and unbelief. Many self-help books are truly sin-help books. We struggle, and we need God's help with our sin to heal the fear and shame causing it.

When we self-harm, like a rebellious child, we harm God. And we harm others who witness our pain because we as a human species are interconnected and impact one another.

A dear woman of God was morbidly obese. To the point I wondered if she got up to go to the bathroom or if she dressed herself. She had whole cakes in her office and ate them all too. She sat behind her desk and ate all day, making strange frog like sounds from her throat randomly. As a supervising counselor she oversaw counseling students. Her death affected her family, her students, her colleagues, and others—just as it had hurt everyone around her to see her destroy herself.

The autopsy report said the cause of death was cancer, but cancer has evidence that it's a result of eating processed foods and toxic ingredients. Researchers put it this way, "Worldwide, we estimate that 481,000 or 3.6 percent of all new cancer cases in adults in 2012 were attributable to high BMI."[5]

Obesity isn't the cause of any death on autopsy reports. Other diseases related to obesity are such as heart disease or diabetes. We instinctively know that sin, over time, when it's full grown, gives birth to death (James 1:15).

Sin is self-induced negligence causing grief, injury, and death to the spirit, soul, and body. The word sin gets a bad rap. But it's followed by one of the most beautiful words, repentance.

To repent is to say, "God, I've mismanaged myself. I've agreed with death. I've agreed with the adversary. I want to agree with you. I want to agree with life. I want to be worthy of life. I choose life."

To repent is to turn from death to life. To repent is to take a spiritual shower. Ultimately, to repent is to say no to an identity rooted in self-harm to one rooted in love—deep love for the Father and yourself as His creation. When we truly turn away, because we've realized our self-harm, we shift our old man from that which agreed with death to our new man which agrees with life, body, soul, spirit care, and love.

To love anyone, including ourselves, requires loving God. When we open up to greater love, we can receive the grace and healing power needed to love ourselves.

> To repent is to take a spiritual shower.

Bottom line: you must learn to love yourself.

A measurement of growth for this is the SEAS self-esteem inventory. See Non-Edible Goodies. Get a score for your level of self-esteem so you can witness how much you'll grow over time into someone who really loves who God made you.

Break Down Fear Walls

We'll need to break down fear walls to increase in love. Fear walls are constructs that create a barrier both to and from our naked soul. They're built by beliefs and interpretations from life's traumas and experiences. Fear walls are built when we've felt unsafe, unprotected, or undervalued for we were. And instead our value was placed in what we've looked like, what we've had, or what we could do.

Fear walls cause us to hide our real self. We can hide anywhere. In our bodies, work, minds, addictions, schedules, emotions, in people, appearances, education, money, and more. Walls create an unconscious push away effect, pushing away the threat of pain and the ability to receive love at the same time.

Fear of the whole self is exposed as we evaluate a few areas. Every time we go for a change, our subconscious evaluates the reflection questions coming up. When these questions don't check out to be safe, we won't be able to sustain the change for long. The fear of the whole self needs some time to allow you and your body to come out of hiding.

And if you're a normal weight but feel bound in your negative thoughts about your body or still binge with food, consider what's on the other side of letting this sabotaging mental behavior go. And step into a greater you with acceptance of your body, ambition, power, anointing, attractiveness, or all of the above.

To fear the Lord over man and especially our carnal man, is the beginning of all wisdom (Proverbs 9:10; Proverbs 111:10). This journey to your whole self is a work in progress.

But this time is different. This time you're facing you, not just your thighs, but all of you. Thank God for the struggle! Thank God for the extra poundage! Thank God for the many attempts to heal this issue. Thank God for revealing it all.

Rejoice! Because of it, you are being made more perfect in love.

> **Rejoice! Because of it, you are being made more perfect in love.**

REFLECTION QUESTIONS

1. What does it mean for you to step into your whole self?

   _____

   _____

2. What criticisms do you fear receiving as you step into your whole self?

   _____

   _____

3. What losses could you experience when you step into your whole self?

   _____

   _____

REFLECTION QUESTIONS
(CONTINUED)

4. What insecurities would be difficult to cope with when you step into your whole self?

_____

_____

5. How does it feel to rejoice for your weight and eating struggles?

_____

_____

PRAYER

Abba Father,

Thank you for bringing the deeper issue of a love deficit in my soul to my attention. Thank you for the weight. Thank you for the struggle. Thank you for my body and all it has endured. Thank you for my soul.

Please help me to face myself and no longer fear the greatness, wholeness, and abundant joy you've placed on the inside of me to reflect more of you. Help me to fear you more and your greatness in me less.

In Jesus' name, amen.

CHAPTER 16

CHUBBOLOGY

Why We're Super Scared to Drop the Weight

"The Lord is my rock, my fortress and my deliverer;
My God, my strength, in whom I will trust; My shield
and the horn of my salvation, my stronghold"

−PSALM 18:2

Losing weight is easy; it's allowing it to go for good that's hard.

A s you step into your whole self, you'll see fitting your soul is more important than those skinny jeans. Who knew? We're going to explore threats to our weight release in what I call Chubbology.

Chubbology
(noun) Chubb-ba-lo-gy
the made up psychological study of why we use weight for self-protection

Like our Inner Glutton's there to help us in strange ways, same is true about our weight. Our *chubby suit* is here for the greater good, but we hate wearing it. We may not *want* the weight or the struggle, but we *need* the weight and the struggle to protect our soul for good reasons.

The depth of intelligence in our psyche ensures that if we didn't have a reason to use weight to self-protect, we wouldn't. This gives us hope for weight release when these reasons resolve in our soul.

191

Losing weight is easy; it's allowing it to go for good that's hard. Excess body weight serves as a form of self-protection. It's nature's natural handgun, armed and ready against any perceived threats to our soul's safety.

We can wear a chubby suit to look less attractive to repel the opposite sex because we feel threatened by our sexuality. We can wear our chubby suit as a barrier from being too close to someone because we don't want to risk our hearts getting hurt again. We can wear it to stay stuck so the real us won't risk failure. We can wear a chubby suit to feel the physical affection missing in our life.

Ever get duped by a prank-can that you open? Our weight release is like a prank-can with a jelly bean exterior. It looks good on the outside. Then suddenly, out jumps a paper snake. We gasp and want to put the lid back on. The snake is the threat triggering fear we didn't know was there or we weren't prepared to handle.

The lid is the weight we've released. And just like that prank-can full of surprise, but packed in a jelly bean exterior, we're frightened. In our chub rationale, we keep our excess weight to protect our vulnerable, unsafe soul.

Try to recall how many times you've both gained and lost more than twenty pounds in your life? Chances are you were confronted with a threat that your soul wasn't ready to handle.

The 7 Threats of Why We Self-Protect with Weight

We can diet all we want, but in the end, if we don't deal with threats to releasing weight, all that's lost will be found again. On the flipside, we can become more accepting of our weight because of the purpose it serves.

A trigger is what sparks a series of actions or self-sabotaging behaviors.

This chapter is focused on *chubbological triggers*, of which the soul experiences a perceived threat to its safety, causing weight to ricochet. Let's look at the seven threats and corresponding fears that make us use weight as a protective barrier. We'll face specific fears we've been hiding in.

I'll warn you, this chapter can stir up tough emotions. Notice your emotional body's responses as you read. If you start thinking about your favorite binge foods, take a deep breath and lean into the Holy Spirit for comfort. If that doesn't work, skip to the next chapter until you're ready. Or go to Chapter 18 to practice an Emotional Fitness Workout™. Each threat may not resonate but rank the ones that do in order of resonance.

CHUBBOLOGICAL TRIGGERS	THREATS
Unwanted Attention	#1 Attractiveness
Unbridled Sexual Lust	#2 Sexual Lust
Vulnerability	#3 Emotional Intimacy
Rejection	#4 Criticism
Loss of Self-Concept	#5 Self-Concept
Loss or Abandonment	#6 Other People's Insecurity
Dealing with Emotional Pain	#7 Deep Life Disappointments

Threat #1 – Attractiveness
Chubbological Trigger – Unwanted Attention

Nancy just finished a successful six weeks at Weight Watchers. Proud of her efforts to drop fifteen pounds, she decided to go out and celebrate with a girlfriend. They went to the local dance school's ballroon party night.

Nancy attracted a creepy guy who insisted she dance with him.

"Hey beautiful, do you salsa?" he asked, as he placed his hand on her lower back.

"Yes, but ...," her words too shy to permeate the loud music.

"It's my lucky day," he said close to her ear. Latin drums blasted the speakers as he swiftly moved into salsa dancing with Nancy.

After a couple songs she mustered the courage to tell him she had to go to the ladies' room. She and her girlfriend grabbed their purses and snuck out the back door.

The next day, Nancy felt funny, but she couldn't put her finger on why. But she did manage to put her fingers all over chocolate bars, and she ate a few daily. Over the next few weeks, Nancy regained all the weight she lost and then some.

Nancy thought she wanted to lose weight, but in losing weight she gained male attention. Digging deeper, she had past sexual trauma. Because of this trauma, she had a tendency to enter into abusive relationships. Her soul wasn't ready to release the weight because releasing the weight gained her attention from men she wasn't equipped to handle.

Intimidated by aggressive men, she didn't have the confidence yet to state her boundaries or preferences. Once Nancy's attractiveness was tested, her army of fat stampeded right back to defend her.

Nancy's scared of unwanted attention. Nancy pondered, *Will he force me to do something I don't want to do? Will he hurt me?*

Probable Causes of the Fear of Unwanted Attention

- We've been sexually abused, molested, or assaulted in some way.
- We've been in physically abusive relationships.
- We feel nervous or intimidated by the opposite sex.
- We've been ashamed of secret, same-sex sexual abuse.
- We don't have established boundaries with the opposite sex.

Reflection Question: Have you fully resolved your past sexual abuse?

With some of these probable causes, it only makes sense to hide in your chubby suit to avoid attention that you're not ready for. We use weight to protect ourselves from the unwanted attention our attractiveness can bring.

Unwanted attention is the kind you don't know how to handle. When our beauty or handsomeness has harmed us, we can hide in a chubby suit because we don't know how to deal with attention from the opposite sex.

We can use our bigness to feel more powerful against threats to our physical safety when we've had negative sexual attention in the past such as molestation, rape, assault, or incest. Studies show twenty percent of females and five to ten percent of males recall sexual abuse from childhood.[1] An analysis of 57,000 females reported twice as much food addiction with a history of childhood sexual abuse than those with no history.[2]

> **We can hide in a chubby suit because we don't know how to deal with attention from the opposite sex.**

To resolve sexual abuse requires regular professional therapeutic care. In a therapeutic relationship, you're empowered to create boundaries, use your voice without being intimidated by others, and heal deep grief. You're not alone. Past abuse is the biggest threat in the weight and eating equation.

A weight loss doctor, Dr. Wendy Scinta, in Manlius, New York, says she now includes questions about abuse when clients utilize her services, and she started a group therapy session because the majority, especially of those with 100 or more pounds to lose, have tragic abuse stories in their past.[3] This doctor understands the chubbological threat, and she knew clients had to deal with their past trauma before they could see lasting results.[4] Research shows that post-traumatic stress, like sexual abuse, leads to obesity.[5]

Take a deep breath. I've had my share of sexual abuse, too. I can empathize. God wants to heal you to a place of full restoration. You'll know when an issue is fully resolved because there's no anger, tears, or emotional charge around it. You can talk about it freely, and it becomes a testimony of Jesus Christ working in your life.

You'll know it's resolved when you've forgiven all involved parties, including yourself. When resolved, you've also overcome toxic beliefs, such as unworthiness, self-hatred, toxic shame or guilt, and any gender related bitterness that took hold during sexual abuse like man or woman hating.

The extraordinary, Joyce Meyer is an exemplary example of healing and wholeness from traumatic sexual abuse all throughout her childhood. I love hearing her stories of restoration. Consider her books as well as the *Victim to Victory* manual for healing sexual abuse by Brenda Clark-Dandridge.

Take peace in the Scripture, "Since you were precious in My sight, you have been honored, and I have loved you" (Isaiah 43:4a). You are clean. You are safe. And you have new discernment you didn't have when you were abused. You have new tools, skills, friends, and community. And if you don't, you can create a life to feel safe and protected.

Threat #2 – Sexual Lust
Chubbological Trigger – Unbridled Sexual Lust

Jim was a lady's man in his earlier days when he played football for his high school team. Years later, he struggled with seventy extra pounds. He pushed memories away of being too sexual with girls and cheating on his girlfriends with football fans. In marriage, his wife was unhappy with his weight. He lost and gained weight several times in their twenty years of marriage.

Jim feared his own sexual lust would be set loose and he'd risk losing his family. Each time he lost weight, he'd get flirtatious attention from women.

He thought, *What if I look like I did back then? Would I act the same? I could make the horrible mistake of cheating on my wife and lose my family. Oh God, would I be a heathen again?*

Judy loved God with all of her heart. She, like many God seekers, attended programs to learn about God and understand who she was in Christ. Over time, her spiritual transformation and learning allowed her to release forty pounds.

Then Reggie came along.

Smitten by his charm and dark features, she struggled with her desire for him and her desire to honor God by keeping her sexual purity. After a while of entertaining her on-again, off-again relationship with Reggie, her sexual lust overtook her, followed by his complete rejection.

Her mistake caused her to regain the forty pounds and then some. Her life regained traction with Christ, she accepted His forgiveness for her sin, but it was difficult to cope with her own sexual lust.

In her past, she struggled with promiscuity and never learned how to relate to men in a non-sexual way. Reggie was her first relationship she had in many years, and it proved her chubbology right.

She pondered, *I can't handle the opposite sex without dishonoring God. How do I interact in a plutonic way with men instead of being so physical? And deeper, what else can I give if I gave myself fully and was still rejected?*

Cecille flirted with an ex on social media. One thing led to another, and she and her ex met up one night at the bar. After several drinks, her inhibitions left, and lust aggressively took over. Ashamed the next day, she confessed to her husband what she'd done. Shame filled her. And weight followed. After two years of marital counseling since the affair, Cecille struggled to let the fifty pounds she gained, go.

"I don't trust myself," Cecille confessed in my office. "What if I cheat again?"

"Ask the weight why it's there," I said.

"I think my weight protects me from myself. I guess at fifty pounds heavier I can't get into too much trouble," she laughed.

Cecille knew at some level her weight repelled sexual advances, as her physical body, needed self-protection from the threat of her sexual lust and the depth of pain the sexual tension had caused in her marriage.

She loved her husband and didn't want to commit another act of adultery. However, her beauty, her physical body, felt safe in her chubby suit because it suppressed the sexual part of herself.

Her internal sense of self didn't trust her own ability to stay adultery free. She wondered, *Could I control myself if I lost weight? What if a man I'm attracted to likes me back? What would I do?*

Probable Causes of the Fear of Unbridled Sexual Lust

- We've harmed another with adultery or cheating in the past.
- We've suppressed our own sexuality.
- We are challenged to trust our own sexual self-control because of previous mistakes.
- We have unresolved sexual self-abuse like chronic masturbation or promiscuity.
- We've been too physical too soon in past relationships.

Reflection Question: Have you reconciled your unbridled sexual lust and the damages your lust has caused?

Watch for my upcoming book, *Stupid Sex!* I'll provide more practical advice to work through sexual history and its impact on relationships with God and our love life. Take a moment to give any fear of unbridled lust to the Lord for full resolution in a time of prayer. Ask Him to heal your sexual past. A trusted counselor can work with you to talk through any part of your soul bound in shame about your sexual past.

Over time, you learn how to trust your sexual self-control as your whole self in Christ becomes firm. Hang tight to the Scripture: "Therefore, if anyone is in Christ, *he is* a new creation; old things have passed away; behold, all things have become new" (2 Corinthians 5:17).

I strongly believe lust is lust. If sexual lust is unresolved, the spirit of lust will transfer to another area like decadent food.

Galatians 5:16 says, "Walk in the Spirit and you shall not fulfill the lust of the flesh." Think about how you've changed in other areas of life by allowing the Spirit of God to lead you. Trust God can heal you in your sexual boundaries as well. Be bold. Heal your sexual history.

> If sexual lust is unresolved, the spirit of lust will transfer to another area like decadent food.

Threat #3 – Emotional Intimacy [Romantic Love]
Chubbological Trigger – Vulnerability

Bob loved to cook. And it was something he longed to share with his wife. He'd lost weight to find Renee, but as soon as he married Renee, he was cooking alright. Within months of the marriage, they were both buying two sizes larger of clothing.

"You've got to stop cooking so many delicious foods. I'm getting fat," Renee said. "I want to be able to fit in my clothes, and it's the second time I'm buying a larger size since I met you!"

"You look great to me, honey," Bob said, mixing the dough for an apple pie as he winked in her direction.

"I don't feel great to me. And you've gained weight, too. I really don't want to be the chubby couple," she laughed, amidst her seriousness. "Babe, I just don't want to set this kind of stage for our children."

Bob felt the same way. But he cooked with her because it was easier to sit and eat than it was for him to sit and talk. He too felt plagued with frustration about his own weight and eating struggles. But marriage was both exciting and uncomfortable. It brought out insecurities of being abandoned.

He wondered, *What if she leaves me? What if she cheats on me? What if she uses my shortcomings as ammunition?*

Katie went through a devastating divorce. Her husband left her with their four children for her to raise on her own. And he went to live in another state with another woman. Food was her comfort from an early age but amplified after abandonment. She decided to get gastric bypass surgery after her youngest went to college.

She quickly slimmed down from a size 25 to 14. Elated, she thought she'd online date to find love again. After her first dinner date with a guy she liked, she came home and chowed down on the doggie bag something fierce.

Liking someone was a threat to Katie. Her mind wrestled with, *What if he only likes me because I'm slim? What if he pretends to love me like my ex did before he left us? Will he call when he says he will? Will he leave me when he gets to know me?*

Probable Causes of the Fear of Vulnerability

- We were emotionally and or physically neglected or abandoned as a child.
- We carry deep shame about who we are or where we come from.
- We believe a lie that we can't be loved for who we are.
- We've experienced a hard loss of love in the past and resist opening our hearts again.
- We fear getting close to others in relationship because they could use our weaknesses as ammunition to hurt us.
- We're not ready to attract a romantic relationship.

Reflection Question: Have you resolved your ability to handle emotional intimacy?

Intimacy, or in-to-me-see, is a sense of closeness when we feel safe enough to be emotionally vulnerable, seen, heard, and known, especially with someone we are attracted to or in a close relationship with.

Much like my increase in cookie consumption when I fell in love with my (now ex) husband, vulnerability caused me to use cookies to help me cope with the threat of heartbreak. I had no exposure to healthy relationship examples, only divorces. Naturally, I didn't feel safe to be vulnerable because it wasn't modeled.

Our chubby suit protects us from the threat of romantic love and intimacy because we use it to reduce our internal sense of attractiveness. Hiding inside of our chubby suit protects us from love getting in and breaking our heart.

The downside is being fearful of love also prevents our love from escaping out and creating the life we've always wanted. When we've not had an upbringing where we were safe to be emotionally vulnerable, we wonder if someone could love us how we are.

We can reduce weight to snag a spouse, but the weight is regained because we haven't learned the skills needed to have an emotionally safe relationship. A relationship that allows you and your partner to be himself or herself is ideal. Together you can heal and grow whole as individuals and as a couple. A lack of emotional safety and vulnerability stems from emotional abuse in the past.

Emotional abuse has a high correlation with obesity and using food. In our first Whole & Free Health course, 84 percent suffered from past emotional and verbal abuse as opposed to 50 percent who suffered with physical abuse.[6]

> **Hiding inside of our chubby suit protects us from love getting in and breaking our heart.**

Emotional abuse is any prolonged time you've felt mistrusted, wrongly accused, ignored, manipulated to feel guilty, or provoked to anger intentionally by someone you should've been able to trust.

We don't feel safe to share in abusive environments. In your own world, you don't have to worry about your heart being exposed or harmed, nor about your dysfunctions harming anyone else. However, within intimate relationships, our insecure secrets are on display, causing a fear of vulnerability.

To be vulnerable is to be in a place open to possible attack, scorn, or ridicule.[7] To be emotionally vulnerable is to open our hearts, hand it to someone else for good keeping, and risk them throwing it in the street only for it to get run over by the 6 o'clock city bus. But be encouraged, our God is the Healer of the broken hearted.

We're to learn from our broken hearts. We learn to open our heart to a wider space of love to handle vulnerability. We're to know we're safe to keep our hearts open 24:7, like a 7-Eleven. Rest in the promises of God. "He heals the broken hearted and binds up their wounds" (Psalm 147:3).

Threat #4 – Criticism
Chubbological Trigger – Rejection

Tina went to her family barbeque. She felt alive, healthy, and vibrant. She glowed with excitement to show everyone her transformed size 8 body. She had lost several pounds since she last saw the crew. And she never felt or looked so good. As she approached the gathering at the local park, family members looked at her, not with excitement for her transformation, but with disgust.

"Tina, you're too skinny! Come over here and eat some of these ribs," her plump grandmother said.

"That's right, Tina, I made potato salad to go with those ribs, and you'll need two helpings looking like that," her uncle chimed in laughing.

Embarrassed by the attacks on her body, Tina soothed herself with large portions of mac and cheese. Her emotions stirred a mix of grief, anger, shame, and surprise. She began her day excited and ended it bloated with both emotions and water retention.

> We're to know we're safe to keep our hearts open 24:7, like a 7-Eleven.

Her family criticized her health progress because it meant Tina would be different. Tina's family members are for the most part obese and plagued with health ailments. Tina's slim body didn't fit in. So, the family made it their business to help her get back up to size.

Tina felt rejected by their negative evaluations of her healthy body. She thought her hard work would win their approval, instead it earned their criticism. Her family made clear attempts to bring her back to a robust waistline so that she was one of the gang.

Tina's mind obsessed, *People don't like my new body. Will they continue to reject me if I don't eat or look like them? I can't handle all the negative comments about my choices and body!*

Probable Causes of the Fear of Rejection

- We don't understand the value of criticism and feedback.
- We make the criticism about us instead of the criticizer.
- We're addicted to people's approval.
- We have an underdeveloped sense of self.
- We've not worked through body shame.
- We've been abandoned or rejected by a parent.

Reflection Question: Have you resolved your fear of rejection?

Criticism can come from those groups we need the most support from in our journey toward a whole and free life. It's scary to consider the idea of being ostracized because of your downsize. However, a part of your freedom is the release from other people's weight issues that are projected onto you as criticism.

Criticisms aren't meant to make you feel rejected or attacked. In fact, comments around your body from someone else aren't your issue.

Comments and criticisms are more about the commentator than you. Romans 2:1 says, "For in whatever you judge another you condemn yourself; for you who judge practice the same things." So, when they criticize what they see in you, they're judging what they can't see in their own self.

Criticisms are especially hard for those who've experienced verbal abuse. Words have the power of life and death, and if words of death were spoken over you, it's difficult to feel comfortable in your soul. Naturally so, because verbally abusive caregivers outright lied to you (your soul) about who you are with their word curses. Verbal abuse creates a heightened sensitivity to negative feedback and is a threat to your soul's sense of safety.

> "Criticisms are especially hard for those who've experienced verbal abuse.

When our own families negatively evaluate our body or choices, we feel threatened because of our human need to belong. And family is the primary place we get this need met. We need family, and we need people to love us unconditionally. So, we unconsciously sabotage positive efforts as to not ruffle family feathers and fit in.

To belong is a major factor in weight and eating because we often feel so alone and isolated in our chubby suits. To move beyond rejection is to first know you belong to the Lord. You're accepted by Him. In Isaiah 43:1, it says, "Fear not, for I have redeemed you; I have called *you* by your name; You *are* Mine."

Threat #5 – Self-Concept
Chubbological Trigger – Loss of Self-Concept

Corinne, a church mother with big hats and sparkling jewelry, went up and down on the scale for many years. Her stocky and wide build seemed to match the brand of strength she represented in the church. She was known as a strong woman of God, and part of her strength was tied to her excess weight.

She associated her motherly image with a large bosom. She wondered, *Don't all mothers have a nice big bosom for weary heads to rest on? How could I be spiritual, motherly, and slim?*

Another fear of Jim's around his football glory days was his loss of self-concept or his identity that was in his size. He was known as "Big Jim" because of his naturally large physique. Two decades later after playing football, eating became his sport.

His Big Jim mantra still played in the back of his mind and was part of how he saw himself. A bigger body helped him believe he was bigger and better. On one hand, he wanted to lose weight, yet, on the other hand, he couldn't reconcile who he would be without it.

His growing body mass, belly and all, helped him to feel bigger than he felt on the inside. He thought, *Who will I be without the weight? Aren't guys supposed to be large and in charge? My husky exterior gives me a sense of power.*

"Man, Harry, is that you?! How much did you lose? You look good, bro!" John, an old friend of Harry's from Bible study approached Harry, who was at the local park. "Come play some hoops. We need a fit guy like you on the team."

Insistent, John swatted Harry on the arm to pull him over.

Nervously, Harry pulled away and made an excuse to leave. That's when the barbeque cravings kicked in, not just for the night but for the whole week.

When he was asked to play ball because he was so "fit" looking, he knew he would make a fool of himself on the team. He was expected to be athletic, but he wasn't. His anxiety that he couldn't be who someone else wanted him to be now that he was fitter triggered his old-time baby back rib special to pop into his mind, then mouth. Harry feared the expectations that came with his slimmer body.

Harry experienced fear of other's expectations. He thought, *Why does everyone expect me to be so good at sports now? I'm not the sports guy even though I look like one now that I've lost eighty pounds. Sports isn't me.*

Probable Causes of the Fear of Loss of Self-Concept

- We've placed part of our identity in weight.
- We associate our roles with being large.
- We're unable to reconcile our roles with our body shape and size.
- We're unsure how we'll participate in our roles at a slimmer size.
- Our sense of self-esteem or bigness as a person is built into our larger size.
- We fear we will disappoint others in our new body.
- We're not sure how to be vulnerable and let others know we can't meet their expectations.

Reflection Question: What part of your self-concept is wrapped up in your body mass?

Roy Baumeister, American psychologist says, self-concept is "the individual's belief about himself or herself, including the person's attributes and who and what the self is."[8] It's necessary to test your chubby suit to see if any part of your self-concept is reinforced in a positive way and then to unravel the self-concept with new possibilities. The transition into our whole self is about us reconciling who we are chubby versus who we'll be slim.

If our self-concept has bigness as a definer, we'll have to reconcile by testing new ideas of what slim could mean for our roles and abilities. For Corinne, she needed to test a new belief that she could be both motherly and slim. For Jim, he'd need to see he's still Big Jim without being at risk for heart disease.

> **The transition into our whole self is about us reconciling who we are chubby versus who we'll be slim.**

Threat #6 – Other People's Insecurity
Chubbological Trigger – Loss or Abandonment

"Hi, honey," I said to my husband, thinking he'd think I looked awesome. I greeted him with a hug and kiss. A cold shoulder met me with a begrudged hello. Then, we argued for the next five minutes, while walking over to the event, about my skirt. My Catholic school teachers would've approved, but he did not.

"Why did you wear that? There will be a bunch of dudes there," he said.

"I thought you'd like it. I wore it to please you. And it's professional," I said, deflated.

After I spoke on health and nutrition to a group of distinguished business professionals (who unbeknownst to me were mostly men), I was met with complete silence. My husband refused to talk with me.

I was forced to mingle with my audience rather than him because he completely ignored me. *Isn't that what he didn't want?* His insecurity and fear of being cheated on and his jealousy of professional men desiring me because of my skirt, fed my fear of being beautiful. He was emotionally triggered, and he couldn't control his rudeness toward me. I was ashamed to have a husband who rejected me.

Less than a year into my terrible, but rather educational, new marriage, I got the hint that my beauty wasn't acceptable on three separate occasions. When it came to men at work, men as friends, or the silence of the skirt. I sabotaged health with boxes of cookies per Chapter 3. My spouse's fear of abandonment created real fat on my body. I was flabbergasted with authentic flab.

His mistrust caused me to feel unsafe in my soul. My lack of soul safety translated into excess fat because of my fear of rejection and jealousy from my own husband. Because I fear God, he had no reason to ever worry about infidelity.

But his past experiences, and to his credit, my past before marriage, made me fear my own beauty. My insecurity and fear of rejection allowed myself to eat over it. Then, I wondered, *Would he leave me? Does he love me? Am I good enough for him?*

For Tamara, jealousy came from her closest family members.

"Oh, now you're a size six and think you're so hot?" Her sister said, shoving the purple dress in Tamara's fitting room.

"Thanks," Tamara said. Jackie, her sister, didn't seem to treat her in the same loving way since she lost seventy pounds over the past year. Their favorite pastime of going shopping seemed like a chore now—a chore of keeping up with her sister's teasing comments. Jealousy saturated Jackie's presence.

"I feel so good. It's great to wear clothes that feel good on me," Tamara said, turning around, happy with the dress and her shape in the three-way mirror. "How do I look?"

"It's alright," Jackie replied, as she rolled her eyes and landed them in the stink eye position.

This didn't only happen when shopping but also at family dinners and in conversations. Tamara knew her sister talked about her to other family members when she wasn't around. She suspected Jackie's jealousy because her sister was always the *thin one* before Tamara lost the weight. Over the next several months, tension grew in the relationship, and Tamara went back to her chubby choices because unconsciously she didn't want to continue to hurt Jackie's feelings.

Tamara wrestled with thoughts like, *I can't seem to make her happy. Is my weight making her so jealous that it'll change our relationship? Will she keep distancing herself from me if I stay in this slim body? We're so close, who else would I confide in?*

Probable Causes of the Fear of Loss or Abandonment

- We're in a relationship with someone who is jealous or controlling about how we look.
- We are in an emotionally abusive relationship.
- We haven't developed boundaries.
- We have a poor sense of self.
- We are in a codependent relationship that doesn't allow us to be a unique, empowered individual.

Reflection Question: Have you resolved your fear of loss?

Jealousy and insecurity from people we love can make us scared of losing them and our relationships, so we put the chubby suits back on to keep us and them safe from this loss. The problem is an insecure spouse can cause trouble for your waistline because they fear losing you to your new possibilities that come with your new trim self.

Jealousy shows up when you're teased, emotionally shut out, accused of cheating and flirting, or other attacks on your character based on your newfound confidence and attractiveness.

I've witnessed some cases where a spouse may fatten their spouse up so other intimate issues are avoided, such as sexual relations. Or to prevent their spouse from being as attractive to other people.

Your loved one's jealousy or insecurity carries an unspoken current as if to say, *If the weight goes, I go.* The weight can be the result of serious marital tensions that need professional as well as pastoral counseling support.

To be clear, please don't divorce your insecure partner! Many underlying tensions can be cleared up as you develop identity security in your whole self. Your spouse's insecurities or jealousies don't have to affect how you treat yourself. If they're not okay, you can still be okay. We are to bear one another's burdens in a sense of prayer and support, not bear their burdens for them to become harmful to us.

In codependent relationships one partner is considered the problem and the other partner acts as the savior. This is unhealthy because for a relationship to be done well, we need to have strong boundaries about who we are in place, so we don't get lost in someone else and take their fears and insecurities out on ourselves.

Be willing to let go of your own fear of their insecurities or jealousies. For Tamara, she learned how to acknowledge the jealousy by directly talking to her sister heart-to-heart. She shared how Jackie's actions affected her.

Tamara encouraged her sister's desire to lose weight. Jealousy is wanting something someone else has but not knowing how to attain it for yourself. Tamara didn't have to make her sister's jealousy her issue and sabotage herself over it.

Don't play small so someone else can feel big. Gain more confidence in your healthy and fit you. Stand in who you are regardless of negativity from others. As you stand firm in your identity, own your stuff and let them own theirs. As we gain a true sense of self, instead of buying other people's insecurities, we can happily return them back to the sender. Your insecurity package was delivered to the wrong person!

If this is a big struggle for you, a fantastic way to honor someone is to pray for them (alone or with them) about their insecurities. Bring their

> " Stand in who you are regardless of negativity from others. "

me insecurities to the Lord as well as your fear of loss of the relationship to Him.

insecurities to the Lord as well as your fear of loss of the relationship to Him.

Also do some work on your personal boundaries, as speaker Barbra Russell says in her mighty little book, *Yes! I said No!* "People pleasing is not a spiritual gift."[9] Books, such as Barbra's for a quick read or *Boundaries* by Drs. Henry Cloud and John Townsend for more depth, are sure to help you create better boundaries to strengthen how you want to be in a relationship with yourself and others despite their insecurities.

The way I've set boundaries is a four-step process.

First, I figure out what I want. I don't want to feel ignored when I look good.

Second, I find a consequence if the person doesn't honor it. When he does that to me, I will insist on meeting with our pastor.

Third, I share my boundary and consequence with the person. "I don't want to feel ignored when I look good, so if that happens again, I'll insist on meeting with the pastor."

Fourth, I do what I say I am going to do if that happens again.

Boundary creation doesn't have to be hard, it just has to be done to manage your own peace well. As Proverbs says, "A sound heart *is* life to the body, but envy *is* rottenness to the bones" (Proverbs 14:30).

Threat #7 – Deep Life Disappointments
Chubbological Trigger – Dealing with Emotional Pain

Peggy, an independent business owner, had undergone significant financial hardships. In a session, Peggy realized that the root of her weight was her failing her own expectations. The weight served as a type of excuse. She thought, *As long as I'm overweight, I can blame my lack of success on it.*

Irrational to say the least, but it was true for her. When she lost weight and couldn't meet her expectations that a trimmer body was supposed to give her—financial business success, she regained it. She gained and lost weight four times over the past two decades. Each time she lost, she understood she'd sabotaged her healthy habits due to using her weight as an excuse.

Her chubby suit served as the reason why she'd been financially unsuccessful in business. If she became her whole self, she would have to be more financially successful.

Not six figures, but seven figures. This unrealistic goal gave her a hidden figure. Her unrealistic expectations of herself stemmed from unresolved unforgiveness. Peggy had to deal with her reality of not being as successful as she had wanted to be at her age and her poor relationship with money; otherwise, she'd stay stuck in her overweight excuse, keeping her broke and big.

Unconsciously she thought, *If I let go of my weight, I'll have to prove myself in other areas. What if I'm a complete failure in life?*

Probable Causes of the Fear of Dealing with Emotional Pain

- We're misaligned with our soul's heart and purpose.
- We're refusing to deal with life's failures, disappointments, and griefs.
- We're misaligned with God's will for our lives.
- We're not learning the lessons life is trying to teach us.
- We have a poor relationship with life.

Reflection Question: Have you come to terms with where you are or what you have been through in life?

> " We cause and create our weight problem to avoid other problems. "

We cause and create our weight problem to avoid other problems. Our weight can be a mask over emotional pain that needs to be addressed. If we use our weight, like Peggy, as an excuse for why we're not as successful as we think we should be, and we lose the weight and are still not as successful as we think we should be, we must face realities of emotional pain that we've avoided with weight drama or we'll create weight drama again to avoid emotional pain.

Fear of emotional pain can accompany previously mentioned threats. Weight can be regained to avoid the emotional pain of dealing with a marriage riddled with years of tension or disagreement or past deaths of loved ones that aren't fully grieved, like my father's loss, or

> **One of the most productive things we can do as eaters, foodies, and Chubby Church members is feel.**

things we feel we should've had but didn't, like a loving parent, child, or spouse.

Perhaps we've had some trouble in life such as drug, alcohol, debt, gambling, or pornography addictions, and we have avoided dealing with the emotional pain of the losses of years, relationships, dignity, or material items our affliction has cost us. One of the most productive things we can do as eaters, foodies, and Chubby Church members is feel.

Feeling is hard because of our dysfunctional past telling us not to feel.

And life can be hard.

We may be seriously disappointed that things didn't work out as planned or expected. We may have to grieve not only the loss or hardship, but also going through the loss and hardship itself. Feeling is the key.

We'll learn how to process these threats and feel as we enact an Emotional Strength Training Plan in the Emotional Fitness Workout™ in Chapter 18. But know God is with you and wants to take your emotional burden from you. Will you give your emotional pain to your healer?

Master Your Chubbology

There you have it. Seven psychological reasons we've been super scared to drop the weight. I've officially got "all up in your business," as they'd say in Jersey. Why? Because if we don't deal with this real stuff, we'll keep stuffing.

> Master your chubbology to break the cycle of using weight to self-protect.

Master your chubbology to break the cycle of using weight to self-protect. And while knowing this insight is good, we need to do something about it. The wonderful Counselor (Isaiah 6:9), and a good therapist can help you to heal them.

We can't and don't need to address everything at once. Just breathe. And pray through any sense of being overwhelmed. Ask the Holy Spirit, "Which of the seven threats should I address right now?" Pick one.

Answer the reflection question of the chubbological threat you sense you're going to focus on right now in your notebook. The same one you're logging observations on Inner Glutton and Diet Nut.

Do your best to pray through the stirring in your heart. Pour out your heart on paper so you're less likely to eat over what's eating you about your chubbology.

Each threat represents excess weight on the body. These and other threats resolve the more we resolve who we are in Christ.

The Lord is our protection. "The Lord is my rock and my fortress and my deliverer; my God, my strength, in whom I will trust; my shield and the horn of my salvation, my stronghold" (Psalm 18:2). And, "Our soul waits for the Lord; He *is* our help and our shield (Psalm 33:20). May God's shield of protection fill your soul with safety and security quickly.

REFLECTION QUESTIONS

1. Which chubbological threat resonated with you the most?

   _____

2. What do you need to believe about the world to feel more safe in your soul?

   _____

3. What boundaries will you need to be successful to let go of excess weight?

   _____

PRAYER

Heavenly Father,

Thank you for confronting what's been holding me back in this chubby suit! Please bring the right person for me to talk to within my budget. Help me not to eat over the depth of emotions stirred in this chapter, but I call upon the power, truth, righteousness, and comfort of the Holy Spirit. Help me to trust you to see me through my chubbology.

Make every threat null and void. I am confident to be my whole self in my right mind, heart, and body! My past doesn't equal my future. I ask for the courage to heal. Please continue to strengthen my foundation to handle great success. Make me completely secure in my identity in you.

Thank you, Father, in Jesus' name, amen!

CHAPTER 17

ADOPT THE FREEDOM MINDSET

Chain #2 - The Dieter's Mindset

"Casting down arguments and every high thing that exalts itself against the knowledge of God, bringing every thought into captivity to the obedience of Christ"

—2 CORINTHIANS 10:5

Our minds are like a dog without a leash.

Diet Nut, the alter ego of Inner Glutton, creates the dieter's mindset. Diets are the American way. It's estimated that 45 million Americans diet regularly and participate in a $66 billion dollar industry.[1] About 97 million Americans try a new fad diet every year.[2] John LaRose, research director of Market Data Enterprise, said, "America's dieters are fickle and shift from fad to fad."[3]

Someone is profiting on diets, why isn't it you?

We've believed lies for too long. Reduce the assault on your results by adopting a freedom mindset and quit being duped into temporary gimmicks.

Chains keep us stuck in bondage. The chain we need to destroy in this chapter is our dieter's mindset.

A mindset is a collection of thoughts that over a period of time influences the way we perceive life. You have a collection of individual thoughts and experiences that over the course of your life has accumulated in your head when it comes to diets, weight, body image, food, and eating. This library of thoughts and images has formed your mindset.

To find out how affected you are by the dieter's mindset, let me ask you a few questions.

DIETER'S MINDSET STRONGHOLD QUIZ

Put a check next to the answer that describes your mindset and add the total points below. The higher the score, the more the dieter's mindset is in motion.

1. How often do you speak or think harshly about your body?

   ☐ (5) ALWAYS ☐ (4) OFTEN ☐ (3) SOMETIMES ☐ (2) RARELY ☐ (1) NEVER

2. How often do you eat without discretion because you've messed up your diet anyway?

   ☐ (5) ALWAYS ☐ (4) OFTEN ☐ (3) SOMETIMES ☐ (2) RARELY ☐ (1) NEVER

3. How often do you search for a new diet?

   ☐ (5) ALWAYS ☐ (4) OFTEN ☐ (3) SOMETIMES ☐ (2) RARELY ☐ (1) NEVER

4. How often do you attempt to diet?

   ☐ (5) ALWAYS ☐ (4) OFTEN ☐ (3) SOMETIMES ☐ (2) RARELY ☐ (1) NEVER

5. How often do you feel guilty or like you've "cheated" when you've eaten what you enjoy?

   ☐ (5) ALWAYS ☐ (4) OFTEN ☐ (3) SOMETIMES ☐ (2) RARELY ☐ (1) NEVER

6. How often do you worry about or count grams or calories?

   ☐ (5) ALWAYS ☐ (4) OFTEN ☐ (3) SOMETIMES ☐ (2) RARELY ☐ (1) NEVER

7. How often is your motive for exercise to lose weight?

   ☐ (5) ALWAYS ☐ (4) OFTEN ☐ (3) SOMETIMES ☐ (2) RARELY ☐ (1) NEVER

8. How often do you eliminate whole food groups because you're on a diet?

   ☐ (5) ALWAYS ☐ (4) OFTEN ☐ (3) SOMETIMES ☐ (2) RARELY ☐ (1) NEVER

9. How often do you eat something you think is "bad"?

   ☐ (5) ALWAYS ☐ (4) OFTEN ☐ (3) SOMETIMES ☐ (2) RARELY ☐ (1) NEVER

10. How often does the number on the scale dictate your mood for the day?

   ☐ (5) ALWAYS ☐ (4) OFTEN ☐ (3) SOMETIMES ☐ (2) RARELY ☐ (1) NEVER

Total Score:

_____

Score Sheet
30–50 | Free your mind and the rest will follow!
20–30 | You've done some mindset work and it shows!
10–20 | You're freeing your mind to the next level!

Adopt the Weight & Eating Freedom Mindset

A healthy mindset will set you emotionally and mentally free from the destructive thoughts that drive weight and eating obsession.

Our results in life manifest *creative inputs,* such as thoughts, emotions, beliefs, and actions. Thoughts both shape and create reality. Think of them as seeds. The mind is fertile ground cultivated by thought seeds. And these seeds can be beneficial or harmful.

Your mind has no judgment around the thoughts. As a fertile ground it grows them with the water of your own behavior, emotions, and beliefs. So, your thoughts yield a crop you can see in your reality—one you like or one you'd rather feed to the birds. If your reality's screaming, "Lord, rapture me now!" to escape itself, we need to look at our creative inputs.

Two Scriptures come to mind that illustrate your part in the creation process: "For as he thinks in his heart, so is he" (Proverbs 23:7) and "A good tree cannot bear bad fruit, nor can a bad tree bear good fruit" (Matthew 7:18). The tree of our thought life produces fruit. For our reality to change, we need to have a change of mind and heart.

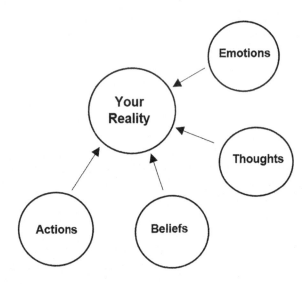

Figure 17.1 Your Manifested Reality

218

Good news, Dr. Carolyn Leaf, a Christian neurobiology researcher, in her book *Who Switched Off My Brain,* confirmed it's possible to reframe the brain by taming the thoughts in your mind in what science calls neuroplasticity. [4]

Albert Einstein said, "We can't change a problem with the same thinking used to create it."[5] And Paul said we're to take every thought captive to make it obedient to Christ (2 Corinthians 10:5) and to renew our minds daily (Romans 12:2).

Can you see how the wrong mindset is a chain that keeps us going in circles in the soul wilderness? A freedom mindset begins with strengthening your mental fitness. Yes, there's a workout for everything.

The Mental Fitness Workout

We're going to eliminate this mental chub by practicing mental fitness. Let's be like Wonder Woman or John Wayne and lasso bondage thoughts. We're going to snatch them up, bring them close to our eyes, and examine the fruit of our reality that our thoughts create and implant new thought seeds and actions.

This workout is hard in the sense that you have an estimated 48.6 thoughts per minute, or up to 70,000 thoughts per day.[6] But easy, because it's only three steps.

First, you identify negative/unhealthy thoughts related to food, dieting, weight, and eating, such as: *I can't eat carbs, I've got to start my diet on Monday,* or *I think this new workout plan will help me lose thirty pounds this month.* Thoughts like these will enter the lasso.

Second, you exchange those thoughts with freedom beliefs like: *I choose not to eat foods that don't provide nutritional value, I live healthy now,* or *Not so fast get-skinny-quick-scheme, I'm onto you and it's one day at a time!*

As a third step, question the thought and the belief it stands on. From now on don't let a thought go by without a question. Ask the

Holy Spirit: *Is this true? What fruit is this producing?* or *Is this helping or hurting me?* Deeper beliefs under the thoughts are usually some variation of I'm not healthy enough, skinny enough, good enough, fit enough, acceptable enough, loveable enough—yada, yada, yada. If we repeat a lie enough times, we accept it as truth.

We'll demolish arguments and every pretension that sets itself up against the knowledge of God, take every thought captive, and make it obedient to Christ (2 Corinthians 10:5).

Once you own these new beliefs, you create a new mindset. But the next step is not only a freedom mindset but also freedom action, which is something you'll do differently going forward. Freedom actions create a powerful punch through the walls of bondage. You'll carry out a freedom action to support your new freedom mindset.

Adopt the Freedom Mindset

Let's expose seven unhealthy mindsets that need to be eliminated from our thinking and the corresponding freedom mindset and freedom actions to slim down mental chub.

Belief #1 – There's a Magic Pill

"There's got to be a solution that makes me lose weight fast."

Shelley couldn't zip her favorite pair of jeans, so she raced to Walmart and filled her cart with protein powders, diet pills, and a bottle of appetite suppressants. At the checkout stand, she added to her purchases a magazine that promised, "Lose 10 pounds in 10 days!"

Last night, Shelley ate half a jar of peanut butter. Anxious, she reasons, *I can't afford to buy a cart load of new clothes to accommodate my expanding muffin top.* Shelley's upset her peanut butter binge caused her clothes not to fit that morning, but in truth, it's her quest for a magic pill to fix the damage that's ill fitting.

220

This scenario is common for dieters. We get deceived because dieting is based in deception. Real diets only work when there's a full lifestyle change, such as vegetarian or gluten free, an acute health issue like diabetes or high blood pressure, or for a short term affair.

A magic pill sounds so soothing, so helpful, so immediate. Think about it, isn't this a cycle that only sets us up for failure?

When we search for a get-skinny-quick scheme, don't we end up relying on that scheme rather than taking responsibility and owning our choices today? In our heroic quest, with a Diet Nut logo'd cape flapping in the wind, we point our finger to the sky, and say, "Where's the next great diet pill. Then, I will eat better!"

Why Magic Pill Hunting Doesn't Work

The get skinny quick belief robs us of *being* healthy now. We tend to postpone good eating habit until later, and engage in poor eating now, because of the hope a magic pill is coming.

The magic pill is knowing there's no such thing as a magic pill because it doesn't exist. The real magic pill is to reject the fantasy of a magic pill and embrace the certainty of the daily body habits, twenty four hours of grace, one day a time. If we don't have a magic pill to pretend to find and struggle to stick to, we can take responsibility for our health today.

When you get duped by the latest diet fad, you make a choice to avoid a true commitment to a lifetime commitment of healthy eating because you're going for the quick fix. True health is a lifelong process. Dieting is a distraction from true health.

Some people set weight loss time frames like they would for other tasks, such as cleaning the garage or finishing a project. It doesn't work well like this for us. What happens if you start a diet plan, believing that in three months you'll lose fifty pounds? You'll eat as though you can lose the weight in days, not daily efforts.

I know because I popped diet pills, tried dozens of diets, and bought all the *National Enquirer* headlined papers that promised me fast weight loss.

A magic pill, the quest for a get-skinny-quick plan, pill, or program distracts from your real success of one day at time healthy habits to create a lifetime of healthy eating.

Freedom Mindset – "I live healthy now"

Ending the dieter's mindset will require you to live a twenty four hour day and get on track immediately, as opposed to waiting to start eating healthy tomorrow or when you find the next *lose weight fast* plan. This also includes not starting your repair diet on Monday or any other day of the week. Why Monday? Forty six percent of diets start on Mondays.[7]

To live healthy now means that no matter what day it is, no matter where you are, and no matter what foods are available or not available, you can still choose wisely that day.

You'll eliminate the holiday or vacation syndrome—when you eat like you're a linebacker trying to make the college team just because it's a holiday or because you're on vacation. Transition your mindset to live healthy now. Allow for one day at a time, a twenty four hour day of grace, moment by moment, choice by choice. Drop the fantasy. It's consistent changes over time that create lasting results.

Freedom Action – Magically Meal Plan

Make a commitment to stop magic pill hunting. Instead, meal plan to reduce the intensive impulse to jump on another diet bandwagon. Meal planning is proven to support healthier eating and healthier families. In one study, researchers found that families who sit down and eat together are less likely to be obese.[8]

Christ said, "Therefore I say to you, do not worry about your life, what you will eat or what you will drink; nor about your body, what you will put on. Is not life more than food and the body more than clothing?" (Matthew 6:25). For us not to worry about Inner Glutton derailing the day and triggering Diet Nut, we need to consider an intentional meal plan.

How to Magically Meal Plan

1. Set your intention on what you'll eat the next day, the night before. Jot down what you intend to eat on a post-it note. If you're wondering what to eat for dinner, you've already lost, and Inner Glutton is more vulnerable to acting out.

2. Decide when to meal plan. Figure out what habit is easier for you to stick with—the night before, at the start of the week, or every two to three days. I prefer the night before, but early on in my journey, I would plan the whole week's meals. It also helps to create a master list of meals. You can make a list on paper, on index cards, with a meal planning app, or on your computer. A list of about five to ten meal ideas for breakfast, lunch, and dinner works.

3. Decide when to grocery shop. Grocery shopping is a nemesis for those who suffer from weight and eating issues. We tend to eat out or neglect our eating, which makes us vulnerable to our Inner Glutton taking over.

    Consider the same day of the week to grocery shop. Lonna reduces the time it takes to grocery shop with an app. She shops on the app, then picks up her groceries at a scheduled time or has them delivered.

Belief #2 – The Drive to Lose Weight

"I've got to lose weight."

I'd been diligent—hired a personal trainer and made five trips to the gym each week. Fifteen rounds of strength building and a boatload of kickbox cardio later, I excitedly anticipated what the scale would show that morning at weigh-in as I walked into the gym.

I stood on the scale wearing a new brown skirt and a lightweight cream jacket that wouldn't add extra ounces. Marilyn, my personal trainer, edged the slide on the scale carefully before she announced the result.

"One hundred ninety pounds," she said in a matter of fact tone.

Then something welled up so fast inside of me I didn't dare try to control it … then it hit.

"Baawaaaaah," an inconsolable tear dam broke, at the gym, in front of innocent, muscular gym rats—unbeknownst to me or them what was happening.

"Why won't it move?" I kicked the scale as I wiped off the mascara trickling down my face.

I worked out with a personal trainer and ate zero calorie products for crying out loud. *Why didn't the scale reflect my efforts? And why was I crying profusely in public?!* I thought hurrying out.

All I thought about was weight loss. I exercised to lose weight, ate to lose weight, but I never seemed to lose much weight.

Out of frustration, I ditched Marilyn and the local health club. Defeated, I spent the next few months paving my way to heart attack city with continual stops at the local Wendy's for a sausage, egg, and cheese biscuit, binge visits for drug store candy, and lonely depressed nights talking to random, way underqualified friend therapists on the phone for hours. Yet my mind still dwelled on losing weight.

I developed a pattern of yo-yo exercise. You know how you exercise one week and then you're off for the next year? I enthusiastically started only to stop again. Why did I do this? Why couldn't I sustain an exercise program? Or an eating program?

Because the only benefit I truly cared about when it came to exercise or eating was weight loss, not better health, productivity, joyful emotions, or world peace—nope, just weight loss for me, my vain self, and I. If weight loss didn't come fast enough, then the exercise and the meal planning was over.

Why the Drive to Lose Weight Doesn't Work

It may be a part of your reality. You may feel you do, indisputably, need to lose weight. The doctor could've told you or your tight jeans (the ones where the button popped off at dinner a few months back). But how long have you thought about losing weight? Is the weight gone yet?

Perhaps, like a driver's manual stick shift, the very thought of losing weight is causing you to stay stuck in "losing weight" gear, never actually shifting to "lost the weight." Mind games are tricky because while it seems like common sense, this thinking doesn't work. Like I said earlier, your mind is fertile ground in which the thought seed will grow.

You tell your mind "lose weight," it takes it presently, losing weight. Your mind only knows what's right now. The difference in thinking is the difference between having to lose the weight and having lost the weight. It thinks, *lose weight, lose weight, lose weight*, so you have a present condition of weight to lose. Make sense?

Freedom Mindset – "I am healthy"

What do healthy people do? We want the results of healthy people, and we know what to do, but we don't believe we're healthy. Dieters don't believe they're healthy, which means the actions of healthy activities are short lived.

Our beliefs impact our actions, and our actions impact our results. We don't need to lose weight, we need to *be* healthy. And we need *to believe* we are healthy now to start doing healthy things. People who think they need to lose weight don't believe they're healthy and deceive themselves into another diet.

God calls Himself the Great I Am—emphasis on am—and He is (Exodus 3:14). He said, "Let there be light"—emphasis on be, and light became (Genesis 1:3). There's power in understanding the sense of the present—to speak things into existence that are not currently in existence—throughout the Scriptures (Romans 4:17).

We're called human beings for a reason. We operate best in the principle of be-do-have versus the other way around. We control by forcing our next diet, attempting to work out for hours or drink gallons of water per day, which is human doing. We body manipulate to force the body to endure our short lived dieting tactics.

The principle be-do-have suggests that out of who we believe we are is what we do. Out of what we do is what we have or the results we get. Being is the essence of our beliefs that underlie our actions.

When we concentrate on being healthy, we tend to become healthier and make better choices. When we believe we're healthy and fit, we'll do healthy and fit things and ultimately have a healthy and less flabby body.

Funny, not in a humorous way, but in an ironic way, the drive to lose weight puts us in a state of being—well, fat.

Freedom Action – Live Like You're Already Your Desired Size

What if you were already the size you wanted to be? How would you be any different? What would you do differently than you may be doing now? Wouldn't those actions lead you to the health you wanted to have? It's a good practice to live as though you're maintaining the weight you've wanted to lose.

Instead of the idea of losing weight, we're going to be and act as though the weight is already lost. What got you to a size 14 won't get you to a size 10. We'll deal with the battles of overeating and food addiction in Book 2, but think about how you've lived in the someday maybe space with your health.

We think because we know we need to lose weight, and weight is driving our thoughts, that we can just lose it later. Yet, later doesn't come, and weight gain is still a reality. Our actions must be based on living at our desired place today.

How to Live Like You're Already Your Desired Size

1. Talk to people at your desired size. Ask what they do to stay healthy. Chances are you could write a book on health material with all the diets you've done over the years. But take some time to find someone at church, Facebook, work, or the local health club whom you admire and pick his or her brain a bit for deeper insights.

2. Do those things. Focus on your vision from the action chapter and practice being at your desired size, no matter what things look like today.

3. Finish this book, take the Whole & Free Health online program, and get the T-shirt. Find out more at *www.WholeNFreeHealth.com*.

Belief #3 – Cheating on Diet with Foods

"I've been good all week so I can cheat just this once."

Ken, a middle aged salesman, loved his quarter pounder with cheese. His demanding job required a lot of road time and fast food provided convenient meals. But Ken hated the belly fat his chubby choices produced, so when he could barely button his pants, he'd ignite his get-skinny-quick diet plan.

And the first thing to go? You guessed it, his quarter pounder with cheese. He knew this supersized meal wasn't beneficial, so he cut it out. As usual, it worked for a few days, but one particularly stressful day at work, he found himself at the drive through window. He told his wife when he got home, guilt ridden, "I cheated." He referred not to her, but to his diet.

Why Cheating with Food Doesn't Work

Cheat. It's not an endearing word, is it? Cheat stirs up dark emotions of shame and deception. The problem with cheating on your own decision to eat well, is an all or nothing definition of the word healthy. As

227

a result, we swing from dieting one day to cheating and possibly to out-of-control the next.

You've tried to rationalize popular diet advice to have a cheat day, but after the so-called cheat day, you still have tormenting guilt and take several days to get back on track from overindulgence.

Not only does cheating on a diet cause you to feel guilty, it also causes you to eat well for a temporary period and disregards your favorite fun foods in a delusional forever fear frenzy. Ultimately you cheat yourself out of mental freedom. This on-again, off-again relationship with healthy eating and living must come to an end.

Freedom Mindset – "I'm in a monogamous relationship with healthy eating and living"

A healthy lifestyle includes having food for pleasure, as well as for nutrition. There's no need to continue to "cheat" or be "off" of your eating. Divorce the concept of diets and explore a new world of options for a true healthy lifestyle. Healthy living is a lifestyle that includes some of the foods you currently reject when you diet.

For example, if you believe having a cupcake is cheating, you're now on a diet, setting yourself up for guilt and failure when you have a cupcake. However, if your mindset shifts to living in a monogamous relationship with health, you can expand your definition of health to include a cupcake occasionally.

Would it be possible to eliminate the word *cheat* from your vocabulary when it comes to diet? And expand your definition of health to include your favorites?

Freedom Action – Expand Your Definition of Health

By expanding your definition of health, you can increase foods that are positively impacting your health and decrease foods negatively impacting nutritional health. Imagine your best foods hit a bullseye. Bullseye foods keep you on track to feel your best energy and confidence.

Occasionally you'll hit outside of the bullseye, hence Ken's quarter pounder. True healthy living includes foods you enjoy. It's the frequency, quality, timing, and size of that choice that changes.

How to Expand Your Definition of Health So You Don't Have to Cheat on Your Healthy Life

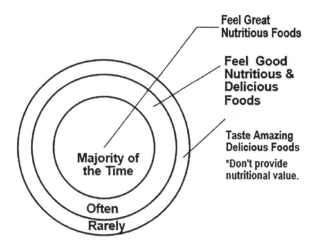

Figure 17.2 Inclusive Healthy Eating

In the next belief we'll discuss the meaning of the three new food groups. But to expand your definition, you can look at what you eat most of the time and include your favorites on occasion. Make your own chart like above and include the foods that meet the descriptions below.

1. The bullseye at the center includes the foods that make you feel great, the ones you consider healthy. They provide your body with value. Eat these foods most of the time.

2. The middle circle includes foods that make you feel good, you consider them healthy, but you need to be mindful of how much of them you eat.

3. The outer circle includes the food and drinks that make you feel like a cheat. But you include a cheat food, as a treat, at a lesser frequency,

better quality, or reduced caloric load. For example, a cookie from refined flour to a whole grain alternative version.

The dieter's mindset can make one cupcake turn into five cupcakes in a nanosecond. In the freedom mindset you can eat a cupcake and have peace about it because you're no longer a slave to the cupcake nor cheating on your diet when you eat one.

The guilt dissipates and now you can bask in the wonderful feeling of food freedom. To sum it up, expand your definition of health to include healthy alternatives of your favorites.

Belief #4 – Food has Morals

"Brownies are so bad."

I once watched a group of women and a group of teenage boys in the same environment, at a friend's Bible study. Without being too weird, I was looking at how they approached eating these little cookies.

The women were selective, only eating one or two. The young men could care less, and they on average ate about five to seven. This was interesting to me because the comments of the women were, "I can't eat too many cookies," or "I don't want to eat like a pig," or "I need to lose weight so I shouldn't be eating these."

Those cookies were plagued by guilt.

The young guys were just thinking, *These cookies look good, so I'll eat some.* They kept it simple, no stories around it, and most certainly no guilt. There's nothing wrong with eating five to seven cookies. What's crazy for us is to eat five to seven cookies with the expectation of losing weight or only having one or two cookies because we're scared to death to gain weight. This isn't freedom.

Why Assigning Moral Value to Food Doesn't Work

Food doesn't have moral value. It's like money. The Scriptures say that the love of money is the root of all evil (1 Timothy 6:10). Is the money evil? No, the people who love money more than what's right are evil. People are the ones who have been divinely made to have moral consciousness and who can operate in good or bad ways. From now on, let go of the thought that any particular food is bad or good.

Freedom Mindset – "There's no such thing as morally good or bad food!"

What happens when you think the chocolate bar is bad? Psychologically, you're validating shame and telling yourself that you're bad because you want something "bad." The cookie is an innocent bystander in the shame and guilt sandwich. When you eat it, you feel bad about yourself!

Deep down inside it comes with feelings of guilt, which is feeling bad! Logically, I'm sure you prefer to feel good. So, why not call food what it is—a chocolate bar that you enjoyed. When you eat "bad" you feel badly that you ate badly, and the demoralization continues to create the same poor eating behaviors.

Humans do have moral consciences; therefore, we can project our deep feelings of shame onto others and inanimate objects like food.

> " *The cookie is an innocent bystander in the shame and guilt sandwich.* "

There's no such thing as a morally good or bad food. There are beneficial and non-beneficial choices for your body, but food itself is neutral.

Freedom Action – Neutralize Food

An Alternative Way to Think about Food

There are three categories of food that we eat:

Nutritious. (N) Nutritious foods have the ability to heal and restore your body's balance. While these foods may not always be the best tasting (Brussel sprouts or liver, for example), —they give your body what it needs to thrive.

Nutritious & Delicious. (ND) Nutritious and delicious foods are foods that feel good to eat and you enjoy the taste. My favorites are mangos, cherries, or a kale salad with salmon. These are flavors you enjoy and that pack a powerful nutritional punch.

Delicious. (D) Delicious foods have virtually no nutritional value, but they make your taste buds dance a jig! While, these foods can be explicit, appealing to your carnal lust nature, it's unrealistic to cut them out completely.

As discussed in the body section, most food is loaded with high fructose corn syrup, sodium, and fat to addict your brain. You can't blame your taste buds for wanting all that manipulated flavor. Nutritious and nutritious & delicious foods won't create a sense of strong craving. You can enjoy them and enjoy the full freedom of your own mind—a mind that isn't captured by your food and weight thoughts.

It's okay to enjoy delicious foods, like cupcakes, cake, crackers, and other tongue rock stars. Just eat them with a frequency that allows you to stay free from food and weight drama. And change from refined versions to better quality. We'll discuss how to eat your delectables in Book 2.

What's great about just calling the food delicious versus bad is that it reflects positively on your self-esteem and your emotions. When you eat delicious food, enjoy it with a smile and savor each bite. It'll feel energetically positive in your soul. You feel good about the delicious choices you made. When you're eating delicious foods, the key is to watch the frequency, quality, timing, and size.

While I am a big advocate for dramatically reducing sugar and refined flour goods due to their negative effects on the brain and body, I think it's unrealistic to expect yourself to never eat delicious foods. Food is for celebration, too. It's meant to be enjoyed.

> When you eat delicious food, enjoy it with a smile and savor each bite.

But per our body habits conversations, if we're a slave to pleasure or only delicious man-made foods, we'll reap great problems in our health.

Are you ready to enjoy your food and take off the good and bad labels?

Belief #5 – Worth as Thinness

"I am worthy of love when I'm thin."

"Listen, you're beautiful and everything, but you need to lose ten pounds for me to be with you," said a man to a woman.

Click, tat, click, tat. The sound of that women's heels walking away.

Conditional love is not love. If anyone treated us as poorly as we can treat ourselves in the weight and worth area, most of us would leave.

Ty, a beautiful young African American woman wanted to be married.

"What's stopping you," I asked.

"My weight! I don't want to attract a guy like this."

"Why not?" I asked.

"Because, Jendayi, I just don't feel like anyone would really love me like this. I feel like any guy would really want there to be less of me to love, you know," she said, laughing nervously.

"So, you want someone who loves you because you're a certain size?" I asked.

Ty furrowed her brow and said, "Well, no, I want someone to love me for me."

"Hmm, does that sound like conditional or unconditional love?" I asked. "Ty, you're beautiful on the outside, and you're shining on the inside. When you get love based on what you look like, you'll fight for unconditional love in the relationship by gaining weight. You've experienced conditional love in the past. It was based on how you looked and how you performed. Is that the love you want for your future?"

Help her see, Lord. Open her eyes.

"No," she replied. She had humbly received the truth that she was worthy of love now, not after she got skinny enough to receive it. The revelation was touching to her as she tried on the new truth.

Rena was told by another believer that it was her weight that made a guy she liked run away. Thankfully, one day when discussing her love life with a friend, Rena admitted she felt she should lose weight so the right guy would come along.

Her loving friend said, "What if you found a man that accepted you as you are and loved who you are, exactly as you are?"

This revelation stirred deep tears from Rena. She accepted herself instead of believing she needed to be anything different to attract her spouse. She's been married for about a decade to her husband who met her at her heaviest weight. He loved her for both who and how she was.

> Your body shape and size have nothing to do with your true worth.

Why Worth in Thinness Doesn't Work

You don't have to be skinny to be approved, loved, valued, worthy, beautiful, or powerful. The truth is you're all of these things right now. Your body shape and size have nothing to do with your true worth.

Remain open, whoever you choose to be with will love you for your spirit and soul expressed through your body. However, how you eat and feel about yourself determines how much worth you feel inside. Eat like you love yourself. You're a child of God.

Freedom Mindset – "I'm worthy of love because I'm loved by God!"

The Father did not send His only begotten Son to die for the cause of both our sin and redemption so that we'd live defeated, worthless, and devalued. When you buy a new television, you want to utilize it for its purpose, right?

You too were bought at a price (1 Corinthians 6:20). You are the son or daughter of God (John 1:12). You're made in His image (Genesis 1:27). Clearly, you have value to God.

He fights for you, encourages you, and comforts you. He does this out of great love. In our understanding of how awesome God is, we know we're nothing without Him, but that does not mean we are nothing to Him.

You are good enough.

You are loved for simply being a human being.

Somewhere down the line you've learned that flaws, wrinkles, and wobbly arms aren't deserving of love, so you place your worth in being better looking.

> **We're perfectly imperfect in Him.**

What I love about our perfection in Christ is that He is perfect and we're perfectly imperfect in Him. The blood of Jesus is priceless, and you were worth that price. Not because of you, but because of who He is in you. The beauty of holiness is what is beautiful to God (1 Peter 3).

Freedom Action – Place Your Worth in Christ

Where do you place your worth? Imagine your soul being like a ball. Your name is on that ball. It's a gorgeous ball, made of gold and silver with rare gems, like pearls or diamonds.

Imagine yourself placing that precious, unique, valuable ball in a bucket that has different labels on the outside of it—labels such as education, ministry title, race, marital status, income, savings, health, weight, or talents.

When we don't feel a genuine sense of worth in who God created us to be, we will look outside of ourselves to the various labels that define worth in our view.

One of my worth buckets was labeled "skinny." Earlier attempts at weight loss caused me to have fleeting self-worth. When skinny, I felt superior, but when chubby, I felt inferior. Inferiority/superiority com-plexes happen when our worth is unstable. If we're pleased with our bucket label of weight, education, income, marital status, or health, it can bring out a superior, arrogant, puffed up, conceited, self-absorbed, and trite side of us.

If we are displeased with our weight and other bucket labels, it can bring out an inferior, depressed, deflated, defeated, isolated, and neglect-ful side. Yet, both fruits of arrogance and depression have the same root in chronically low self-worth or lack of self-value.

> "Inferiority/superiority complexes happen when our worth is unstable."

Where have you placed your soul's worth?

How to Place Your Worth in Christ

1. Speak to the label that's been stealing your worth. For example - You can take your self-worth out of the scale by speaking to it. Speak to the scale and tell it who's boss. It sounds something like this, "Scale, the Lord is my boss, not you! I have worth in Him, you are not going to predict my mood any longer. I am enough! I am more than what I weigh."

2. Keep growing your identity in Christ. Read Scriptures on who you are in Christ. And seek the Lord about your worth.

Belief #6 – Thinness Equates to Happiness
"I can't be happy, until I lose weight."

Danielle participated in a healing retreat I lead called *The Hungry Soul*. During our discussion time, as I led a teaching on the interrelationship between body, soul, and spirit, Danielle revealed her true belief: if she was overweight, she was destined to be unhappy.

She insisted and almost yelled at me.

"Jendayi, how in the world can I be happy being seventy five pounds overweight?! You can't be happy and fat!" her voice echoed in the large great room of my Denver condo.

We sat at the dining room table as I taught on giant post-it notes on the wall of our intimate retreat.

"What's bigger, Danielle, your soul, which is who you are, or your body?" I replied. We don't get who we are, so we're often limited by the sight of our bodies.

Danielle studied the flipchart at the front of the room that contained a diagram of interlocking circles to represent body, soul, and spirit as she pondered my comment. She looked that diagram up and down several times. Tears clouded her eyes.

"Isn't the body an instrument for my soul?" she asked.

"So, which is bigger?" I repeated.

"My soul?" she asked.

"So, where does happiness come from?" I asked.

"My soul?" she asked again.

"Danielle, who makes you happy?" I asked, driving the lesson home.

"I do," Danielle said as her frown turned into a smile, revealing her newfound understanding.

Why Waiting to Lose Weight to Be Happy Doesn't Work

Waiting to lose weight to be happy puts your life on hold. In exchange for an adventurous life out and about in God's beautiful creation, you're stuck watching television, watching YouTube videos, watching everyone's wall on Facebook, and watching your own life go by.

And while you're watching, waiting to be slim so you can be happy, you've got to have your popcorn, right?

Don't postpone living any longer. Weight isn't your problem. Your discontentment is. Unhappy people are people who don't know who they are or whose they are yet.

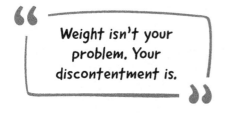

> **Weight isn't your problem. Your discontentment is.**

You put off doing fun things, meeting new people, and doing what you've always wanted. We're suspended on hold until this weight problem goes away. The problem is that it never seems to go away—for good anyway.

A lack of contentment in body produces an unsafe feeling in the soul, and an unsafe soul—that isn't feeling good enough to be happy now—will create a self-protection barrier in weight on the body. Oh, and more than 43 percent of people with depression are obese.[9] And 38 percent of obese people are depressed.[10] It's time to think and do something differently.

Freedom Mindset – "I choose to be happy in my size now!"

Marci Shimoff, author of *Happy for No Reason: 7 Steps to Being Happy from the Inside Out*, said, "To become happier we have to snap out of the trance that our happiness rests in 'more and better' which we'll get 'someday.' No matter what we have, *Happy for No Reason* exists only now, not later."[11]

Create a life you enjoy and love, just put the weight thing on the back burner, and put loving yourself and being content with who you are on the front burner. Better soul care leads to a healthier, happier body.

Your soul has been oppressed because of the whole weight and eating thing. It wants to come out and play. Make happiness a choice in your current size to produce soul safety to let the weight go as you embrace more of you—and more of life.

When you're unhappy at your current weight with unresolved roots, it's only a matter of time before you'd be unhappy at a new weight. With weight and eating obsession, if we're unhappy, we eat! So eventually the same problem will happen again.

Happiness is a choice.

> **When you're unhappy at your current weight with unresolved roots, it's only a matter of time before you'd be unhappy at a new weight.**

Joy is fruit of your spiritual transformation in Christ (Galatians 5:22).

Paul was content in all circumstances because Paul's joy came from the inside out (Philippians 4:11–12). Life is guaranteed to have problems, but in Christ, happiness is a choice to honor all that God has given you. He gives us peace (John 16:33). And to shout joyfully unto the Lord is how we defeat the enemy of our soul.

Prophesy over yourself like David did: "The King shall have joy in Your strength, O Lord; and in Your Salvation how greatly shall he rejoice!" (Psalm 21:1). Rejoice! You're coming out of weight and eating bondage.

The Lord has delivered you and will see you through. Joy is your portion. "This is the day the Lord has made; We will rejoice and be glad in it." May God's overflowing joy fill you! And pray the joy of the Lord will be the source of joy in your life!

Freedom Action – Celebrate and Enjoy Your Life

If there have been activities you haven't done because your weight has stopped you, it's time to do them. Begin to live your life fully, despite your current weight condition. As you cultivate happiness in soul and joy in spirit, you'll see weight release from your body. Do this daily to create a genuine state of happiness and joy.

Choosing happiness and focusing on what's good, pure, holy, and worthy of good in your day can become your new normal. Go try a new Bible study, join a small group, go hiking, buy clothes you like, take a vacation, and wear a bathing suit. As you break free of discontent by doing what you haven't done because of weight, you'll break free.

Will you make a choice to be happy despite your body shape or life circumstances?

How to Celebrate and Enjoy Your Life

1. Make a list of all the things you'd like to do in life, then do them.
2. Cross things off the list after you complete them.
3. Meditate on Scriptures to direct your unhappiness to happiness.
   - Don't be dejected and sad "for the joy of the Lord is your strength" (Nehemiah 8:10b).
   - "The Lord *is* my strength and shield; My heart trusted in Him, and I am helped; Therefore my heart greatly rejoices and with my song I will praise him" (Psalm 28:7).
   - "Not that I speak in regard to need, for I have learned in whatever state I am, to be content" (Philippians 4:11a).

Belief #7 – One Mistake Defines the Whole Day

"I messed up my eating, so I might as well eat whatever I want."

Jenna sabotaged her efforts almost daily. She'd get up with Diet Nut at her side, focusing on the perfect breakfast meal. But by lunch she couldn't resist the smell of freshly baked Danishes near her small town workplace. Jenna got her Danish and threw the rest of her healthy eating plan out the window, devouring any refined carbohydrate that crossed her path.

Candy, office birthday cake, extra mashed potatoes at dinner—nothing could escape Jenna's mouth. She thought, *I already messed up, so why bother eating well now?*

Diet Nut owned the morning, but her Inner Glutton dominated lunch through bedtime. Out of control and discouraged Jenna repeated

240

this Groundhog Day until she changed her mindset and figured out her track.

Why One Mistake Defines the Whole Day Doesn't Work

This mindset doesn't work for obvious reasons. Health results will be delayed every time that we make a mistake and decide to wallow in it by making a dozen more the rest of the day. In the twenty four hours of grace we get each day, we'll make some mistakes, but wild eating delays our progress.

Your life isn't defined by this one area. Usually when we mess up there are other factors at work like sleep quality, things on your heart, or inadequate time with God. Think of your whole life as being on or off track so you can see when you are tracking well with God or when you're off.

Freedom Mindset – "I get back on track immediately!"

You're riding a bike down a long street and you fall off, but you still want to get home. Would you just stop riding the bike? Would you roll around on the street making your scratches worse?

It's the same case here. Dust yourself off, get back on the bike, and keep going. The bike is your commitment to freedom choices. There's no falling off the wagon in a healthy relationship with food. Be committed to your best life, no matter what bumps you hit along the road.

The sooner you get up and get back on the bike and keep riding, the more you will see the transformations take place. You can and will achieve health, but you don't throw out the whole day or night based on a mistake or two or three.

Freedom Action – Figure Out Your Track

Study yourself over the next few weeks to develop your personal on track and off track understanding. You're in the process of looking deeply at your soul, lifestyle, patterns, and environment to find out what supports you thriving.

There's a saying, "The secrets of your future are hidden in your daily routine." To find out what works best for you, start thinking about what an on track, great day looks and feels like so you can enjoy more of them.

- What does it mean to be on track in your life?
- What does it mean to be off track?
- When did you last feel great in your joy and body?
- How do you get yourself to feel good again after you've felt down?

Table 17.3 Example of Jenna's Life On and Off Track

JENNA'S LIFE ON TRACK	JENNA'S LIFE OFF TRACK
Eating according to bio-individual food plan	Eating wildly without discretion
Morning devotional completed	Skipped morning devotional
Clean house	Messy house
Exercising 4 to 6 times per week	Exercising less than 3 times per week
Planning fun activities to look forward to	Watching excessive television
Drinking water	Drinking coffee like it is water
Showing up for work on time	Late for work
Logging Inner Glutton findings as needed	Binge eating and not learning from it
Emotionally Clearing on a regular basis	Wallowing in negative emotions and thoughts
Bills are paid on time	Overspending, missing payments
Sense of contentment	Sense of overwhelm, feeling anxious or negative
Taking vitamins and supplements	Skipped vitamins and supplements
Kind toward others	Rude toward others

> **Your life on track feels good. Really good.**

These questions help to describe what your life, on track, looks and feels like. We can create our lives and our outcomes.

Your life on track feels good. Really good. Words like calm, balanced, happy, fun, light, encouraging, positive, and energetic come to mind as feelings of being on track. Your life off track feels bad. Words like anxious, unbalanced, scattered, sad, dull, heavy, discouraging, negative, and drained describe being off track.

It's up to you to do the self study to find out what makes you happy and energetic. You deserve to feel great on a consistent basis. And

> **It's up to you to do the self study to find out what makes you happy and energetic.**

from this day forward, in your committed, monogamous relationship with healthy eating and living, you can refer to yourself as being on or off track. And when off track, get back on track quickly by asking the question, *What's the best thing for me to do right now?*

How to Figure Out Your Track

1. Make a two column chart. Put 'My life on track' on one side and 'My life off track' on the other side.

2. Review the questions above Table 17.3 and describe what each track looks like.

3. Going forward, refer to being on or off track and do your best to get on track quickly.

Renew Your Mind

Do you feel the heaviness lifting from your soul? The dieter's mindset is weighty. You can put the freedom mindsets on index cards or post-it notes to repeat them in your mind. We walked through the seven strongest beliefs in the dieter's mindset and exchanged them for a freedom mindset.

To strengthen this even further, add a scriptural boost. We're to renew our minds daily, Paul said, "And do not be conformed to this world, but be transformed by the renewing of your mind, that you may prove what *is* that good, acceptable, and perfect will of God" (Romans 12:2).

We've taken a break from heavy lifting in chubbology and practiced mental fitness. Coming up next is the Emotional Fitness Workout™ to heal chubbology, as well as emotional eating.

REFLECTION QUESTIONS

1. Which dieter's mindset belief is most difficult to release?

   _____

   _____

2. Which new freedom mindset belief resonates the most?

   _____

   _____

3. What new freedom action will you try?

   _____

   _____

PRAYER

Heavenly Father,

You're the Source of all creation, the Source of my strength, and the Creator of my mind, please overhaul my dieter's mindset and help me to walk in a freedom mindset. Help me to break free into a whole and free person for your glory!

Help me to take erroneous thoughts captive and know that you're with me to unravel my identity as I let go of the old and welcome the new ways of being. Help me to believe and to act healthy now. Give me greater discernment with ways I have been duped into thinking I need a diet plan. Lord, free me from the bondage of weight and eating for your good purpose in my life.

In Jesus' name, amen.
It is so!

CHAPTER 18

ENACT AN EMOTIONAL STRENGTH TRAINING PLAN

Chan #3 – Emotional Eating

"Jesus wept"

−JOHN 11:35

Out of the heart the mouth eats.

O*h, God! What did I just do?* I reached for the phone and dialed a therapist as though calling 911.

Thankfully, I got an appointment with Kali the next day. We exchanged greetings as I entered her office. I sat on a cream colored cushioned chair. Nervous, I glanced at the wooden floors and a fireplace. The blue and cream walls matched the Denver sky. Proper degrees that hung above her desk provided me with a sense of security in her ability to help me. I exhaled a sigh of relief.

"So, what's happening with you?" she asked.

"I keep having overeating episodes," I said.

"What's that like?" she asked.

"Oh, you know, two oversized slices of pizza, a huge cinnamon roll, and a pint of butter pecan ice cream all in one sitting." Ashamed, my eyes could've burned a hole in the wooden floor.

"Why do you think you're doing this to yourself?" she asked.

"Well, I'm married, but I feel like I'm all by myself. My husband hasn't been attentive the past few months. I know he loves me, but I feel abandoned by him," I said on the brink of tears. "I keep overeating when he doesn't come home from work or prioritizes his friends over me. Do you think he's avoiding me?"

The words stung my heart as they rolled off my tongue. I felt pathetic and ashamed. I reflected on my move to Denver a year prior and tapped the iceberg of my suppressed pain of not having close friends and family around. My husband was closest to me, but it was unfair to think he could meet all my needs.

Kali proceeded to walk me through a meditation to stir up emotional memories. She asked questions to help me tap into beliefs that drove me to stuff myself.

"What's the earliest memory of feeling lonely and abandoned?" she asked in her soothing tone.

Holy Spirit, help me, I prayed.

A wellspring of grief flooded my heart as a vivid image of the scene emerged in my mind. "My father's funeral at twelve years old. He's lying in the casket and I'm looking over the casket at his sleeping face," I said.

"What do you need to say to your dad," she asked.

"I never knew you," an unconstrained shout took flight toward my dead dad, "I never knew you." I repeated several times louder and louder, as grief completely overtook my eye sockets.

Kali urged me to say all that was in my heart to say to him in my active memory movie.

This emotional baggage was completely forgotten until I confronted the matter.

My twelve-year-old self believed his death was because she was defective. His final departure created a sense of confused identity.

The revelation, *I never knew him,* meant I didn't know a part of myself. Who knew all of that unresolved baggage sticks around until we decide to unpack it? If we don't unpack it, we'll eat it.

Inner Glutton Revealed

We went deeper.

"What other memories do you sense?" she asked after my stream of tears slowed.

"I'm six years old eating sauerkraut at my grandmother's house. I stuffed myself with it." An agonizing, heart-wrenching sob emerged, and choppy words persisted with an aha! moment, "Oh my goodness, my parents just got divorced. I had no one to talk to even though my family was right there!"

Kali handed me tissue after tissue for several minutes. She helped me to understand again my younger self believed she was defective. The divorce benefited my mom and dad but left me with a fear I'd be abandoned and rejected in intimate relationships.

I'd sauerkraut'ed my emotions that day to the point of vomiting. Until that moment, I was unaware of where my deep dependency on food began.

I worked with Kali and the Holy Spirit over time to reshape my thoughts and beliefs to internalize the truth; I'm never alone. God's always with me.

Emotional wounds drive emotional eating.

Childhood drama and its unpredictability gets recreated with inner drama with weight and eating. My little girl self at various ages needed to experience and release these emotions so I could successfully move forward to weight and eating freedom.

Binges contain messages about our identity. My Inner Glutton was my hurt little girl self that I had to embrace to heal.

I still had a lot of work to do, but I left her office a new woman.

Binges contain messages about our identity.

249

Healing Emotional Eating

Everyone emotionally eats. The question is to what degree? Is it a binge to the tune of 200 calories or 5,000? Does it happen multiple times per day or once in a blue moon?

Emotional eaters eat from an ***emotionally triggered*** place. That place is our emotional wounds. Emotions we'd rather not feel or aren't comfortable feeling, we manifest as a hearty lasagna, then eat our feelings masked by the lasagna.

My present situation, my husband's absence, triggered an *implosion*—an episode of Inner Glutton overeating. This particular episode I called, Death by Sticky Buns.

Our past impacts our present reactions and choices. To my surprise, the trigger of loneliness, which spurred an eating binge over my husband's absence, wasn't about my husband at all.

It was about unresolved pain from the same emotion of abandonment ungrieved by my father's absence. In other words, when I felt lonely or abandoned in the present, I ate from the past abandonment of my father.

My friends, this is the golden key to healing our emotional eating. We eat excess because Inner Glutton is an unhealed child within, trapped inside of an erroneous belief about who he or she is. Our child inside needs to be heard, loved, and affirmed by us, their caregiver. It takes processing difficult emotions to heal. And it's a tough to process without tools.

Out of the heart the mouth speaks (Luke 6:45b). And I say, out of the heart the mouth eats. Because in my episode, Death by Sticky Buns, I ate from the soul wound of abandonment. Once healed, I

> We eat excess because Inner Glutton is an unhealed child within, trapped inside of an erroneous belief about who he or she is.

could no longer eat from or out of that emotional wound, because the abandonment of not knowing my dad was no longer *there* to eat from.

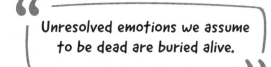

Unresolved emotions we assume to be dead are buried alive.

Unresolved emotions we assume to be dead are buried alive.

For the first time in my life, I allowed myself to fully cry out my grief over my dad's death without holding back. And boy did I cry. I cried for hours, everywhere I went, for days!

After my consuming wonder of why on earth I hadn't made my emotional 911 call years sooner, a remarkable strategy birthed. *The Emotional Fitness Workout*™, a five step inner workout.

EMOTIONAL EATING STRONGHOLD QUIZ

Put a check next to the answer that describes your emotional strength and add the total points below. The higher the score, the more emotional wounds are present.

1. How often do you use food to alleviate negative emotions and stress?
☐(5) ALWAYS ☐(4) OFTEN ☐(3) SOMETIMES ☐(2) RARELY ☐(1) NEVER

2. How often can you recognize emotions that sparked the reason(s) you used food?
☐(1) ALWAYS ☐(2) OFTEN ☐(3) SOMETIMES ☐(4) RARELY ☐(5) NEVER

3. How often do you identify what you're feeling when you're feeling it?
☐(1) ALWAYS ☐(2) OFTEN ☐(3) SOMETIMES ☐(4) RARELY ☐(5) NEVER

4. How often do you differentiate physical hunger from emotional hunger?
☐(1) ALWAYS ☐(2) OFTEN ☐(3) SOMETIMES ☐(4) RARELY ☐(5) NEVER

5. How often do you divert your actions from harming yourself with food?
☐(1) ALWAYS ☐(2) OFTEN ☐(3) SOMETIMES ☐(4) RARELY ☐(5) NEVER

6. How often do you take time to feel your feelings?
☐(1) ALWAYS ☐(2) OFTEN ☐(3) SOMETIMES ☐(4) RARELY ☐(5) NEVER

7. How often do you judge or criticize the way you feel?
☐(5) ALWAYS ☐(4) OFTEN ☐(3) SOMETIMES ☐(2) RARELY ☐(1) NEVER

8. How often do you blame your poor eating choices on how someone made you feel?
☐(5) ALWAYS ☐(4) OFTEN ☐(3) SOMETIMES ☐(2) RARELY ☐(1) NEVER

9. How often do you make yourself feel better with things besides food?
☐(1) ALWAYS ☐(2) OFTEN ☐(3) SOMETIMES ☐(4) RARELY ☐(5) NEVER

10. How often do you use a process or strategy to clear your negative emotions?
☐(1) ALWAYS ☐(2) OFTEN ☐(3) SOMETIMES ☐(4) RARELY ☐(5) NEVER

Total Score: | **Score Sheet**
30–50 | You're in the right place!
20–30 | You've done some hard work and it shows!
——————— | 10–20 | Handle this weight and eating thing and you're golden!

What Are Emotions?

Miriam Webster describes emotion as a conscious mental reaction (such as anger or fear) subjectively experienced as strong feeling usually directed toward a specific object and typically accompanied by bodily physiological and behavioral changes.[1]

Emotions have the root word motion, which means action, and are intertwined with our thoughts, actions, and beliefs per Chapter 17. And while emotional states tend to be transient, what we do as a result of emotional eating sabotages our health. To graduate from emotional eating, we need to become emotionally savvy.

Your Choice to Become Emotionally Fit

Emotional healing is like a hotel in your soul. The more painful the past, the larger the number of rooms. These rooms carry labels, such as "rejected at sixteen at the school dance" or "criticized in front of friends by Mom" or "men." These times in your past shaped your mindsets and thoughts today.

You make the choice to open the door to each room and allow the Holy Spirit to come in and clean it out. After it's clean, the Holy Spirit fills it up with God's love and truth, then moves into another room as you unlock permission.

Before a miracle like what took place in Kali's office, my soul had to go through prep work. Along my journey, I found the book *Feelings Buried Alive Never Die* by Karol Truman.

It helped me realize that I gave my power to emotions, money, food, my mother, my circumstances—basically anything as an excuse to eat whatever I wanted despite the negative effects on my body.

We're victimized and tormented by emotional wounds until we deal with them.

Healing is a part of our spiritual path. Healing is the tough, real work of a maturing believer.

> **Healing is the tough, real work of a maturing believer.**

The more fruit of the Spirit evidenced in our lives, the more we know we've been healed (Galatians 5:22).

It's up to you to invite the Holy Spirit into your healing. It's your

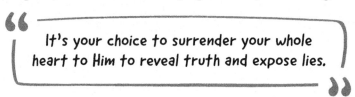

> **It's your choice to surrender your whole heart to Him to reveal truth and expose lies.**

choice to surrender your whole heart to Him to reveal truth and expose lies. This process is lifelong, there's no end date, but it gets easier.

We'll learn how to do the Emotional Fitness Workout™, then enact an Emotional Strength Training Plan to grow bigger than running to food like it's our grandmama with our emotional problems.

Will you make the choice to become emotionally fit?

What Is Emotional Fitness?

The five step Emotional Fitness Workout™ is a tool to help you process painful emotions that affect your emotional eating choices. Emotional fitness is your skill of what you feel, connected to why you feel that way. To strengthen our emotional body, reduces our need to protect and defend with chubby suits or Inner Glutton sabotage.

Emotional fitness strengthens the emotional body to handle offenses, upsets, disappointments, and overall feelings effectively when they occur so we're not eating over them. Wouldn't you love to get over an offense sooner? How about a disappointment in less than five minutes?

The power of emotional fitness is you get to take your power out of the hands of others, circumstances, and food. Emotional fitness for weight and eating strengthens your emotional body as a foundation for better physical and spiritual health.

When to Start an Emotional Fitness Workout™

Just as an alarm goes off to start your day, a trigger is the alarm to start an Emotional Fitness Workout.™

We Know We're Triggered When

- We have an overwhelming urge to find food. We seek out fast food, raid the kitchen cabinets, run to the convenience store for junk food, or tap into a secret stash of candy.

- We feel strong emotions such as loneliness, defeat, anger, grief, guilt, and/or embarrassment. We may also feel fat or ugly.

- We feel fearful, unsafe, threatened, or uncomfortable (chubbological triggers).

- We shut down all emotions, numb them, and isolate with excess screen time (the Internet, movies, television, or social media) and mindless eating.

- We're about to overeat, want to overeat, or have just overeaten.

- We're sabotaging progress, regaining weight, and/or choosing poorly.

Have any of these signs affected you in the past week? Moving forward, look for signs that you've been triggered and start the Emotional Fitness Workout™.

THE EMOTIONAL FITNESS WORKOUT™	
Step #1: Stop	How can I disengage in self-harming pursuits?
Step #2: Pinpoint	What triggered me and what emotions am I feeling exactly?
Step #3: Evaluate	Why am I feeling this way?
Step #4: Experience	How can I best process my feelings right now?
Step #5: Release	What or who do I need to let go of?

Step 1 – Stop

How can I disengage in self-harming pursuits?

"Stop," the officer said, "Put the knife and fork down." Couldn't you use the food police from time to time to help you put excess food down? The first step in the Emotional Fitness Workout™ is to stop. To stop is to consciously disengage your Inner Glutton when he or she's tempted to excessively eat. This step strengthens your emotional impulse control muscle.

- Ben cruised angrily down the road after work. He pulled up to Wendy's drive through, as he savored the number 4 combo. By the time his turn came at the window, he drove away.

- Amanda knew if she bought the chocolate cake, she'd eat it all. She walked past the bakery section and continued grocery shopping.

- Tina crunched the corner of a tortilla chip, then threw it and the rest of the bag out. She caught herself before the whole bag ended up featured on her belly.

- Sarah stared at the banana bread while home alone. She went outside to get fresh air to ward off the desire to devour it.

In the above examples, each person practiced step one. Like a Corvette can go from zero to sixty miles per hour in about three seconds, so too can our negative emotions drive us to food.

Before we look up, our Inner Glutton has already acted, and we're throwing out candy cartons. "She's quick," a Whole & Free Health course participant admitted, "Sometimes Inner Glutton's so fast I didn't even see what happened."

We turn to food as fast as we flip on a light switch. *Switch* and you've derailed your efforts. To stop, is to slow down the process from trigger point to an emotional eating episode.

As we increase our emotional pain tolerance, we gain impulse control. When we stop the behavior, we find reasons behind what's driving it. Next time think through what's going on behind the compulsion. This skill and first step is the hardest skill to learn, be gracious with yourself.

Ben didn't want to stop, no one really does, but he realized if he kept surrendering to his cravings telling him to get a burger, he'd get the same high blood pressure, frustration with his burger belly, and intimacy issues with his wife. All of which, came from his stops for fast food.

> " *As we increase our emotional pain tolerance, we gain impulse control.* "

He needed to change. If it wasn't now, it would be later. Per his doctor, one more bite could propel him into a heart attack. Ben's eaten hundreds of fatty burgers in his forty years. When was enough, enough?

Aren't you inspired every time you choose life?

Temptation and the Tempter

Temptation comes from the tempter. Now when the tempter came to Him, he said, "If You are the Son of God, command that these stones become bread" (Matthew 4:3). Jesus knew who He was and what was on the other side of His obedience. As our identity in health strengthens, we're not tempted by food anymore. And we can trust the rewards of victory that exist on the other side of obedience.

We have everything we need to overcome temptation. Paul said, "No temptation has overtaken you except such as is common to man; but God *is* faithful, who will not allow you to be tempted beyond what you are able, but with the temptation will also make the way of escape, that you may be able to bear *it*" (*1 Corinthians 10:13*).

As Peter Scazzero says for the subtitle of his book *Emotionally Healthy Spirituality*, "It's impossible to be spiritually mature while remaining emotionally immature."[2]

We're to increase our emotional pain tolerance, and we can only do this with practice. A low emotional pain tolerance is guaranteed to throw us into the arms of a soft pretzel whenever we don't get what we want.

A low emotional pain tolerance thrives on self-destruction. When you stop the damage, your self-confidence increases. Would Ben have felt better or worse about himself if he had eaten fatty fast food? Each time we stop, we strengthen the "yes, I can do this" belief muscle.

Every time you succeed at step one, you rebuild from the demoralization you've taught yourself over the years by breaking your own agreements. Instead of saying yes to self-harm, self-destruction, and shame, you can say "yes!" to your true identity in Christ.

To strengthen the most difficult emotional muscle of all, impulse control, allows us to learn delayed gratification—also known as the spiritual practice of patience. Our flesh loves to get what it wants when it wants, but this very nature is anti-progress in the kingdom of God.

As long time emotional eaters, we'll always make excuses and rationalize eating more. Always! Food is how we cope. Food is our favorite reward. It's our default modus of operandi.

How to Stop

To stop, do the following:

- **Pray for God's help immediately.** Try simple prayers like, "Holy Spirit, I need your help right now to stop my compulsion to go to food. Please help me to stop and do the right thing in this moment." Or "Satan, the Lord rebuke you. God hasn't given me any temptation I cannot get away from."

- **Reflect on three reasons you want to stop from your Action Plan.** Ben reflected on his biggest reasons:

  1. I want to love God with all of my heart, soul, and strength, not food.
  2. I want to see my children grow up.
  3. I want to pay for one airline seat, not two.

- **Cheerlead yourself to stop.** King David encouraged himself in the Lord. Ben did, too.

  Ben said to himself, *I can do this. My boss isn't worth more negative health reports. I can drive home and eat leftovers. I can change. The same power that raised Jesus from the dead lives in me.*

- **Think about three negative consequences of chubby choices.** Give thought to the repercussions of poor decisions. The consequences of our choices must become harder to swallow. These are the opposite of what you want.

Ben's negative consequences were clear:

1. I'll dishonor my temple.
2. I won't reverse heart disease.
3. I could risk not seeing my daughter grow into a woman and walking her down the aisle when she gets married.

- **Recite the Scripture you chose to stand on and say it out loud.** Ben stood on Philippians 4:13 and spoke, "I can do all things through Christ who strengthens me!"

- **Speak to the food itself.** Ben spoke to the food temptation directly, with attitude. He said, "Number 4 burger you're not my god. I let you go." It does help to say "stop!" out loud, too.

  You have the power of the Holy Spirit inside of you to stop the impulsivity to go to food when emotional. So, when fast food screams your name, use it.

What If You Can't Stop?

You can stop before, during, or after going to food. Once you stop, go onto step two. But sometimes, we can't stop. This happens when we're overcome by something physiological, such as food addiction or when the emotion is deeply rooted. Be patient with yourself and move on to step two to support uncovering the source of the binge.

REFLECTION QUESTIONS ?

1. What foods do you go to when you have a negative emotional reaction?

    _____

    _____

2. What have you done in the past to stop a chubby choice?

    _____

    _____

3. From the ideas above, what's one thing you can do when triggered to emotionally eat?

    _____

    _____

Step 2 – Pinpoint
What triggered me and what emotions am I feeling exactly?

Whether you succeed at step one or not, implement step two. Step two, pinpoint, is recognizing your trigger(s) and emotions to strengthen your emotional literacy muscle to find the emotions you've been eating from.

Think about your last emotional eating episode. What made you want to eat in the first place? Whatever the answer—a fight with your adult child, a surprising performance review, or a break up—we call this a trigger.

Figure out what happened. Then ask yourself, what am I feeling?

- Ben relied on God to get him through the past two years of reporting to Aaron. Aaron, a demanding and egotistical type, couldn't help but blast Ben in front of the team. Ben recognized his trigger was Aaron's words in front of other colleagues.

  Aaron said, "Ben, you're late and inconsistent. This report is not up to standards for our client. You need to redo this before next Tuesday."

  Ben pulled away from the drive through window as he recognized his anger toward Aaron. Ben pinpointed his feelings. Underneath Aaron's harsh words, Ben felt undermined and humiliated.

- For some time, Amanda craved chocolate cake after romantic dinners with her husband of forty years. The chocolate cake obsession after dinner was replacing Amanda's deep grief from unresolved pain of how terribly her husband treated her in the first three decades of their marriage. To stop the desire for chocolate cake's comfort meant processing the emotions of hurt, betrayal, and grief from her husband's numerous affairs, as well as the lost years of happiness she'd never get back.

- Marie discovered her excessive ice cream binges at night were triggered by financial stress. She was underpaid and wasn't eligible for promotion. Her anxiety caused her to eat over fear of her financial future.

We need to know what spurred the food reaction, then embrace our emotions without judgment.

When you're looking for a store in the mall you find on the map the red dot that says, "You are here". To pinpoint your emotions is to figure out where you are emotionally. Emotional literacy is an important step toward emotional fitness. We need to be able to put a name to the way we're feeling.

Like my father's story, which represented only a sliver of the wounds

> " Emotional literacy is an important step toward emotional fitness.

I emotionally ate from, we're emotionally stunted until we deal with it. These wounds don't just go away. We must decide *to feel them and heal them*. And we can't do that until we know how to identify them.

How to Pinpoint

To pinpoint, do the following:

- **Find your trigger.** Ideally, we have a clear scenario that compels us to eat. Figure out what that scenario is. If you tend to have a fast paced life or feel it's difficult to process emotions, consider everything happening in your life, then consider where there might be emotional charge to explore.

- **Study emotional vocabulary.** Most people identify about ten emotions they feel on a consistent basis, but there are 34,000 emotions.[3] Growing your emotional literacy also grows your emotional strength. Check out names of various emotions online.

- **Name your feelings.** You're not limited to one feeling. You can have five feelings happen at once. You can have a new feeling you haven't experienced before. Learn what your emotions are trying to tell you.

The most common places we're eating from are:

- **Anger.** Anger can also feel like injustice, resentment, disrespect, betrayal, or contempt.
- **Grief.** Grief can also feel like sadness, dejection, defeat, despair, loneliness, or abandonment.
- **Guilt.** Guilt can also feel like regret, sadness, anger, or fear.
- **Shame.** Shame can also feel like embarrassment, rejection, guilt, self-doubt, or insecurity.
- **Fear.** Fear can also feel like worry, anxiety, uncertainty, incompetency, or inadequacy.
- **Boredom.** Boredom can also feel like emptiness, meaninglessness, purposelessness, or restlessness.

- **Ambivalence**. Ambivalence can also feel like anxiety, insecurity, stagnation, pressure, or avoidance.
- **Overwhelm**. Overwhelm can also feel like insufficiency, fear, loss of control, or numbness.

According to Myers' Briggs Type Indicator, a personality assessment with years of indepth research on how people process emotions, people are classified to varying degrees as thinkers or feelers.[4] For thinker types that make decisions more objectively than subjectively, emotions can be difficult.

So, thinkers may take a day or two to realize what emotions they're feeling. I'm this type of person, which is why I had to do extra work to heal my emotional body. Stay hopeful. As you rehearse your last food binge episode, you'll find insights and connect the dots.

REFLECTION QUESTIONS

1. What triggered you in your last binge?

   _____

   _____

2. How exactly did you feel about the situation?

   _____

   _____

Step 3 – Evaluate
Why am I feeling this way?

To evaluate, is to find causal reasons to your emotional button and connect the past to the present. After you identify what you're feeling and what happened that may have caused the feelings, ask the Holy Spirit, "Why am I feeling this way?" or "When have I felt this way before?"

Wendy Buckland, co-owner of Hope International Ministries and author of a great quick read *Victorious Emotions*, says, "Emotions do not validate truth; they validate what we believe." She goes on to say, "We need to understand there's a difference between what we want to believe and what we subconsciously believe."[5]

To evaluate our emotions we're getting to what we believe consciously and subconsciously.

- As Ben evaluated his trigger, a memory came to mind of his teenage self.

    In the memory, Ben, his dad, and his brother Mark were in the garage. As Mark and Ben worked on a toy plane, Ben shared his idea to paint the plane burgundy.

    Ben tested the burgundy paint on the wing. Ben's dad's alcoholic anger spiraled out of control, and in a split second, the atmosphere went from peaceful to hostile.

    "Ben, why'd you do that?! So stupid!" Ben's dad slapped the plane wing off and raged out of the garage.

    Ben and Mark followed, crushed.

    Ben remembered the shattering he felt in his soul that day. He was older than Mark, and Mark looked up to Ben. Nonetheless, Ben's dad had the habit of having these outbursts in front of Mark. Aaron's rude outburst about Ben's performance hit a button in Ben's emotional body of feeling undermined.

- Tina argued with her husband. Afterwards, she typically ate a bag of tortilla chips to stuff the anger down. She discovered her trigger in a session. When Tina took extra care to dress up for her husband, he didn't offer her any positive affirmation of her beauty, even though she was stunning.

His lack of validation stirred up arguments about trivial things. She longed for his words of affirmation like, "You're beautiful" or "You look great tonight, honey." But instead, her seething anger drew her to chips and guac while her husband got the silent treatment.

Tina wondered, "Why wouldn't he give me a kind word when he knows that's my love language?!"

After evaluating, Tina recalled memories of her mother never being validated by her father. It seemed the family had some sort of curse of beauty without validation.

She also remembered a time when she dressed up in a beautiful ballerina outfit at age five. Her dad was interested in television more than in her. She twirled to get his attention, but he stubbornly watched television and ignored her beauty and twirls.

Tina's hurt created emotional wounds of being unvalidated, not pretty enough, and unworthy of attention. She needed to process her feelings to forgive her husband and dad for not validating her beauty.

- Sarah processed through her emotions and found a memory where she came home from school and ate candy and junk food to the point of sickness in her room while watching television. She ate the loneliness away. She ate away the belief that she wasn't wanted.

After you take time to figure out what emotions you're feeling, evaluate all the reasons you're experiencing them. This is figured out best by questioning yourself in what I call *episode interrogation*. Perform one until you find a connection from the past to the present.

Be prayerful in the evaluating process. Our Creator can dig into the soul and spirit and pull out memories and reasons for our behavior. The Spirit knows all.

How to Evaluate

To evaluate, do the following:

- **Perform an episode interrogation.** Ask yourself the following questions to reveal the root of the emotion or the memories about how you're feeling.

  1. Why do I feel this way?

  2. When have I felt this way before?

  3. When is my earliest memory of feeling this way?

  4. What am I saying to myself?

  5. What am I afraid of? What's the worst that can happen?

  6. What am I believing right now that's making me feel or behave this way?

  7. Why am I so offended?

- **Pray for the root memory.** Ask God to "locate the source" of the emotions you're feeling. Memories such as pictures, thoughts, words, or past situations may seem disconnected at first, but are a part of the answer in locating the source.

- **Talk it out with a good friend, family member, or your accountability partner.** The act of sharing our emotional self can help to evaluate and experience our feelings.

REFLECTION QUESTIONS ❓

1. What memories from your past are connected with your present eating episode?

   _____

   _____

2. Perform an episode interrogation from your last emotional eating event. What did you discover?

   _____

   _____

Step 4 – Experience

How can I best process my feelings right now?

Up until now, you've judged, criticized, and condemned your emotions. You've made excuses to eat over them. And you may even wallow in them during lonely weekends as you couple up with cookies, or at least I did.

Feeling has been difficult.

You've numbed yourself with food and other things that may have allowed you to escape emotions. But the true test of our healing is our willingness and ability to feel our feelings instead of eating them. Step 4 is all about feeling your feelings. And we won't be able to skirt this with an emoji.

- Ben processed his anger toward Aaron while driving home. He spoke out what he would've said if he could've said it without getting fired.

> But the true test of our healing is our willingness and ability to feel our feelings instead of eating them.

"Aaron, you're a bad boss! I hate having you as a boss. How dare you speak to me like that in front of my colleagues?! I'm sick and tired of you undermining my authority and talent! You're a jerk! The Green report was good enough! You just want to nitpick and look for things to harass me about!"

Ben went on for half of his thirty five minute commute home. So what if the other drivers on the road thought he was a nut case. Ben felt good about getting the anger out of him.

- Tina wrote her husband a letter to express her frustration about him not validating her beauty. Through writing out how angry and hurt she felt, she released words stuffed down with tortilla chips. She then prayed for herself and her mother to release the anger about not feeling validated. Tina didn't give her husband the letter.

- Marie sat with the deep fear of not being able to cover her bills. She continued to process her emotions and discovered a link to her childhood poverty. It was difficult as a child to get what she wanted. She made the connection from her present financial anxiety to her past financial poverty.

Underneath the mountain of difficult emotions like anger, fear, or grief is a great reservoir of love and joy. But to attain emotional treasures you've got to process your feelings. Feeling your feelings on the front end will reduce your body's backend.

Because we're body, soul, and spirit, we know there are emotional causes that need to be addressed, since what's toxic physically or emotionally will manifest.

As Peter Scazzero says, "To minimize or distort what we feel is a distortion of what it means to be image bearers of God." And, "to the degree that we're unable to express our emotions, we remain impaired in our ability to love God, others, and ourselves well."[5] I couldn't agree more.

How To Experience

To experience, do the following:

- **Sit still.** Sit with your feelings. You may find a need to pray, cry, or scream. All is acceptable. Turn off the distractions, quiet all noise, and be with your own soul. Emotions surface as you get quiet. If you have family in the house, ask for alone time, sit in your car, or reserve a room at the library.

  The seas of feeling can feel choppy at first, but I promise an emotional shark won't devour you. You'll get good at exercising your emotional body. What we do is avoid feeling by eating because we think it's so hard to feel, but then we deal with the hardship of our poor choices. So, go ahead, bust out the tissues and skip the shenanigans.

- **Heal the memory**. When a memory comes up for you, speak the truth to it.

  - Speak to the younger version of yourself in the memory and say what you needed to hear at the time. Be kind and gentle. Tina spoke the validation she needed to her five-year-old self, "You're so pretty! Look at you! You're beautiful!"

  - Speak the truth to others involved. Say what you've wanted to say, even if it's ugly. This can be done on paper. Tina confronted her dad, "I'm much more interesting than the television. You should've given me a word of affirmation. I needed it as your little girl. Because I didn't get your affirmation, I looked for it wrongly from men!"

— Allow a greater positive memory to be imagined. Tina imagined what her dad should've done and said to her when she came into the living room dressed up as a ballerina. She allowed herself to feel the joy and excitement of his imagined validation and affirmation.

- **Write a letter directly to the situation.** When angry, you can write directly to who or what you're angry at. It can be sugar addiction, your spouse, yourself, your job, or the scale. You can write a letter to a rock! Deal with it directly on paper. This helps you to clarify your feelings to understand yourself in the matter. When angry or upset, write a letter directly to the person or circumstance that's making you upset. Tell them directly your raw feelings and thoughts. Do not give the person the letter.

- **Speak it out loud.** If you don't enjoy writing, speaking it out loud has the same results. Like Ben in his car, speak to the issue directly. It's healthy to learn how to express yourself in less awkward, rude, and passive aggressive ways. When you speak it out, you'll get words to interact healthier in person.

- **Journal.** Journaling is the best way I find to process emotions. Journaling on a consistent basis has been instrumental in my process because journals are a place to share freely. If you're concerned about someone finding your journals, find a secret place to store them.

- **Hit something.** An anger workout was popular in the 70s and involves getting your anger out honestly by using a plastic bat against the sofa and screaming out what you're upset about as though you're talking directly to the person or problem.

    You can yell into a paper bag or stomp and scream. While this may be nutty to onlookers, you'll be the doing a happy dance that those ugly emotions are out of your heart.

It's Your Human Right to Feel

When King David asked God, *Who can dwell in Your Holy Tabernacle?* God's reply was, *He who walks uprightly, works righteousness, and speaks the truth in his heart* (Psalm 15:1-2). The human heart is the seat of emotions, and it's the truest part of you. In emotional fitness, we look at how we can speak the truth of our heart for healing.

The greatest stories ever written in the Bible or anywhere are filled with emotion. When Jesus saw the upset of Lazarus's death, He wept. When Joseph's years of bitterness around his brother's betrayal were confronted, he wept and had to sort through his emotions before he could properly deal with what needed to be dealt with in the famine.

Feeling is your God given right.

To devalue or repress them, as Peter Scazzero says, is also to deny being "human and made in the image of God."[7] Embrace your humanness for a whole and free life in Christ.

Feeling is your God given right.

REFLECTION QUESTIONS ❓

1. How do you procrastinate feeling?

   _____

   _____

2. What feelings are you uncomfortable with experiencing?

   _____

   _____

3. Pick a technique for feeling your feelings and try it on your last emotional eating episode.

   _____

   _____

Step 5 – Release

What or who do I need to let go of?

By definition, to release is to allow (a person or animal) to leave a jail, cage, prison, etc.; to set (someone or something) free; to stop holding (someone or something).[8]

- To release Aaron would free Ben from the resentment that drove him to Wendy's. Ben followed the steps and released the three parties that were held in contempt in Ben's heart: Aaron, his dad, and himself.

  He parked the car in the driveway of his suburban home.

  Okay, I can do this, he thought to himself as his inner man relied on God's help. "Aaron, I release you from my judgments against you—for being rude, inconsiderate, undermining me, and being disrespectful to me in front of my colleagues. Because of your words, I felt hurt, rejected, embarrassed, ashamed, and undermined. God is the Judge, and I forgive you fully and completely. I will honor you and respect you in spite of how you have treated me. Aaron, I let you go. God bless you and forgive me for my resentment and judgments."

He was on a roll, "Dad, I release you from my judgments against you—for being a horrible dad, for being abusive, harsh, and mocking me in front of Mark. You made me feel hurt, angry, disrespected, embarrassed, and dishonored. I'll honor you and respect you in spite of how you've treated me. God bless you and forgive me for my resentment and judgments."

Ben took a deep breath and looked into the drop-down mirror.

"Ben, I release you from my judgments against you—for your lack of thoroughness in the Green report, for not standing up for yourself, for being a coward, for going to food to help you, and for not preventing that situation with a third review. You should know by now what Aaron wants. You made yourself feel undermined, stupid, disrespected, angry, resentful, upset, and targeted. I forgive you."

Ben felt an inner release as his ten-year-old son ran out from their house to see what his old man was talking to himself about. Ben, relieved and proud, grabbed his computer bag, locked up the car, and hugged his boy. "I love you, son."

- Tina made the executive life decision that she would validate herself. After writing letters to her husband and father, she wrote one to herself to let go of her need for affirmation from anyone else. She was free. Shortly thereafter, her husband and others started complimenting her on a frequent basis. The underlying resentment was resolved. She released her husband, and the crazy cravings for chips and guac were a distant memory.

- Marie let go of her financial worry by turning it into positive actions. Instead of eating ice cream, she put her energy into changing her financial story. She texted friends for job openings, looked into getting a bachelor's degree, and updated her resume over the next several nights. Action in the right direction took the cravings away.

Forgiveness Isn't an Option

The very nature of spiritual wellness is forgiveness. God gave us Jesus Christ as an act of the Father's forgiveness toward mankind. Without Jesus we wouldn't be reconciled to the Father. And Jesus gave us the Holy Spirit to empower us to forgive the unforgiveable. The Holy Spirit is the leader when it comes to processing and releasing emotions.

As believers, forgiveness is the very thing that sets us apart from the world. We need the mercy of the Father. As Matthew 6:14 tells us, "For if you forgive men their trespasses, your heavenly Father will also forgive you."

And Jesus acknowledges that sometimes forgiveness is extra difficult. He taught to forgive seventy times seven times (Matthew 18:21–22) or until the matter is fully resolved.

The Lord's daily prayer reminds us that we need to be in a constant state of forgiveness, "And forgive us our debts, as we forgive our debtors" (Matthew 6:12). We're also to forgive the man in the mirror, as we hold ourselves in much condemnation and contempt over our chubby choices.

> **The Holy Spirit is the leader when it comes to processing and releasing emotions.**

Practice the art of forgiveness and receive the scientific benefits as well. A study of married couples showed that when the victim in the situation forgave the other person *both* experienced lower blood pressure.[9] And *not* forgiving someone is associated with more anger, anxiety, and sadness.[10]

Spiritually, to release is also beneficial. "Let us lay aside every weight, and the sin which so easily ensnares us" (Hebrews 12:1b). These weights or issues prevent us from freely moving forward.

You may wonder, what if a heinous act was committed, such as rape or incest? How do you forgive in situations like that? Process your emotions and ultimately release until you feel peace.

Christ said on the cross, "Father, forgive them, for they know not what they do" (Luke 23:34). I believe this is the case with any perpetrator. Forgiveness doesn't mean you agree with the act that was done.

But to stay victimized, the perpetrator still has power over your life, because holding onto unforgiveness is like eating a cream-filled donut on a regular basis and expecting the other person to buy the bigger underwear.

Make the tough decision to forgive in all circumstances, in advance.

> Holding onto unforgiveness is like eating a cream-filled donut on a regular basis and expecting the other person to buy the bigger underwear.

The *fore* in forgive, means beforehand. When we release our needs or the people involved, we take back our health.

How to Release

To release do the following:

- **Get clear.** First clarify what you need to let go. Ask:
  - Who or what do I need to let go of?
  - Where do I feel "right" or judgmental?
  - What do I think about myself, my circumstance, or the person (people) involved?
  - What emotion do I need to let go of?
- **Speak it out.** Like Ben's example, confess aloud or write I forgive you (person or thing) for (what you feel they did, how they are, and how you judge them) and making me feel (your feelings about it). Be as descriptive as possible.

- **Write a thank you letter to the situation or person upsetting you.** Thank them for all the positive things they've done for you. This fosters forgiveness and perspective.

- **Write the rest of the story.** Create a narrative of yourself in the midst of the circumstance or situation that you're dealing with. Write it as though a story and finish the story with a better ending.

- **Remember to forgive yourself.** Heal your emotions and the pain caused by your own acts of stupidity, overeating, indulgence, or whatever else. We all make significant mistakes, it's an undeniable fact of the human experience, forgive it, and move on with your life.

- **Look in the mirror.** Do the work above in the mirror. It adds a layer of healing you can only get looking into your own eyes. Try it.

- **Take action.** One thing we may need to release is our inaction or wallowing in the emotions. Because emotions stir action, what actions do you need to take next? What actions can support a better decision?

  Instead of eating over what's eating you, take action in a positive direction. Make a list of actions that would relieve you from negative emotions. You may need to have a conversation with someone to resolve things fully or figure out how to do something you've never done. But get to work. And, remember prayer is an action, too.

REFLECTION QUESTIONS ❓

1. What triggers/buttons cause you to overeat?

   _____

   _____

2. How often does this happen?

   _____

   _____

3. What can you do to prevent the button/trigger?

   _____

   _____

Your Emotional Strength Training Plan

What triggers can I heal before they happen?

An **Emotional Strength Training Plan** is the practice of emotionally clearing and completing Emotional Fitness Workouts™ when triggered. Your emotional chub gets ripped by being intentional about strengthening your emotional body.

To enact an Emotional Strength Training Plan, do the following consistently:

1. **Complete an Emotional Fitness Workout™ as soon as you feel triggered.** Practice the five steps to fully process your emotions and heal the button being triggered. You'll get really good at it, and people around you will notice your change on the inside and the outside.

2. **Emotionally Clear.** Often once a day or every few days, complete an emotionally clearing exercise. Grab a pen or ponder the responses. You can even say, "In regard to life ..." or "In regard to my marriage ..." or "In regard to my weight ..." to dig up and clear more negative feelings.

   - I feel mad because ...
   - I feel sad because ...
   - I feel glad because ...
   - I feel bad because ...

3. **Get good at identifying your buttons.** Put language to the trigger that causes an emotional over-reaction or impulsion by writing them down. List the things that currently upset you or give you the urge to eat.

4. **Hire a therapist to work through your emotions.** One study found that 190 overweight or obese persons lost on average 13 percent of body weight over the course of a year by using acceptance-based therapy methods.[11] Dialectical Behavioral Therapy (DBT) helped 40 percent of participants release weight in a twenty week study receiving treatment and materials, versus only 3.3 percent of the wait list who didn't receive support.[12]

   Other studies show that Cognitive Behavioral Therapy (CBT) supported a 5 to 8 percent reduction in body weight over the course of the year.[13] Either way, many studies show that psychotherapy positively affects your personal health and wellbeing. Therapists also help you process difficult feelings.[14]

5. **Keep learning about emotions.** Books mentioned: *Feelings Buried Alive Never Die* by Karol Truman, *Victorious Emotions* by Wendy Buckland, or *Emotionally Healthy Spirituality* by Peter Scazzero help our knowledge and wisdom in healing the emotional body. Also look out for my upcoming book *Emotional Fitness for Spiritual Strength*.

6. **Boost your mood to gain a better perspective.** To boost your mood after processing through negative emotions try the following strategies to switch to a more positive emotional channel.

- **Listen to music.** Music can increase feel good neurotransmitters to elevate your emotional state in minutes. Put on your favorite music and dance like David danced for an even greater effect.
- **Take a hot bath.** It helps muscles and the soul relax.
- **Exercise.** We covered this in Habit 5. Nothing beats a natural anti-depressant like exercise. Go for a walk.
- **Attend church or an inspirational program.** You don't have to leave home to find some motivation and inspiration on YouTube. Tune in to your favorite televangelists online.
- **Pray for those you love.** Praying for others helps us to move through our own upsets, and gets us into a more benevolent frame of mind.

Encouragement

When we choose to do this soul work, inner breakthroughs become a part of the adventure of living life with God. Emotional eating episodes become less frequent and calorically

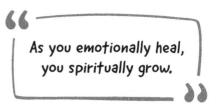

As you emotionally heal, you spiritually grow.

destructive. As you emotionally heal, you spiritually grow. And, as you emotionally heal, you physically improve your health.

But just like you can't run a mile this week and expect to be fit for a marathon next week, the same is true here. Emotional strength isn't built in a day. It's built from years of doing Emotional Fitness Workouts™ trigger after trigger, button after button, until very few, if any, buttons can be pressed.

An Emotional S.P.E.E.R.

An acronym for the steps is: S.P.E.E.R. When triggered, take a spear (SPEER) to kill emotional eating at the root.

S: Stop
P: Pinpoint
E: Evaluate
E: Experience
R: Release

Alrighty, take a few minutes to memorize it.

This workout does for the emotional body what exercise does for the physical body and what the Word of God does for the spiritual body. When you're triggered, don't let it fester. As often as you can, get to the bottom of your emotional eating pit.

Take your healing process one day, one hour, and one moment at a time. Implement the Emotional Fitness Workout™ frequently. I remember as I worshipped God one morning, I thought, *How will I ever get through this? Will I ever overcome?* Never forget, we're overcomers. And we'll be whole and free, inch by inch, insight by insight, step by step, skill by skill.

REFLECTION QUESTIONS

1. What step in the Emotional Fitness Workout™ is most difficult for you? Why?

_____

_____

2. What emotions do you need to process?

_____

_____

PRAYER

Dear Father,

Thank you for this insight. Please help me to get spiritually, emotionally, physically, and financially fit! Please help me to locate the source of negative beliefs about myself. Help me to believe I can handle life because I can do all things through your Son, Jesus Christ. I am strong and have courage in you.

Thank you for helping me to look at my past and heal me at times I want to run to food. Convict me by the power of your Holy Spirit to stop this behavioral pattern as I trust you to comfort and heal me. Help me to memorize and apply these steps to become emotionally healthier and happier!

In Jesus' name I pray, amen.

CHAPTER 19

SUPERSIZE YOUR POWER SOURCE

Chain #4 – Going It Alone

---

*"But seek first the kingdom of God and His righteousness,
and all these things shall be added unto you"*

–MATTHEW 6:33

We'd like to talk to you about cheeses.
—THE MICE EVANGELIST TEAM (ANONYMOUS)

Y ou know those plugs with six outlets? Yes, that's what I mean by supersize. Jesus is the greatest source of power there is. He shines like the sun (Psalm 84:11). He is the Son. He's the Light of the World. We're going to magnify that power with a power surge into Jesus by seeking the kingdom of God and our King (Matthew 6:33). To plug in is to be in tune with His kingdom and partner with the resources of our King in this battle, instead of Going It Alone.

The Kingdom of God

In the Lord's Prayer He specifically says to pray, "Your kingdom come. Your will be done, on earth as *it is* in heaven" (Matthew 6:10). And Jesus came as a King to set motion to His kingdom on earth. And kingdoms come with rights to their citizens.

Jesus's ministry was all about the gospel of the kingdom. He wanted us to experience a greater level of freedom in the Father. The kingdom is inside of us and is being established on earth by the power of the Holy Spirit through Him.

Jesus taught us that a world existed beyond what we could see and that the heavenly realm could be plugged into and brought to earth. We also have access to this realm as we partner with Him and seek His kingdom.

A benevolent king takes care of His people. Our will, fully surrendered and submitted to our King, is a loving relationship filled with trust, honor, respect, and mutual benefits. You get God's protection and the covering of His kingdom as a kingdom citizen, and in turn God gets to speak into your life, give you assignments, and cause you to be a blessing to Himself and others.

> **We also have access to this realm as we partner with Him and seek His kingdom.**

Breaking the Chain of Going It Alone

What's super important in the journey for weight and eating freedom is that your life—your very life—depends on your relationship with God and family. How deep are you willing to go with Him? How deep are you willing to go with others? How much are you willing to plug in and partner? Not because you should, but because you see the amazing source He is for your life.

The fourth chain that keeps us stuck in soul wilderness is Going It Alone. From the very beginning, it wasn't good for man or woman to be alone. God wants to fully partner with you for your emotional, physical, mental, and spiritual growth. He wants a relationship with you. He wants to be involved, like your best friend with the details of your life.

He wants to help you to repair your relationship with Him, yourself, your body, food, and people. To partner with Him for the building of His kingdom defeats the chain of Going It Alone. There's no way to win this battle without a strong adoption of your kingdom rights. We're to partake in the resources of our King.

GOING IT ALONE STRONGHOLD QUIZ

Put a check next to the answer that best describes your spiritual life and add up the total points below. The higher the score, the more spiritual chub is present.

1. How often do you prioritize time with God?

☐ (1) ALWAYS ☐ (2) OFTEN ☐ (3) SOMETIMES ☐ (4) RARELY ☐ (5) NEVER

- -

2. How often do you read your Bible?

☐ (1) ALWAYS ☐ (2) OFTEN ☐ (3) SOMETIMES ☐ (4) RARELY ☐ (5) NEVER

- -

3. How often do you engage with worldly television, music, or other media?

☐ (5) ALWAYS ☐ (4) OFTEN ☐ (3) SOMETIMES ☐ (2) RARELY ☐ (1) NEVER

- -

4. How often do you engage the Holy Spirit?

☐ (1) ALWAYS ☐ (2) OFTEN ☐ (3) SOMETIMES ☐ (4) RARELY ☐ (5) NEVER

- -

5. How often do you express your praise to God for everything?

☐ (1) ALWAYS ☐ (2) OFTEN ☐ (3) SOMETIMES ☐ (4) RARELY ☐ (5) NEVER

- -

6. How often are you motivated to please people more than God?

☐ (5) ALWAYS ☐ (4) OFTEN ☐ (3) SOMETIMES ☐ (2) RARELY ☐ (1) NEVER

- -

7. How often do you fellowship in a small group?

☐ (1) ALWAYS ☐ (2) OFTEN ☐ (3) SOMETIMES ☐ (4) RARELY ☐ (5) NEVER

- -

8. How often do you engage in worship or prayer at home?

☐ (1) ALWAYS ☐ (2) OFTEN ☐ (3) SOMETIMES ☐ (4) RARELY ☐ (5) NEVER

- -

9. How often do you connect with a Godly support system?

☐ (1) ALWAYS ☐ (2) OFTEN ☐ (3) SOMETIMES ☐ (4) RARELY ☐ (5) NEVER

- -

10. How often do you feel offended by others or God?

☐ (5) ALWAYS ☐ (4) OFTEN ☐ (3) SOMETIMES ☐ (2) RARELY ☐ (1) NEVER

- -

Total Score:

Score Sheet

30–50 | You're in the right place to get rid of spiritual chub!

20–30 | You've done some great work, and it shows!

_____ 10–20 | You're spiritually fit!

Spiritual Triggers

A *spiritual trigger* is caused by neglecting a kingdom resource. When triggered spiritually, we're vulnerable to overeat, emotionally eat, negatively obsess about body weight, shape, or size, and make other unwanted chubby choices, just like with physiological, emotional, chubbological, and circumstantial triggers.

Spiritual triggers also cause us to go astray from God's best in our lives. Kingdom power plugs energize us when we connect to the kingdom of God. We need to use the resources God has for us to defeat spiritual triggers. There's seven spiritual triggers and seven kingdom power plugs we'll discuss.

SPIRITUAL TRIGGERS	POWER PLUGS
Emptiness	#1 His Presence
Disconnection	#2 His Family
Legalism	#3 His Grace
Spiritual Starvation	#4 His Word
Discouragement	#5 His Spirit
Demonic Interference	#6 His Authority
Worldliness	#7 His Godliness

Power Plug #1 – His Presence
Spiritual Trigger – Emptiness

"You will show me the path of life; In Your presence is fullness of joy; At Your right hand are pleasures forevermore" (Psalm 16:11).

Every relationship gets stale. Married people know this well. It's natural to get complacent.

When you first get married, you hide your ear hairs and natural tendency to throw socks on the floor. When you're married for some time, your spouse reminds you to cut your disturbing ear hairs and pick your socks up—and not in the most loving tone.

When you're married for longer than that, your spouse cannot care less about your ear hairs because she has her own to deal with. And the socks? Well, they've mysteriously disappeared from the laundry, and you don't have any socks for her to be annoyed about anymore.

Our relationship with Christ can be like this, we can get complacent. We know we need to read our Bible and pray more, but we don't. And like a spouse after many years, you can forget why you were so in love with the Lord in the first place if you're not intentional.

Couples that make it will tell you that they're intentional. Jim and Ruth Sharon wrote *Secrets of a Soulful Marriage: Creating and Sustaining a Loving, Sacred Relationship*, which is about intentionally deciding to create a great relationship. That's the secret: you must decide it, work toward it, plan it, and make time together happen.

In our relationship with Christ, we also need to be intentional to have time in His presence. Intention is a powerful word, it means having the determination to act in a certain way.[1]

It's in His presence that the lies shake off, the strongholds are torn down, and the yoke is broken. In Jesus' name, we can speak to the mountain, and it'll be cast into the sea.

Our spiritual freedom is contingent upon our relationship with our heavenly Father, Jesus Christ, and the Holy Spirit as a triune force. The Godhead is our primary family and wants to be in deep relationship with us. To not do so would be cutting off our power supply at its source. This relational aspect of God is throughout the Scriptures. It's why He created us in the first place. As Genesis 1:26 says, "Let Us make man in our image."

It's in His presence that the lies shake off, the strongholds are torn down, and the yoke is broken.

When I think about friendships and people in my life, I think about character. I think about what they value. What I don't understand is how someone wouldn't want to be friends, and I mean really good friends—best friends—like married type friends with someone who cares about orphans, widows, the sick, and the poor; who makes time to meet their needs and gives hope to the hopeless; who can't stand adultery, dishonor, stealing, lying, or cheating; and who would never do any of those things.

This friend is someone who also forgives quickly and completely, hates evil, speaks up, is honest, loves deeply, encourages, and refuses to leave even when times are rough. This friend would never reject or abandon you and constantly intercedes for you. And lets you make your own choices.

Not only that, this friend is loaded. He has resources that reach beyond the heavens. He doesn't drive a fancy car. He doesn't need one. He doesn't live in a fancy house. He owns the whole earth. . . the universe. He took care of all your debts and your legal bills.

Who wouldn't want this type of friend?

In our right minds, we would love to be friends with a person like this. We'd marry a person like this. We'd fight for a person like this. We'd die for a person like this.

But Jesus died for people like us. People who fall short. People who can't stick to their word. People who cheat, even if it's with a donut on a diet. People who do stupid things for stupid reasons, like grapefruit diets and diet pills to look good in a bathing suit for people they don't even like or know.

Yet, He did. There is no greater friend. There is no greater Bridegroom. And there is no greater path in life to follow. He is our ultimate source. He is our power. He is our strength. He is our bread.

And my friend, oh my friend, we need to be more intentional about cultivating our knowledge of Him, our love of Him, and our understanding of Him because it's that knowledge and that heart for our King that heals like nothing else can.

Much of the emptiness or the vacuum-like feeling we try to fill with food is a desire for more of His presence. In His presence we're fulfilled because there's a fullness of joy (Psalm 16:11). It's challenging to get into His presence with so much life happening, isn't it?

> **Much of the emptiness or the vacuum-like feeling we try to fill with food is a desire for more of His presence.**

In heaven, we don't have the cares of this world. We get to enjoy God all the time there because we're not bound by time constraints in eternity. So, think of it like this: remember the whole self? Well, how about our heavenly self? Can you imagine what heaven will be like? Can you feel that boundless joy? For a heavenly jolt, connect with God in prayer from that place.

His presence and His kingdom bring forth our true identity. As William Paul Young, author of *The Shack* said, "If you want to hold onto your false self, the presence of God will feel like hell to you. If you want to let it go, it will feel like heaven to you."[2] We can connect to His presence anytime. We can cultivate it as a part of our lives to bring heaven to earth.

Our relationship with food has displaced our identity in Christ. Food has been a place of dependency and comfort. Eve wanted wisdom from the food offered to her by Satan. Food was an innocent bystander to her desire for wisdom. She didn't feel like she could get enough wisdom from God. She didn't even ask Him first. To strengthen our relationships with God we need to share our needs, desires, and emotions with Him first and get food out of the way.

Our relationship with God has to be paramount in our lives. We're to operate as a family of one. There's no separation of Jesus, God, and the Holy Spirit, like the body, soul, and spirit operate as one with different functions, or water, ice, and steam are one but have three different functions, so is God, Jesus, and the Holy Spirit.

We have a powerful team. As William Paul Young also said, "We're never alone. Aloneness is an illusion. You always have the Father, Son and Spirit with you. So, at the very least, you have a party of four in perfect oneness that we don't understand."³ That four is you, Jesus, the Holy Spirit, and the Father. So, at any time, we can fill up on His presence to dispel our emptiness.

Plug into His Presence

1. Prioritize daily prayer. During a daily prayer time, share with Him all your heart's concerns, hopes, desires, and challenges. To involve Him in all the details of your weight and eating journey may seem odd. But, because it's a part of the process of growing in freedom, He welcomes it.

2. Fill your home with worship and praise Him. He fills our emptiness with our worship. He inhabits our praise. We don't need music to praise but playing worship music conditions our heart to God's presence. Our worship is for us to stay connected to our Source of strength in a world of temptation and deception.

Power Plug #2 – His Family
Spiritual Trigger – Disconnection

"By this, all will know that you are My disciples, if you have love for one another" (John 13:35).

Remember earlier when I mentioned how we have an out-of-control identity crisis? And that we can go to food as though a hamburger mistaken for our mom or dad? Well, food becomes the family we wish we had. The family bond is strong. And it's within the context of broken families that we have a broken identity, and it's within whole healthy family that we can also heal our identity.

Family bonds matter more than we know. The bible says, "Honor your father and mother, which is the first commandment with promise: that it may be well with you and you may live long on the earth"

(Ephesians 6:2–3). So, the reason for compulsive eating goes beyond the natural realm issues of problems. There's a connection to family and long life, perhaps because if we don't have a good relationship with parents, we'll fill our deficit with excess food which shortens life.

This battle isn't about food as much as it is a deficit of truth and connection with God and others. Our food turmoil reflects our relationships with others.

> **Our food turmoil reflects our relationships with others.**

Our past wounds in the dad or mom department, or people, or church—in the form of hurts and disappointments—are projected onto our relationships, which includes relationships with God, food, and body image.

To heal, we'll need to plug into our spiritual family. For several years, I participated in my first small group ministry that met frequently. Families and singles attended, and it was an amazing experience. This home group didn't replace church, it complimented it. The home group was a safe space to do life with others in a practical manner.

In it were spiritual parents, aunts, uncles, brothers, and sisters in Christ. These family bonds with spiritual family helped to restore broken bonds from my natural family. It provided a safe, fun, and Holy Spirit-sensitive place for me to seek God, ask questions, grow, and operate in the gifts of the Spirit.

> **These family bonds with spiritual family helped to restore broken bonds from my natural family.**

Dr. Timothy Johns provides Christ-centered families with a manual, *Micro Church: Families on Mission*, to create a culture of the kingdom within small home groups to effectively nurture relational bonds. The early church had home groups and practiced spiritual family in Christ and relationship. Regular connection with spiritual family is critical to our weight and eating freedom.

Dr. Johns said, "Every problem is an attachment and relational issue. At a neurological level, our brains must function with attachment and love bonds. Once we get a high level of attachment, the group family – tells us who we are, and they fill us with affection."

> Regular connection with spiritual family is critical to our weight and eating freedom.

He goes on to say, "If nutrients of relationship affection such as kind words, encouragement, truth, prayer, and acceptance are missing, there's hoarding—because there's a vacuum in our lives, that we attempt to fill with an essential pleasure such as food, that chemically replaces relational intimacy."[4]

We need to connect with one another. If we don't, we'll keep connecting with food and beating ourselves up over weight. In the kingdom there isn't eating and drinking, but tremendous joy (Romans 14:16-17). We get this joy through relational intimacy.

And while people are a source of great joy, we're also a source of great pain. We hurt each other, because our past relationships hurt us. To undo our relationship damages is essential to freedom, and it can only be done in the context of a relationship with God and others.

Matthew Kelly, author of *The Seven Levels of Intimacy*, says, "Relationships are for the purpose of the best version of ourselves."[5] All relationships face obstacles. The highest level of intimacy is expressing our needs and overcoming challenging times together.

A Holy Spirit-led family group with a strong understanding and knowledge of the Word of God is the fastest way to heal and grow.

Drs. Jack and Judith Balswick, authors of *The Family*, said, "Among the hurting behaviors in a family environment are conditional love, self-centeredness, perfectionism, faultfinding, efforts to control others, unreliability, denial of feelings, and lack of communication. With such behaviors, the focus is on self rather than on the best interest of the other family members. In hurting families, each individual is affected on the personal level."[6]

Their thoughts resonated deeply in my childhood experience. The Balswicks also said, "Hurting families are characterized at the individual level by their members not being in touch with their feelings. Their fear of rejection keeps them in denial of their emotions. What they need most is a safe atmosphere in which they can express their feelings, thoughts, wants, and desires and be heard and understood by the other family members."[7]

A recreated spiritual family that meets regularly, provides a safe atmosphere to express our heart, and be validated in our whole self.

Dr. Peter Young, Pastor of BridgeWay Church in Denver said, "Family is the greenhouse that produces safety, love, affirmation, and acceptance. It's the place we call forth destiny."

He continues, "Within family, we learn character, values, significance, security, faith, and relationships. God intended to raise up spiritual family within the body of Christ to breed wholeness. The enemy has been content to see the church of Jesus Christ build programs, structures, finances, and count numbers, conversions, and baptisms, provided they don't know how to do life-on-life discipleship in family."[8]

> A recreated, spiritual family that meets regularly, provides a safe atmosphere to express our heart, and be validated in our whole self.

We can't expect breakthroughs without strong, godly relationships in our lives. Per Pastor Peter, we thrive in that greenhouse of family with other believers to nurture our transformation.

For it's our love for one another that we're known as Jesus' disciples (John 13:25). Despite what social media promotes, in no way are we to be isolated, disconnected, or neglectful of our development of human face-to-face relationships. Spiritual family connections help us to defeat disconnection that makes us isolate with food and hibernate in shame about our bodies.

> Spiritual family connections help us to defeat disconnection that makes us isolate with food and hibernate in shame about our bodies.

Plug into His Family

1. Pray and seek out mentors and spiritual family to build relationships with include mature spiritual parents, brothers and sisters, and aunts and uncles in the Lord.

2. Find or create a small group for a weekly or bi-weekly gathering to connect. Because there are still dysfunctional spiritual families, it's necessary to have the right training on mental, emotional, and relational health. Kingdom missional families from RockTribe.org or JesusTribes.org provide resources to build and nurture a healthy spiritual family.

3. Commit to stronger and deeper relationships. Conflict is inevitable, but our strength in Christ is being able to get through conflict without eating over it or abandoning the relationship.

4. Read 1 Corinthians 13:4–8, and where it says "love," replace it with your name. This is your new relationship building protocol. "Love suffers long and is kind; love does not envy; love does not parade itself, is not puffed up; does not behave rudely, does not seek its own, is not provoked, thinks no evil; does not rejoice in iniquity, but rejoices in the truth; bears all things, believes all things, hopes all things, endures all things. Love never fails" (1 Corinthians 13:4–8a).

Power Plug #3 – His Grace
Spiritual Trigger – Legalism

"For the law was given through Moses, but grace and truth came through Jesus Christ" (John 1:17).

We've probably had a time or two in our past where we've counted every last calorie, fat gram, or carbohydrate. Or if the scale didn't say a certain number, as discussed in Chapter 17, we would basically melt down or have a temper tantrum about it.

Or we have felt a rigid need to follow the diet or the eating plan to its exact specifications. This is the legalistic side of the weight and eating matter. We're not to partner with condemnation or control but with God's unfailing grace and mercy.

Legalism with food and in life sets up a performance mindset. And we inevitably fall short because legalism in food, eating, and weight spurs bingeing behaviors. The spirit of legalism is about control, force, and manipulation.

It's based on the false, broken, and bound self we've discussed. It's an attempt to prove to be worth something based on the ability to follow rules and is not of the kingdom of God. Whenever we condemn, obligate, or guilt ourselves, we've misread grace.

There are 613 ordinances in the Torah or Old Testament. Moses delivered God's statutes that were specific and difficult to follow. People tried and fell short or faked it because no one could.

But God knew something the people didn't know. He knew of His own unfailing mercy, grace, love, and compassion. He sent Jesus for us to see it in action. "For the law was given through Moses, *but* grace and truth came through Jesus Christ" (John 1:17).

In weight and eating, we can miss partnering with God's grace. We try to get it all right and perfect. It's good to partner with the power plug of God's unfailing grace and mercy. There's no specific eating plan to follow, except that bio-individual one you can work with the Holy Spirit to create. That way you're aligned with Spirit for your body's health.

295

All is well. All is going to be okay. It's okay to experiment with food plans, test workouts, or water spritzers. But some things are just a test to learn what you need to learn as you continue your wellness path.

His grace includes alternative healthier or homemade options of all your favorites. Grace is being okay with the fact that you may not be your desired size, but you're still loved, even when you've disappointed yourself. It's so wonderful to have grace with ourselves.

> **Grace is an extension of time to do what you need to do, learn what you need to learn, and be who you're to become.**

Grace is an extension of time to do what you need to do, learn what you need to learn, and be who you're to become.

In our relationship with God, we can rest in His grace. The grace that He's working with us to perfect us. Psalm 138:8 says, "The Lord will perfect that which concerns me; Your mercy, O Lord, endures forever; Do not forsake the works of Your hands."

His grace is sufficient and shines in our weaknesses (2 Corinthians 12:9).

Let Him know when you're vulnerable to chubby choices, obsessive thoughts, or feelings of inadequacy. And as you make mistakes, let His hand help to get you back up. You're free to make as many mistakes as you need to make to get where God is calling you to go.

Going forward, plug into God's amazing grace and mercy that you can have with foods, your body, your weight changes, and your body image.

> **You're free to make as many mistakes as you need to make to get where God is calling you to go.**

Plug into His Grace

1. Whenever you feel condemnation, obligation, fear, or guilt, pray for release of God's grace.

2. Accept the fact that God made you a certain way for a specific reason that's beneficial to your life and identity.

3. Always check your motives to make sure you're doing things for the right reasons.

4. Don't hide. Share your truth and be honest with your accountability partner. The opposite of grace is condemnation, shame, ridicule, and criticism. Do your best not to retreat when you feel any of these, but instead use it as an opportunity to confirm your identity in Christ. You're more than your mistakes.

5. Pray as much as you need to for whatever reason you're concerned about.

Power Plug #4 – His Word

Spiritual Trigger – Spiritual Starvation

*"And Jesus said to them, 'I am the bread of life.
He who comes to Me shall never hunger,
and he who believes in Me shall never thirst'" (John 6:35).*

If I were to bring you a barbeque brisket, you'd probably dig right in, especially if you missed a meal. Better than barbeque brisket, the Word is food. Jesus is the Word (John 1:1). The way we abide in Him is to take Him in or to let His body be as bread.

"For the word of God is living and powerful, and sharper than any two-edged sword, piercing even to the division of soul and spirit, and of joints and marrow, and is a discerner of thoughts and intents of the heart" (Hebrews 4:12).

Spiritual food penetrates body, soul, and spirit in ways we can't fully comprehend. And that's okay. All we need to do is eat, which we're very good at! And the more we eat spiritually of Jesus, the more we will heal from things that aren't of Him.

The Word of God sustains. The Lord's Prayer says, "Give us this day our daily bread" (Matthew 6:11). He's not just referring to physical food but also spiritual food. We have daily needs for our body, and we have daily needs for our spirit.

Most of us Chubby Church members, don't miss a meal. But we can misplace our need for spiritual food for natural food, similar to how we confuse signals of poor sleep or dehydration that can cause us to overeat. Well, spiritual starvation will cause us to overeat too. If we've missed adequate time in the Bible feasting, then we can guarantee we're spiritually famished.

Feast on the Word. After a meal of the most tangible form of Jesus Christ, His Word, we're nourished. The Word of God is described as milk, meat (solid food), water, and bread. That's a whole meal!

The word can clean, cut, divide, conquer, heal, deliver, reveal, and provide direction. It's a potent medicine to all of life's situations. It strengthens us. It removes the shame, the lies, and the doubt. In the kingdom, it's a daily meal.

As we've discussed Jesus referred to Himself as the Bread of Life, which sure beats Wonderbread®. His bread has spiritual nutrients, such as vitamins of faith of which we need several grams per day to sustain us. "So then faith *comes* by hearing, and hearing by the Word of God" (Romans 10:17). Without faith it's impossible to please God (Hebrews 11:6). The Word helps us to find faith in days of doubt on the weight and eating journey.

Jesus wants to join you for dinner. "Behold, I stand at the door and knock. If anyone hears My voice and opens the door, I will come in to him and dine with him, and he with Me" (Revelation 3:20). Bring the Word to the table and eat with Jesus to ward off spiritual starvation.

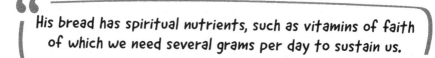

His bread has spiritual nutrients, such as vitamins of faith of which we need several grams per day to sustain us.

Unlike junk foods where we can't eat just one because it doesn't satisfy, the Word fulfills.

Plug into His Word

1. Feast on the Word of God. When we feast on the Word, we'll be feasting less on other things. Sometimes I'll do a Word binge day and read and study for hours. Try it.

2. Delight yourself in His Word (Psalm 119:16). Try a Bible study group or class.

3. As a morning practice, eat the Word of God before you eat.

4. Use a Bible app that reads passages to you aloud while you're doing other things, like exercising or the laundry.

5. Study the Word according to your interests. For example, if you're a new parent, study the Word on parenting. "Be diligent to present yourself approved to God, a worker who does not need to be ashamed, rightly dividing the word of truth" (2 Timothy 2:15).

Power Plug #5 – His Spirit
Spiritual Trigger – Discouragement

*"The Spirit of Truth, whom the world cannot receive,
because it neither sees Him nor knows Him; but you know Him,
for He dwells with you and will be in you" (John 14:17).*

We're to value what the King values. And our King, highly values His Spirit over Himself (Luke 12:10).

The Holy Spirit is our helper, teacher, and comforter and is sent by the Father as a governor to establish the kingdom on earth for Jesus Christ (John 14:26). It's exciting to live and operate by the power of the Holy Spirit. We're to worship God in Spirit and Truth, and the Spirit is our leader in all things for a successful life. We're to be quick to hear, obey, and do what we sense from the Holy Spirit.

And all we need to do to access this is to genuinely ask. "If you then, being evil, know how to give good gifts to your children, how much more will your heavenly Father give the Holy Spirit to those who ask Him!" (Luke 11:13). The Holy Spirit is the ultimate gift to encourage us and walk out kingdom principles.

We need the Holy Spirit in a really big way. The Holy Spirit acts on behalf of our King and sets us in order. "Nevertheless I tell you the truth. It is to your advantage that I go away; for if I do not go away, the Helper will not come to you; but if I depart, I will send Him to you" (John 16:7).

Dr. Miles Munroe, my mentor through his books and teachings, wrote *The Most Important Person on Earth*. He said, "Our entrance into the kingdom of heaven, results in the restoration of our legal authority as rulers on earth. Then, our baptism in the Holy Spirit results in restoration of our power or ability to carry out that authority."[9]

Yes, we need the power and ability to carry out our authority. And the Holy Spirit is available to us to comfort, help, fill, prophesy, convict, lead to righteousness, judge, edify, discern, provide answers, and help us manifest the God placed dreams in our hearts. The fastest way to break through bondage is to operate in the power and gifts of the Holy Spirit.

The Holy Spirit gives lots of gifts but pray for the spiritual gifts of prophecy and tongues as they support the edification and encouragement of your spirit man to walk out your victory in every area of life (see 1 Corinthians 14).

Every kingdom has a language that unifies, a culture, values, and territory.[10] The kingdom of God is no different. A part of that language is the gift of tongues, which is a nuclear weapon to the kingdom of darkness and is a direct line to heaven. Don't be scared, instead study.

The fastest way to break through bondage is to operate in the power and gifts of the Holy Spirit.

Learn about the Holy Spirit's gifts and authority.

The Spirit of Truth provides hiking boots over the mountain of weight and eating bondage. I urge you to ask the Father for a greater increase of the Holy Spirit in your life. And to lean on Holy Spirit for encouragement. When we're filled with the Holy Spirit, it's much harder to fill ourselves with creamy alternatives.

Plug into His Spirit

1. Repent and be baptized by the power of the Holy Spirit for the remission of sins and by water. Make sure when you're baptized that it's done solely in the name of Jesus Christ. He's the one who signs the check on our entrance into the kingdom.[11]

2. Attend Holy Spirit-filled churches and events that are also grounded in the Bible not emotionalism.

3. Don't limit God. Allow the Spirit to offer His gifts in dreams, prophecy, words of knowledge, healing, and more to you for the benefit of the kingdom's establishment.

4. Learn about the Holy Spirit. A great resource is *The Most Important Person on Earth* by Dr. Miles Munroe.

Power Plug #6 - His Authority
Spiritual Trigger – Demonic Interference

"Behold, I give you the authority to trample on serpents and scorpions, and over all the power of the enemy, and nothing shall by any means hurt you" (Luke 10:19).

Why is the battle of weight and eating so fierce anyway? Why has it taken up so much mental, emotional, and physical space? Do we have clogged spiritual arteries? Are we spiritually myopic? It's because it goes directly against the primary commandment, which is to love God.

One of the first and most blatant attacks from the enemy has always been food. Food is powerful. Food agriculture over the last several decades has changed. When the Lord told man to till the soil, eat all the green plants for food, and work six days a week, He provided order to us about our agricultural practices. But we've lost the practices in honor of the convenience food that corporate giants felt we needed. Deceived, we need drugs to fix us from food that is breaking us.

> **One of the first and most blatant attacks from the enemy has always been food.**

Food, a Celebration Gone Wrong

God has several ways that food is used throughout Scriptures, but primarily it was for our enjoyment. God is good, and all that He made is good.

Food is a pleasure we get to enjoy as human beings. He told us we'd have problems in life, and life is kind of tough, isn't it? The least we can do is enjoy our meals. "I know that nothing is better for them than to rejoice, and to do good in their lives, and also that every man should eat and drink and enjoy the good of all his labor—it is the gift of God" (Ecclesiastes 3:12–13).

> **Deceived, we need drugs to fix us from food that is breaking us.**

It's also for celebration. Feasting is about celebrating the holy days of the Lord, marital unions, and other special events.

And food is for our strength. In Scriptures when David or one of the prophets was weary, he was instructed to eat.

Holy Spirit-filled, Registered Dietitian, Laura Woodard says, "With food, we can view it through a lens of fear and how it could harm us, or we can remember that it is actually God's gift to us because He loves us."[12] How has what used to bring enjoyment and great pleasure now become ridden with guilt and shame? When did it become so harmful?

Health as Spiritual Warfare

Steve Wohlberg, host of the *His Voice Today* television show, came to revelation of our health as warfare when his three-year-old son was plagued with seizures that medication made worse and doctors provided no answers for his cure.

After seeking God in heartfelt prayer, he found the right nutritional support and heavy metal detox for his son's brain. His son healed. Steve sensed that we're at war. In his book, *End Times Health War*, he said, "It's an end time war against our health because cancer, heart disease, liver, kidney, and autoimmune disease are killers."[13]

You might not have thought of your health as spiritual warfare, but it is. Think about it: if you had to devise a diabolical plan to distract people from loving God first, what would you go after? Not much contributes to our energy and spiritual practices more than food. Food is a spiritual matter. Just as the serpent tempted Eve in the garden, so the tempter whispers in our ears to eat more than we should.

We're in a spiritual battle for our health. Michael Moss, author of the award-winning book, *Salt, Sugar, Fat,* exposes the food industry as well as the United States Government on the crime against Americans that surrounds processed food.

The food industry's processed food crime is likened to the tobacco industry's cigarettes crime.[14] The tobacco industry was able to market their lethal products that caused addiction to boost sales, which led to cancer and early death.[15]

Michael Moss exposed executives in high places who knew their foods caused obesity in adults and children, heart disease, hypertension, diabetes, and decided that it isn't their responsibility.

For example, Coca-Cola®, measures success by how many "heavy users," they have. This implies that Coke makes stuff intentionally addictive for profitability.[16] Coca-Cola's® not alone, cereal makers, and all kinds of boxed food companies subscribe to the

> We're in a spiritual battle for our health.

addictive food methodology. Behind the food and drug industry are spiritual wars for you and your family health.

Deliverance

Ephesians is very clear that we're not fighting flesh and blood battles (Ephesians 6:11–12). We fight unseen things—spirits. There're many examples of Jesus casting out spirits. There are also spiritual doors open to spirits that we need to shut giving way to physical ailments and disorders. For example, read Deuteronomy 21:20-21.

"And they shall say to the elders of the city, 'This son of ours is stubborn and rebellious; he will not obey our voice; he is a glutton and a drunkard.' Then all the men of his city shall stone him to death with stones; so you shall put away the evil from among you, and all Israel shall hear and fear" (Deuteronomy 21:20–21).

This example in Deuteronomy is not about the gluttony, but gluttony was a spiritual symptom of stubbornness and rebellion, spiritual yokes.

Now in those days, there may not have been family therapy offices around the corner. And

> **Deliverance ministry is definitely not unicorns and rainbows, but it's necessary.**

who knows, the parents may not have been great parents, but this child was responsible and in agreement with evil. Before the revelation of Jesus Christ, some sins were worthy of death. Jesus saved us from the law of sin and death. Can I get an amen?!

Gene Moody of Deliverance Ministries in Louisiana, said, "A Christian can be tormented or afflicted by evil spirits in some area of his life and still be a sincere Christian; just as he can be tormented by physical sickness and still be a sincere Christian."[17] He also said, "The Holy Spirit is able to coexist with these unconfessed sins."[18] Demonic interference needs to be, "detected, hated, renounced, and expelled" in the name of Jesus.[19]

Deliverance ministry is definitely not unicorns and rainbows, but it's necessary. And we can't ignore Jesus's many teachings on demonic interferences. The devil or demons aren't to be feared by believers. As we have the ultimate authority given to us by Jesus Christ. And it's only in His name that we have authority over the kingdom of darkness that is hellbent to destroy our progress and knowledge of Jesus Christ.

Pastor Joshua "Tayo" Obigbesan, Pastor of Christ Liberty Restoration Ministries in Colorado, is what I call a spiritual doctor. His discernment for spiritual warfare and everything of the Spirit is remarkable. I trained under him to learn about spiritual warfare and deliverance ministry.

When I received deliverance, I was excited because all I've ever wanted for Christmas is the kingdom. See, Jesus said, "But if I cast out demons with the finger of God, surely the kingdom of God has come upon you" (Luke 11:20). When we do get deliverance in a manifested way, such as a scream, burp, yawn, or other strange noises and happenings, we know that the kingdom of God has come upon us and our victory is guaranteed.

Earline Moody struggled with weight and eating bondage. She went through normal deliverance protocols such as forgiving anyone who caused her to go to food and deliverance from any places of bitterness and rebellion, but she said she was delivered from a demon called, don't laugh, "I like to eat".[20]

Yes, the love of food has similar consequences to the love of money. Greed for food, money, or anything is not of God. Use your spiritual authority and rebuke gluttony, indulgence, resentment, fear, and whatever else the Holy Spirit leads you to rebuke. When I sense a desire to binge, I'll openly rebuke a spirit of gluttony. And I always pray this when forced to go to a buffet! It may be weird, but it works every time.

If you've got the heebie jeebies, check out Howard Pittman on YouTube. He's the author of *Placebo*, a testimonial pamphlet of an experience with God that outlines the basics of what happens in the spiritual realm. [21]

In it he describes how the kingdom of darkness works. Demons have rank, hierarchy, and variety like an army. They represent one word, such as lust, fear, gluttony, or doubt. And there's more of them than humans.

These demons, such as a spirit of lust, enter humans through any gate of the body via our thought life (words). Gates of the physical body are the eyes, ears, nose, mouth, genitals, and anus. He describes witnessing a man and woman talking in a break room while at work. Talking turned into flirting and a demon spirit of lust circled the couple and jumped into the man. Lust is a spirit.

> "We've got to use our authority as a weapon against real demonic interference of mind, emotion, and spirit to empower our health."

Jesus commanded many demons to flee, which is a part of Scripture that we deny because we may not be able to reconcile the natural and spiritual realms in our minds. But Jesus said, we're to trample over serpents and scorpions, and take authority (Luke 10:19).

When we struggle, sabotage, and commit blatant disobedient acts with food, we've got to recognize that we're in a spiritual battle and speak to the matter with authority. But if we don't believe we're in a spiritual battle, we won't fight it. Furthermore, if we don't know who our enemy is, how can we really direct our prayer words appropriately? We've got to use our authority as a weapon against real demonic interference of mind, emotion, and spirit to empower our health.

Plug into His Authority and Power

1. Learn and practice the discipline of spiritual warfare on a regular basis and don't be afraid to use your authority to rebuke the spirits of lust, rebellion, and gluttony in Jesus's name.

2. Check out training tools for learning, such as Moody's *Deliverance Manual* and Dr. Ed Murphy's *The Handbook for Spiritual Warfare*.

3. Use strong prayer books for spiritual warfare prayer at least a couple of times per week. Pastor Obigbesan's *Power and Prayers to Destroy the Means of the Wicked* has an excellent easy read combination of prayer and teachings. I love this book as a resource. And anything by John Eckhardt, such as *Prayers that Rout Demons, Prayers that Break Curses,* or *Prayers that Bring Healing* are effective.

4. Keep your life right before God and your conscience clean.

Power Plug #7 – His Godliness
Spiritual Trigger - Worldliness

"Teaching us that, denying ungodliness and worldly lusts, we should live soberly, righteously, and godly in the present age" (Titus 2:12).

The opposite of godliness is worldliness. Worldliness is a goal of that speedo or bikini I mentioned earlier. This is why I'm not interested in people sending photos of themselves in bathing suits. If you send photos, please be fully dressed. Worldliness is all over the body image area. We are beautiful. We're made in His image.

Media contradicts God's goodness and wholeness. And sadly, too many of us partake in things we shouldn't. We need discretion, not only over our mouths, but also over our eyes, ears, and minds.

We increase in godliness when we're more open to His ways or what He says versus what everyone has taught us or what our culture has said.

The fruit of the Spirit is the best guide for godliness. And as my mentor says, be a really good fruit inspector. Because as we discussed in Chapter 4, if we're looking at the fruit and it's not looking good, we need to look at the roots.

Worldliness is one of those roots. Worldliness is a desire for things that are vain or without substance. We're not to be conformed to the world's mindset but to God's will (Romans 12:2).

If He's made us unique all on our own, with unique finger prints, hair, voices, then who are we to say we're imperfect.

> " *Worldliness is a desire for things that are vain or without substance.* "

If you or the world sets standards for how you should look, then you'll never measure up because the world's standard is photoshopped and artificially contrived—also known as a lie. And there we go again listening to the lies and rejecting the truth that what God made is very good. Can you imagine Mary being worried about her breast size or waistline all day? Or Jesus being worried about his biceps or chest strength?

These thoughts totally defeat godliness.

Since He is our Creator, He also gets to create the standard. You're one of a kind, whole and unique as a human being. You're fearfully and wonderfully made (Psalm 139:14).

Something one of a kind is immeasurable because the only thing to measure against is itself. That means whatever your size or shape doesn't matter. There's beauty in you, in everything about you. Are you willing to stop comparing to the world's standards? Are you willing to let go of

> " *Something one of a kind is immeasurable because the only thing to measure against is itself.* "

your own standards for ideal beauty? How about vanity and the insatiable hunger for physical perfection?

Your beauty is a nonnegotiable truth of creation. Therefore, your perception of beauty must be the truth. There is only one standard, and it's whatever you are. Your eyes, nose, hair, and bone structure are a perfect blend. For a body image boost, I'll look forward to sharing more with you in Book 2.

> " *Our beauty is a nonnegotiable truth of creation.* "

Come Out of the World

To bear my soul with you, if I could wave a magic wand and get one wish, it would be for us to love Him more. For us to be so intentional about the lover of our souls.

For us to stop being partially devoted and to become sold out. A bought-in attitude says, "That's it. I'm done with the things of the world. I'm coming out of the world on every side. I'm getting my character, attitude, mouth, music, and entertainment out of the world."

Well, I don't want to ruffle feathers, but I do want you to really think about it. Do you live for you, or do you live for God? Do you live out of fear, or are you motivated by God's love? Do you feel obligated to serve Him, or do you feel excited that you get to serve Him? Do you feel married to Him, or are you a cheater?

We need to know God—the One who gives back, who's alive, and who speaks to His people. The One who guides with a loving open hand. The One with arms wide open when we're riddled with shame. The One who gives us a map on how to do life and relationships. The One who works by His Spirit through people. The One who offers truth. That One. Let us increase in godliness and not deny its power (2 Timothy 3:5-7).

Plug into His Godliness

1. Study and cultivate the fruit of the Spirit in yourself and others. "But the fruit of the Spirit is love, joy, peace, longsuffering, kindness, goodness, faithfulness, gentleness, self-control. Against such there is no law" (Galatians 5:22–23).

2. Renounce vanity and explore how your body image and weight have been tainted with a worldly mindset or worldly desires.

3. Ask yourself, "Is what I'm doing okay with God?"

4. Pray for an increased affection for God and His ways.

God is supernatural. He breaks the laws of physics. He supersedes our limitations. He is an all-consuming fire, filled with the energy, power, and the wherewithal we need to be, do, and have anything we need in our lives. It's in this power, Elohim—the intensification of all power, that we must allow ourselves to surrender for healing, breakthrough, and more. Ultimately, I charge us all with loving God more and loving the world less. With Jesus we win. With our God, we can leap over a wall (Psalm 18:29).

He's coming as King!

REFLECTION QUESTIONS

1. Which of the kingdom power plugs ministered most to you?

   _____

   _____

2. What practices will you adopt this week?

   _____

   _____

3. How can you increase your kingdom power plugs to overcome weight and eating bondage?

   _____

   _____

PRAYER

Heavenly Father,

Forgive me for any way I've misunderstood who you are. Thank you for the mighty acts of love and encouragement you've given to me in my health and life. Thank you for seeing me through this far. I praise you for your unfailing love, abundant mercy, and unmeasurable grace in my life. I ask you to increase my love for you. Be my daily feast.

Fill me with your love so much so that it overflows! I realize I fall short in loving myself, and loving others, and loving you. Make me a vessel of your love. Help me to stand in my truth that I am a child of the Most High God and that with you I can leap over wall. May I worship you in spirit and in truth. May I intentionally nurture my relationship with you. I love you so much, Father. I love you so much, Jesus. I love you so much, Holy Spirit.

Thank you for healing my body, soul, and spirit. Thank you for calling me your friend. Thank you for your character. Thank you for being at work in all areas of my life. Thank you for empowering me by your Spirit to finish this book. Hallelujah!

Bless your holy, matchless name.

In Jesus's name, amen.

CHAPTER 20

COMING RIGHT UP, AN ORDER TO WIN

"But thanks be to God, who gives us the victory
through our Lord Jesus Christ"

−1 CORINTHIANS 15:57

Your weight and eating giants are going down.

P ain consumed me. I couldn't eat. I couldn't sleep. I could barely
drive my car.

"Abba! Have mercy on me!" I cried out to God over the
past week.

It was nine years ago when I first felt the sting of a gallbladder attack.
It felt like my gallbladder would burst. Almost a full week in pain went
by before I had my ultrasound appointment on a Friday morning.

I went into the ultrasound office. The technician applied the cold
wet gel as I squirmed in pain.

The results on the monitor were dismal.

"You'll need to have surgery right away. You're scheduled for first
thing on Monday morning," the technician said.

"Okay," I mumbled. I felt humbled by my overeating habits that led
me to lose organs. I thought to myself, *not cool, Jendayi, not cool at all.*

The next day my spiritual family met for an already scheduled discipleship meeting. I came in late and slipped in the back. A group of

313

about twelve people or so were gathered in the large, partially finished basement of our spiritual directors.

I ached in pain, hugging the right side of my body. I bopped back and forth. I stood up and sat down. I tried anything to ease the needle-like stabs of pain.

"Jendayi, come up here, and let's pray for you," my mentor, Debbie, said at the break.

I went up to the front grateful to receive prayer and care. I didn't want to lose my gallbladder, I just really prefer to keep all of my organs.

She prayed healing over me. And before I knew it, I felt a tangible, invisible presence, like a wind, come inside my mouth, down my esophagus, and through my body to my gallbladder's pain. I felt the power of God so strong, it scared me.

My brain couldn't catch up to what my heart and body was receiving. My arms had to stay opened wide under this powerful force. All I could do was surrender as my gallbladder received the Spirit's surgery. The spirit moved like a hockey puck intricately in the gallbladder area.

All I had to do was receive, but it was harder than one would think.

I had prayed the whole week repeatedly, "Heal me, God!" I had pleaded and pleaded before His throne on my knees and on the bed as I tossed and turned the past five nights. When healing rushed in like a wind—powerful, strong, real, and tangible, I was in awe. I felt, firsthand, the amazing wind of the Holy Spirit.

"He's healing me!" I exclaimed "He just did the surgery!"

At His touch I was healed! I was enveloped by the wind of God's love.

At that moment, I knew the profound, miraculous healing power that Jesus walked in daily for healing people.

I found myself in a mental struggle with the supernatural healing that had just taken place. One moment my mind would think, *I'm in pain, I have surgery Monday*, then my spirit would remind me, *I'm healed*, and I felt no pain at all.

I went back and forth this way as we all rejoiced over the forty-five minutes or so, until I was in full agreement with no pain. Then I had no pain. We

God is a
supernatural healer.

rejoiced and prayed over everything—and I mean everything—because the presence of God overpowered the place.

I was healed by the greatest Physician in the universe.

My pending surgery never happened. We all saw my pain, we all saw my healing, and we all felt His presence in the room. A true and total miracle showed itself. I could and couldn't believe it.

God is a supernatural healer.

And yes, I had to also end my relationship with excess butter and matzah.

I'm amazed too, at the work you've accomplished so far. I'm so proud of what the Holy Spirit is doing! You've read twenty chapters and several reflection questions. Wow. Thank you, Jesus!

But like my pleading, we've got to stay before the Father on our knees, crying out for our healing miracle, our mindset shift, our emotional freedom, and our spiritual strength!

We need to lean on Him for an absolute transformation of body, soul, and spirit.

And while the sudden disappearance of weight never happened, and I had to walk it out step by step, it's faith that sees us through. We'll need His wind of the Spirit to keep our momentum strong and our faith believing we can get to the promised land. And you're so close…

We need to lean on Him for
an absolute transformation
of body, soul, and spirit.

You, on Top of the Mountain

You're standing at the very top of a mountain. The wind is blowing through your hair or slightly cooling your skin if you're bald. The sky is bright, blue, and beautiful. The striking mountain sun is shining on your face. You look out over the land from where you came, but that place is far removed.

You've crossed your Red Sea. You've climbed several thousand feet to the summit of the weight and eating freedom mountain. And you bask in the wonder of the Lord for taking you this far, for reading through this big ole book, and for the changes you're already making. You've found more peace within and stirred up new inner conversations.

Embrace all you've just experienced. Release the pain of weight and eating that you've been through. Think about the ideas, actions, tips, and strategies you've learned.

Ponder the healing He's doing, and life He's renewing. And prepare yourself for the descent and the giants we must battle ahead. Giants of compulsive overeating, sugar and junk food addiction, generational weight and eating strongholds, body image, and more.

To win this battle, you'll need to be willing to do whatever it takes to reach the end.

In worship one day in my living room, I listened to Israel Houghton's song *Take the Limits Off*. I heard, "Are you willing to take the limits off?" I sensed I was playing life too small.

The Holy Spirit exposed my self-imposed limits. I was willing to crouch down at the base of the mountain, but I feared ascending the mountain.

After a few moments I heard Him say, "Are you willing to go great with me?" I knew at that moment it could cost me everything—my relationship, money, ego, and time—and it did.

But no matter what it costs, as children of God, we can't keep playing small. Take hold of the promises of God for the abundant life. Don't allow the enemy or flesh to take your future. I wish weight and eating bondage wasn't so complex. But because it is, we still have work to do. Be determined. Your weight and eating giants are going down.

It is the fear of the Lord and your willingness to do whatever it takes, that brings out our greatness. We can't protect our egos when we rise higher in Christ. It's got to be about Him. We must rise above our false concepts of identity and our false comforts. We're taking back our health, but we're also taking spiritual territory, our family, and generations with us.

> You're an overcomer by the blood of the Lamb
> and the testimony of Jesus Christ (Revelation 12:11).

Stay committed to win the battles and get to your promised land. You're an overcomer by the blood of the Lamb and the testimony of Jesus Christ (Revelation 12:11).

Known as The Drill Sergeant of Life, Beatrice Bruno—a Christian motivational speaker extraordinaire, one of my mothers in the Lord, and author of *How to Get Over Yourself and Let Go of the P.A.S.T.*—said, "Your future is here for you. It's been designed to benefit you and your generations to come. Don't let anyone or anything stand between you and your future you were created to have! Go forward and apprehend your future and challenge it."

You heard her. Keep going.

Coming right up ... an Order to Win.

REFLECTION QUESTIONS ❓

1. Do you believe God is a supernatural healer? Why?

_____

_____

2. What chapters do you need to re-visit?

_____

_____

3. What are your biggest learnings from this book?

_____

_____

PRAYER

Holy Spirit,

Thank you so much for helping me to read and absorb this content to work for me. I pray to win the battles ahead for good. Thank you for taking me to my promised land! I will trust you to guide me there!

I confess today that I trust God! I will manifest my destiny! All things will work for my good, because I love you and I'm called according to your purpose. Thank you for this book! Thank you for my weight and eating freedom. I am free indeed!

In Jesus's name, amen!

INVITATION TO CHRIST

"Nor is there salvation in any other, for there is no other name under heaven given among men by which we must be saved"

−ACTS 4:12

Churches are like restaurants: you've
got to try them until you find a favorite.

Have you ever had a house guest ruin your home's atmosphere? Maybe he or she criticized every little thing or brought nasty music, nasty food, nasty ways, and a nasty attitude into your dwelling space? This is how I liken a holy God—our God, who is love.

Certain people just can't understand, receive, or interpret the presence of God. Like that house guest, who couldn't get your loving atmosphere, needed to go, so also the cancers of hate, negativity, pride, and other stinky attitudes would need to depart from an atmosphere of holiness, peace, and love.

God sent Jesus for us to be able to reconcile with God through Jesus because the Father is too holy for us to bear. He is so holy that we would die in His presence unless He sent us a redeeming branch to cover our unholiness and ridiculousness so that we can be reconciled to the Holy One. Jesus is our olive branch.

We get to be adopted to a heavenly, holy Father, through His Son, by the power of the Holy Spirit.

One thing is for sure: "For God so loved the world that He gave His only begotten Son, that whoever believes in Him should not perish but have everlasting life" (John 3:16). God absolutely loves you and is excited about you! He wants you on His team. He wants to help you with this thing called life. He wants to teach you how to love, grow, and help yourself, your family, and others.

He gives the free gift of salvation, which is an invitation to His kingdom. He's already Lord, but we just want to acknowledge Him in our lives and come into alignment with the true Lover of our souls.

Douglas Groothuis, researcher and author of *Christian Apologetics* said, "He [Jesus] entered the world supernaturally, accredited Himself with unparalleled signs and wonders, possessed an impeccable character, made claims only befitting God Himself, and died with the purpose of redeeming humanity. The best account of the historical facts is that He was who He said He was. If this is so, we should respond to Him on His terms[1]... Other gods are prophets, not messiahs, avatars, not incarnate, sages, not saviors."[2]

And because God is so good, all you need to do is bring your words and heart into alignment by confession, then seek out a church to get baptized as soon as possible for the remission of sins in the name of Jesus Christ—who signs the check on our salvation.

Baptism is a sign that you've now entered the kingdom of God and are partnering with the Holy Spirit to bring about your true identity and purpose in the earth.

Will you pray the prayer on the next page to acknowledge the Lord? As Romans 10:8-11 instructs, "If you confess with your mouth the Lord Jesus and believe in your heart that God has raised Him from the dead, you will be saved. For with the heart one believes unto righteousness, and with the mouth confession is made unto salvation. For the Scripture says, 'Whoever believes in Him will not be put to shame'".

DAYSTAR NETWORK'S PRAYER FOR SALVATION[3]

"Dear Lord Jesus,

I know that according to your Word in John 3:3, I must be born again to see the kingdom of God. Father I know I am a sinner. I believe Christ died for me. I believe that you shed your blood, died on the cross for me, and rose again from the dead. I repent and turn from my sins. I need you, Jesus.

I no longer want to be in control of my life. Please come into my heart, forgive me of my sins, and be my personal Lord and Savior from this day forward. Please give me the strength by your precious Holy Spirit to live for you.

Please forgive me of my sins ... I want to turn from my sins.

Jesus, thank you for the gift of salvation. I promise to obey you with the help of the Holy Spirit and to follow you all the days of my life. In Jesus's name, amen."

For resources for your confession go to:

https://howtoknowjesus.joycemeyer.org/
http://www.daystar.com/prayer/know-jesus/

Check out various churches in your local area until you find one that feels right for you. Churches are like restaurants: you've got to try them until you find a favorite. Get a good Bible that you can understand and enjoy your new adventure with the Lord!

Congratulations! Your life will never be the same again.

Welcome to the team! If you've prayed this prayer, please email:

info@wholeandfreepress.com.

ACKNOWLEDGEMENTS

I am deeply thankful to the many people that have prayed over this work, contributed to this work, supported me in the work, and who received the work. I could not have done this without your prayers, love, encouragement, kindness, beta reading, proof-reading, editing, teaching, training, patience, coaching, and generosity that saw me through. I'll trust you know who you are. Few days go by that I don't thank God for laying me on your heart for prayer or support to see His plan through.

I love you.

Thank you! Thank you! Thank you!

NON-EDIBLE GOODIES

SEAS - Self-Esteem Inventory

DIRECTIONS: For each of the statements below, rate what is your level of exhibiting these behaviors in your life. Use the following rating scale and circle the number of your rating for each item:

1 = never   2 = rarely   3 = sometimes   4 = frequently   5 = almost always

1. I seek approval and affirmation from others, and I am afraid of criticism.

           1   2   3   4   5

2. I guess at what normal behavior is, and I usually feel as if I am different from other people.

           1   2   3   4   5

3. I isolate myself from and am afraid of people in authority roles.

           1   2   3   4   5

4. I am not able to appreciate my own accomplishments and good deeds.

           1   2   3   4   5

5. I tend to have difficulty following a project through from beginning to end.

           1   2   3   4   5

6. I get frightened or stressed when I am in the company of an angry person.

           1   2   3   4   5

7. In order to avoid a conflict, I find it easier to lie than tell the truth.

           1   2   3   4   5

8. I have problems with my own compulsive behavior, e.g., drinking, drug use, gambling, overeating, smoking, use of sex, shopping, etc.

 1   2   3   4   5

9. I judge myself without mercy. I am my own worst critic, and I am harder on myself than I am on others.

 1   2   3   4   5

10. I feel more alive in the midst of a crisis, and I am uneasy when my life is going smoothly; I am continually anticipating problems.

 1   2   3   4   5

11. I have difficulty having fun. I don't seem to know how to play for fun and relaxation.

 1   2   3   4   5

12. I am attracted to others whom I perceive to have been victims, and I develop close relationships with them. In this way I confuse love with pity, and I love people I can pity and rescue.

 1   2   3   4   5

13. I need perfection in my life at home and work, and I expect perfection from others in my life.

 1   2   3   4   5

14. I seek out novelty, excitement, and the challenge of newness in my life with little concern given to the consequences of such action.

 1   2   3   4   5

15. I take myself very seriously, and I view all of my relationships just as seriously.

 1   2   3   4   5

16. I have problems developing and maintaining intimate relationships.

 1   2   3   4   5

17. I feel guilty when I stand up for myself or take care of my needs first, instead of giving in or taking care of others' needs first.

| 1 | 2 | 3 | 4 | 5 |

18. I seek and/or attract people who have compulsive behaviors (e.g., alcohol, drugs, gambling, food, shopping, sex, smoking, overworking, or seeking excitement.)

| 1 | 2 | 3 | 4 | 5 |

19. I feel responsible for others and find it easier to have concern for others than for myself.

| 1 | 2 | 3 | 4 | 5 |

20. I am loyal to people for whom I care, even in the face of evidence that the loyalty is undeserved.

| 1 | 2 | 3 | 4 | 5 |

21. I cling to and will do anything to hold on to relationships because I am afraid of being alone and fearful of being abandoned.

| 1 | 2 | 3 | 4 | 5 |

22. I am impulsive and act too quickly, before considering alternative actions or possible consequences.

| 1 | 2 | 3 | 4 | 5 |

23. I have difficulty in being able to feel or to express feelings; I feel out of touch with my feelings.

| 1 | 2 | 3 | 4 | 5 |

24. I mistrust my feelings and the feelings expressed by others.

| 1 | 2 | 3 | 4 | 5 |

25. I isolate myself from other people, and I am initially shy and withdrawn in new social settings.

| 1 | 2 | 3 | 4 | 5 |

26. I feel that I am being taken advantage of by individuals and society in general; I often feel victimized.

	1	2	3	4	5

27. I can be overresponsible much of the time, but I can be extremely irresponsible at other times.

	1	2	3	4	5

28. I feel confused and angry at myself and not in control of my environment or my life when the stresses are great.

	1	2	3	4	5

29. I spend a lot of time and energy rectifying or cleaning up my messes and the negative consequences of ill-thought-out or impulsive actions for which I am responsible.

	1	2	3	4	5

30. I deny that my current problems stem from my past life. I deny that I have stuffed-in feelings from the past which are impeding my current life.

	1	2	3	4	5

Scoring and Interpretation

Add the ratings for all 30 items in your journal. This score indicates the degree to which you are affected by low self-esteem.

Score Interpretation

0-30 | Not affected by low self-esteem.

31-45 | Traces of low self-esteem. Take preventive action to reduce its impact on your life.

46-61 | Presence of mild low self-esteem in your life. Take steps to treat this.

62-90 | Presence of moderate low self-esteem. Take steps to treat this as soon as possible.

91-120 | Presence of severe low self-esteem. Take steps to treat this immediately.

121-150 | Presence of profound low self-esteem. Take immediate step to treat this and seek out professional help to assist you in this process.

http://coping.us/seasmanual/selfesteeminventory.html

A Prayer of Gratitude for the Body

- Lord thank you for my toes and feet. Thank you for giving me feet that take me in the direction you send me. Thank you that I have feet to stand on. Thank you that my feet are blessed and shod with the gospel of peace.

- Lord thank you for my legs. Lord I could not have any legs to stand on. Thank you for giving me legs to help get me where you want me to go. Thank you for my knees that help me to sit and bend. Thank you for my thighs, help me to accept them as they are, and see them as the strength that they are for my body.

- Lord thank you for my hips. Thank you that I am able to sit comfortably. Thank you that I get to have this body and the ability to move and choose clothing that helps me to feel confident.

- Thank you Lord for your protection over my body and over my shape and size as it is. Thank you that you accept me for the body I have. Lord help me to accept this body you gave me. Help me to love what you have created in me and in this body. Thank you, Father, for anointing me with the grace and strength to honor my body.

- Lord I repent for harm and abuse to my body and I ask you to help me to treat it as a Holy Vessel of your spirit. I ask you to help me to appreciate it and to value it. Thank you, Lord, for this temporary home of my body that helps me to implement your will on earth.

- Thank you Father for my stomach. Thank you that I have digestion and organs that are working. Thank you for the stomach I have, it could be bigger, it could be flatter, but it's functioning and its mine. Please nourish me from your spirit and help me to love my stomach. I ask you to help me accept my stomach exactly how it is.

- Thank you, Father, for freeing me from criticism of my body! Thank you for helping me to stop negatively evaluating my body shape and size. Thank you for helping me not to dwell on worldly things.

- Thank you, Father, for my arms. Thank you that they help me to pick things up, hug those I love, carry my bags, and put myself in more comfortable conditions. Thank you for the arms that give me strength. Thank you for my hands Father! Thank you for my fingers and my nails. Thank you that I can work with these hands, I can feel with these hands, I can Facebook with these typing fingers. I can cook and eat with these hands. I can praise your name with these hands! I can lift my hands up to you.

- Thank you for my neck that turns my head.

- Thank you for the weight I have on my body. Thank you that I am not being carried out of my house due to obesity. Thank you for increasing my appreciation for my current body size and shape exactly how it is. Thank you, Father, for setting me free from weight and eating bondage. Thank you for setting me free from valuing myself based on my weight! Thank you for freedom from being weight obsessive. Thank you that my body can hold weight. Thank you that my body can release weight.

- Thank you that the head is the authority over the body. Thank you for my brain that communicates to my body and organs what to do and when to it. Thank you, Father, for my face. Thank you for my eyes, eyebrows, lips, and nose. Thank you for the senses I get to experience that involve my head. Thank you for my head's shape and size. Thank you for the value of my brain, that I can do things, and help others with it.

- Thank you, Body, for all of your remarkable service to my soul and spirit. Thank you, my Body, for forgiveness for the damage I've done to you. You are alive! I will treat you with love and care!

- Thank God for those parts of the body that you struggle to fully appreciate, value, and accept. Thank God for the hair on your head, or the hair you may have left, or your head shaped for baldness. Thank God even for your private parts. Thank God for your organs, your heart, liver, and kidneys for example. Thank God even for those unique birthmarks, beauty marks, and scars. Turn around your body hatred to body appreciation.

Emotional Fitness Workout™ Worksheet

Use this worksheet to move through the steps in Chapter 18.

1	Stop

2	Pinpoint

3	Evaluate

4	Experience

5	Release

Emotional Fitness Workout™ Worksheet

Use this worksheet to move through the steps in Chapter 18.

1	Stop

2	Pinpoint

3	Evaluate

4	Experience

5	Release

UPCOMING BOOKS

Join Jendayi's mailing list for upcoming books
at *www.jendayiharris.com*

Did you enjoy *The Chubby Church*?

Many others are struggling and dying before
their time because of weight and eating bondage.

We must get the word out.

Will you help?

Your review helps others decide to purchase this book on
www.Amazon.com.

Thank you!

Post your review today!

Ready to win?
In Book 2 you'll:

- Defeat the 7 giants in the weight and eating battle
- Get strategies for sugar, junk, and other food addictions
- Figure out how to make health work for your lifestyle
- Learn strategies to avoid recapture in weight and eating bondage

You didn't think you could conquer a decade long problem with one book, did you? In *The Chubby Church Book* 2, we'll have to deal with food addiction, compulsive overeating, isolation, body image, generational strongholds, and more.

Book 2 is smaller, but still power-packed to help you win for good!

Available Late Summer 2019.

Too busy to read?
Listen to Jendayi instead on:

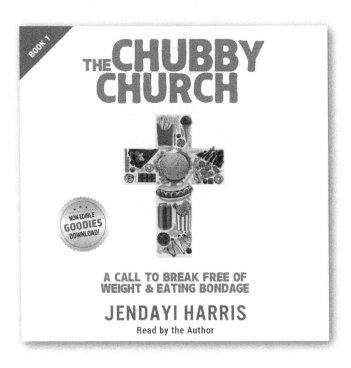

www.audible.com

For Moms Who:

- Have regrets from early experiences raising their children
- Feel hurt or distant from her adult child
- Need strategies to stop beating herself up with guilt
- Want to improve her relationship with herself and her adult child

Are you a mom with regrets from early experiences as mothers, and who feel the consequences in their current relationships with their adult child?

This book is a big hug for you! In this book, I talk about an 8-step strategy your adult child needs to repair your relationship.

Instead of beating yourself up with guilt, feeling angry that your adult child is disconnected from you, or worrying about seeing your grandchildren – Take Action! The book and workbook together pack a powerful strategy to take back your family!

Available Fall 2019.

Are You Emotionally Fit?

You'll learn:

- How to understand emotions and get ego out of the way
- The 5-step Emotional Fitness Workout™ for inner strength to feel happy, healthy, and whole for life
- Why so many religious people fail to show the love of God
- How to navigate the triggers that sabotage relationships

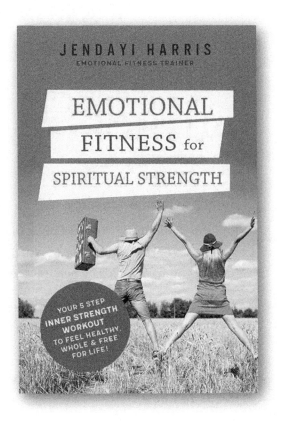

Spiritual and religious communities know that something is missing when a person isn't willing to work on their character, reactions, and general personal development.

Using Biblical principles, stories, and practical tips, this book will help build your emotional body to ward off offense, fear, and anger, and to develop more connected conversations and a loving presence.

Available Summer 2020.

Is God calling you to write?
If so, get started with:

Author Audience Academy

Join this community of Christian authors and get access to the proven step-by-step plan you can use to write, publish and market your book (even if you have no idea where to start).

Find out more here:
http://www.authoraudienceacademy.com/

3 Proven Book Writing Formulas Every Nonfiction Author Needs to Know

By the end of this free training, you will have chosen a book topic, created a basic outline, and decided on the technique you will use to write your next book.

Get started with this free training here
http://trainingauthors.com/formulas/

Join Whole & Free Health to:

- Share in *The Chubby Church* reading experience
- Have a place to share your successes
- Find products that work for others for cleansing and supplementation
- Share recipes
- Share and receive devotionals, prayers, and encouragement
- Get accountability
- Meet others who share the journey
- Join optional paid courses – Whole & Free Health Body, Whole & Free Health Soul, or Whole & Free Health Spirit. You can choose online and live workshops as available, to focus on applying *The Chubby Church* book contents and more
- Join optional paid audio-visual book club for Jendayi to read to you

It's FREE!

On your smart phone:
Find **Mighty Networks App**,
then search for **Whole and Free Health**

Online go to:
www.WholeNFreeHealth.com

Jendayi Harris is a minister of practical advice on how to do life in Christ well. She has a Bachelor of Science in Business Administration from Seton Hall University as a part of the distinguished Martin Luther King Scholarship Association. She received her Master of Arts in Counseling Psychology from Colorado Christian University. She's a Nationally Certified Counselor, as well as a Licensed Professional Counselor in Colorado. After a health revelation in her early twenties, she became a Board-Certified Health Coach with the Institute of Integrative Nutrition.

From a Ministry standpoint, she has been mentored by Rabbi Ralph Messer of Simchat Torah Beit Midrash, Pastor Tayo Obigbesan of Christ Liberty Restoration Ministries and is now an active member of BridgeWay Church under Pastor Peter Young and Apostle Bill Johnson of Bethel Church.

Jendayi is certified as a DiSc instructor with TTI and a Certified Emotional Intelligence facilitator from industry leader, Talent Smart. In her leisure time she enjoys teaching, writing, family, running, and her two baby-dogs.

Her unique background and experience in many areas as well as incredible life experience makes her a source of Godly practical advice and wisdom in an age of information and great confusion.

As a Soul Freedom Author & Teacher, she speaks on a range of topics and issues of soul and family restoration. In her opinion, to love God, your self, and others, is the most productive response to our daily insanity.

To hire her for speaking or to hear about her latest releases, visit her site at

www.jendayiharris.com.

Photograph by Kymora Jaxson Photography

NOTES

Introduction

1. Stephanie Averkamp, "Diet and Weight Loss Statistics," fitnessforweightloss.com, accessed March 16, 2019, *http://www. fitnessforweightloss.com/diet-and-weight-loss-statistics/.*

Chapter 2: Are You a Member of The Chubby Church?

1. Eric A. Finkelstein et al., "Obesity and Severe Obesity Forecasts through 2030," American Journal of Preventive Medicine 42 (6) (2012): 563–70, *https://doi.org/10.1016/j.amepre.2011.10.026.*

2. Alexandros N. Vgontzas et al., "Obesity and Self-Reported Short Sleep Duration: A Marker of Sleep Complaints and Chronic Psychosocial Stress," Sleep Medicine Clinics 4, no. 1 (2009): 65–75, accessed April 24, 2018. doi:10.1016/j.jsmc.2009.01.001.

3. "Adult Obesity Facts | Overweight & Obesity | CDC," Centers for Disease Control and Prevention, accessed March 16, 2019, *https://www. cdc.gov/obesity/data/adult.html.*

4. Claire Y. Wang et al., "Health and Economic Burden of the Projected Obesity Trends in the USA and the UK," The Lancet 378, no. 9793 (August 27, 2011): 815–825, doi:10.1016/s0140-6736(11)60814-3.

5. Jessica Glenza, 2017, "Only One in 10 Americans Eat Enough Fruits and Vegetables, CDC Study Finds," The Guardian, Guardian News and Media, November 17, 2017, https://www.theguardian.com/us-news/2017/nov/17/ just-12-of-americans-eat-enough-fruit-and-vegetables-cdc-study-finds.

6. Federation of American Societies for Experimental Biology (FASEB), "Highly Processed Foods Dominate U.S. Grocery Purchases," Science Daily, March 29, 2015, *http://www.sciencedaily.com/ releases/2015/03/150329141017.htm.*

7. Fox News, "Fat in Church," Fox News, January 4, 2013, accessed March 16, 2019, *http://www.foxnews.com/opinion/2012/06/03/obesity-epidemic-in-america-churches.html*.

8. Marla Paul, "Religious Young Adults Become Obese by Middle Age," Northwestern University, accessed March 23, 2011.

9. Kate L. Lapane et al., "Religion and Cardiovascular Disease Risk," SpringerLink, Kluwer Academic Publishers-Plenum Publishers, June 1997, https://doi.org/10.1023/A:1027444621177.

10. "Denial," Merriam-Webster, accessed March 17, 2019, *https://www.merriam-webster.com/dictionary/denial*.

Chapter 3: Welcome to Burger King – My Story

1. Kevin Trudeau, *Natural Cures They Don't Want You to Know About* (Elks Grove Village, IL: Alliance Publishing Group, 2004).

Chapter 4: Do You Want Freedom with That? – Freedom in Body, Soul, and Spirit

1. Watchman Nee, *The Spiritual Man* (Anaheim, CA: Living Stream Ministry, 1998).

2. Sanctify." n.d. Merriam-Webster accessed April 28, 2019. *https://www.merriam-webster.com/dictionary/sanctify*.

3. Nicholas Bakalar, "37.2 Trillion: Galaxies or Human Cells?" *The New York Times,* December 21, 2017, *https://www.nytimes.com/2015/06/23/science/37-2-trillion-galaxies-or-human-cells.html*.

4. Watchman Nee, *The Spiritual Man*, 198.

5. American Psychiatric Association, *Diagnostic and Statistical Manual of Mental Disorders: DSM-5.* 5th ed. (Arlington, VA: American Psychiatric Association, 2013).

6. Henry Wright, *A More Excellent Way* (New Kensington, PA: Whitaker House, 2009).

Chapter 5: The Call to Weight & Eating Freedom Action Plan

1. Stephanie Averkamp, "Diet and Weight Loss Statistics," fitnessforweightloss.com, accessed March 16, 2019, *http://www.fitnessforweightloss.com/diet-and-weight-loss-statistics/*.

2. Lysa TerKeurst, Made to Crave: Satisfying Your Deepest Desire with God, Not Food: Six Sessions: Participants Guide (Grand Rapids, MI: Zondervan, 2011), 11.

3. Amy Osmond Cook, "Healthy Living: Defeating the Couch Potato," Orange County Register, October 23, 2014, *https://www.ocregister.com/2014/10/23/healthy-living-defeating-the-couch-potato/*.

4. Ibid.

5. William Arthur Ward, "If You Can Imagine It, You Can Achieve It. If You Can Dream It, You Can Become It," accessed March 17, 2019, *https://www.quotes.net/quote/6643*.

6. *Alcoholics Anonymous* (New York: Works Pub., 1948).

7. Ibid.

8. Swimcoachpro, "Increase Your Chances of Achieving Your GOALs by up to 95%," Swimcoach, October 17, 2018, *https://swimcoach-pro.com/2018/04/30/increase-your-chances-of-achieving-your-goals-by-up-to-95/*.

Chapter 6: Habitize Body Stewardship – Physical Freedom

1. National Center for Chronic Disease Prevention and Health Promotion (NCCDPHP), "Health and Economic Costs of Chronic Diseases," Centers for Disease Control and Prevention, February 11, 2019, accessed February 27, 2019, *https://www.cdc.gov/chronicdisease/about/costs/index.htm*.

2. Ibid.

3. CDC Newsroom, "Up to 40 Percent of Annual Deaths from Each of Five Leading U.S. Causes Are Preventable," Centers for Disease Control and Prevention, May 1, 2014, accessed February 27, 2019, *https://www.cdc.gov/media/releases/2014/p0501-preventable-deaths.html*.

4. "Introduction," Dietary Guidelines 2015–2020, accessed February 27, 2019, *https://health.gov/dietaryguidelines/2015/guidelines/introduction/nutrition-and-health-are-closely-related/*.

5. Pam Belluck, "Children's Life Expectancy Being Cut Short by Obesity," *The New York Times,* March 17, 2005, accessed March 25, 2017, *https://www.nytimes.com/2005/03/17/health/childrens-life-expectancy-being-cut-short-by-obesity.html*.

6. "Mental Illness," National Institute of Mental Health, November 2017, accessed February 27, 2019, *https://www.nimh.nih.gov/health/statistics/mental-illness.shtml.*

7. "50% of Mentally Ill Untreated," Mental Illness Policy Org, accessed February 27, 2019, *https://mentalillnesspolicy.org/consequences/percentage-mentally-ill-untreated.html*

8. Rosalynn Carter, Rebecca Palpant Shimkets, and Thomas H. Bornemann, "Creating and Changing Public Policy to Reduce the Stigma of Mental Illness," *Psychological Science in the Public Interest* 15, No. 2 (September 3, 2014), 35–36, accessed February 27, 2019. doi:10.1177/1529100614546119.

Chapter 7: Habit #1 Nutrient Load – Am I Malnourished?

1. Stacy Simon, "World Health Organization Says Processed Meat Causes Cancer," American Cancer Society, October 26, 2015, accessed January 27, 2019, *https://www.cancer.org/latest-news/world-health-organization-says-processed-meat-causes-cancer.html.*

2. Federation of American Societies for Experimental Biology (FASEB), "Highly Processed Foods Dominate U. S. Grocery Purchases," Science Daily, March 29, 2015, accessed January 20, 2019, *http://www.sciencedaily.com/releases/2015/03/150329141017.htm.*

3. Agence France-Presse, "Unhealthy Eating Linked To 400,000 US Deaths Per Year: Study," NDTV, March 10, 2017, accessed January 20, 2019, *https://www.ndtv.com/health/unhealthy-eating-linked-to-400-000-us-deaths-per-year-study-1668102.*

4. Kimberly Hartke, "Violent Behavior Linked to Nutritional Deficiencies," *Well Being Journal*, January/February 2014, 33–34.

5. Ocean Roberts, "The Anti-Cancer Powerhouses," *What Doctors Don't Tell You: Helping You Make Better Health Choices*, March 2019, 44–53.

6. "Dying for a Burger?" *Nutrition Action Healthletter*, July/August 2017, 7.

7. Ibid.

8. Elizabeth Lipski, *Digestive Wellness*, 3rd ed. (New York: McGraw Hill, 2005), 24.

9. Michael Via, "The Malnutrition of Obesity: Micronutrient Deficiencies That Promote Diabetes," *ISRN Endocrinology* 2012 (January 05, 2012): 1–8, doi:10.5402/2012/103472.

10. Jayson Calton and Mira Calton, The Micronutrient Miracle: The 28-day Plan to Lose Weight, Increase Your Energy, and Reverse Disease (Melbourne, Victoria.: Black Books, 2016), 26.

11. Michael Greger and Gene Stone, How Not to Die: Discover the Foods Scientifically Proven to Prevent and Reverse Disease (London: Pan Books, 2018).

12. Ibid.

13. Sarah Gottfried, The Hormone Cure: Reclaim Balance, Sleep, Sex Drive, and Vitality Naturally with the Gottfried Protocol (New York: Scribner, 2013).

14. Lisa Oz, "The Oz Rx: Eat for a Long Life," Dr. Oz: The Good Life, 2017, 66.

15. Carolyn Costin, The Eating Disorders Sourcebook 3rd ed. (New York: McGraw-Hill, 2007), 224.

16. Arne Astrup and Susanne Bügel, "Overfed but Undernourished: Recognizing Nutritional Inadequacies/Deficiencies in Patients with Overweight or Obesity," International Journal of Obesity 43, no. 2 (July 06, 2018): 219–232, accessed March 03, 2019, doi:10.1038/s41366-018-0143-9.

17. Jayson Calton and Mira Calton, "Obesity and Its Connection to Micronutrient Deficiency – the Evidence Is Becoming Stronger," Calton Nutrition, September 29, 2015, accessed January 08, 2019, https://www.caltonnutrition.com/obesity-and-micronutrient-deficiency/.

18. Donald R. Davis, Melvin D. Epp, and Hugh D. Riordan, "Changes in USDA Food Composition Data for 43 Garden Crops, 1950 to 1999," Journal of the American College of Nutrition 23, no. 6 (May 07, 2004): 669–682, doi:10.1080/07315724.2004.10719409.

19. Ibid.

20. Calton and Calton, "Obesity and Its Connection to Micronutrient Deficiency – the Evidence Is Becoming Stronger."

21. Astrup and S. Bügel, "Micronutrient Deficiency in the Aetiology of Obesity," International Journal of Obesity 34, no. 6 (2010): 947–948, doi:10.1038/ijo.2010.81.

22. Michael Moss, Salt, Sugar, Fat How the Food Giants Hooked Us (London: WH Allen, 2014), 42.

23. Ibid.

24. Joseph Mercola and James DiNicolantonio, "The Healthy Brain: Fattening Up the Brain," *What Doctors Don't Tell You: Helping You Make Better Health Choices*, February 2019, 44–49.

25. *What the Health*, directed by Kip Anderson and Keegan Kuhn, performed by Kip Anderson, Garth Davis, and Dr. Neal Bernard, What the Health, 2017, accessed September 01, 2018, *https://www.amazon.com/*.

26. Ibid.

27. Calton and Calton, The Micronutrient Miracle, 90.

28. Fox News, "Survey Shows 74 Percent of Americans Living with GI Discomfort," Fox News, November 24, 2013, accessed March 08, 2019, *https://www.foxnews.com/health/survey-shows-74-percent-of-americans-living-with-gi-discomfort*.

29. Lipski, *Digestive Wellness*, 23–24.

30. Cate Montana, "Magic Bullets," What Doctors Don't Tell You: Helping You Make Better Health Choices, May 2018, 58–64.

31. Josh Axe, "7 Signs and Symptoms You Have Leaky Gut," Dr. Axe, May 08, 2018, accessed March 08, 2019, *https://draxe.com/7-signs-symptoms-you-have-leaky-gut/*.

32. Julie Malacoff, "The Surprising Way Your Brain and Gut Are Connected – Shape Magazine," Amare Blog, December 21, 2017, accessed March 08, 2019, *http://blog.amare.com/the-surprising-way-your-brain-and-gut-are-connected-shape-magazine/*.

33. Ibid.

34. Josh Axe, "Leaky Gut Diet and Treatment Plan, Including Top Gut Foods," Dr. Axe, July 30, 2018, accessed March 08, 2019, *https://draxe.com/leaky-gut-diet-treatment/*.

35. Ibid.

36. Josh Axe, "7 Signs and Symptoms You Have Leaky Gut."

37. Edward Group, "The Ultimate Candida Diet Program," Dr. Group's Healthy Living Articles, November 09, 2017, accessed March 08, 2019, *https://www.globalhealingcenter.com/natural-health/ultimate-candida-diet-program/?msclkid=4460dc92d02213d8c68b8010700e5693&utm_source=bing&utm_medium=cpc&utm_campaign=Mycozil NB Blog - Search&utm_term= candida fats&utm_content=Mycozil Candida Diet Avoid NB Blog*.

38. Ibid.

39. Laura Paris and Garland Oka, "SIBO Is the New Candida," Laura Paris, February 27, 2017, accessed March 09, 2019, *https://www. parishealingarts.com/sibo-new-candida/*.

40. William Davis, Wheat Belly: Lose the Wheat, Lose the Weight, and Find Your Path Back to Health (London: Harper Thorsons, 2015), 25.

41. Davis, *Wheat Belly*, 25.

42. Ibid.

43. John Douillard, "5 Things You Never Knew About Gluten . . . But Should," John Douillard's LifeSpa, September 24, 2016, accessed March 08, 2019, *https://lifespa.com/5-things-never-knew-gluten-but-should/*.

44. William Davis, Wheat Belly Slim Guide: The Fast and Easy Reference for Living and Succeeding on the Wheat Belly Lifestyle (Emmaus, PA: Rodale, 2017), 4.

45. Davis, *Wheat Belly*, 70.

46. John Douillard, "Do Low-Gluten Diets Increase Type 2 Diabetes Risk?" John Douillard's LifeSpa, May 31, 2017, accessed March 08, 2019, *https://lifespa.com/do-low-gluten-diets-increase-type-2-diabetes-risk/*.

47. Yoko Watanabe et al., "Skipping Breakfast Is Correlated with Obesity," *Journal of Rural Medicine* 9, no. 2 (June 17, 2014): 51–58, doi:10.2185/ jrm.2887.

48. Sid Kirchheimer, "Breakfast Reduces Diabetes, Heart Disease," WebMD, March 06, 2003, accessed March 08, 2019, *https://www.webmd.com/diabetes/news/20030306/ breakfast-reduces-diabetes-heart-disease#1*.

49. Greger and Stone, *How Not to Die,* 157.

50. Diana Kelly, "21 Ways to Lose a Pound a Week," *The Complete Guide to Diets That Work* (New York: Centennial Living Media, 2018), 20–23.

Chapter 8: Habit #2 Cleanse – Am I Toxic?

1. Lindsay Wilson, *Genetically-Modified Foods: Your Right to Know* (Lakewood, CO: Natural Grocers, 2013).

2. "Man: The Chemical Ape," *nursingschoolhub.com*, accessed January 11, 2019, *https://www.nursingschoolhub.com/chemical-ape/*.

3. Ibid.

4. David Schardt, "Kicking the Can: When Food Containers Become Part of Your Meal," *Nutrition Action Healthletter*, November 2017, 8–11.

5. David Schardt, "Safe at the Plate," *Nutrition Action*, December 2017, 3–6.

6. "Parasites – Toxoplasmosis (Toxoplasma Infection)," Centers for Disease Control and Prevention, October 02, 2018, accessed March 02, 2019, *https://www.cdc.gov/parasites/toxoplasmosis/gen_info/faqs.html*.

7. Joseph Hattersley, "How Chlorine Is Detrimental in Our Water," *Well Being Journal*, May/June 2006, 18–24.

8. Lindsay Wilson, Trust Us, It's Harmless: Could the Popular Herbicide Glyphosate Be Destroying Our Health? (Lakewood, CO: Natural Grocers, 2015).

9. Ibid.

10. Lynne McTaggart and Bryan Hubbard, "Cell Phone Radiation Could Explain Diplomats' Mysterious Illness," *What Doctors Don't Tell You: Helping You Make Better Health Choices*, January 15, 2019.

11. "The Problem with Parabens," What Doctors Don't Tell You: Helping You Make Better Health Choices, February 2019, 72–73.

12. Don Colbert, MD, Toxic Relief: Restore Health and Energy through Fasting and Detoxification (Lake Mary, FL: Siloam, 2012).

13. "Colon Cancer Facts," Colon Cancer Coalition, accessed March 02, 2019, *https://coloncancercoalition.org/get-educated/what-you-need-to-know/colon-cancer-facts/*.

14. Ibid.

15. Karol K. Truman, *Feelings Buried Alive Never Die* (Phoenix: Olympus Publishing Company, 2003), 238.

16. Anna Medaris Miller, "8 Myths about Constipation," *U.S. News & World Report*, April 05, 2015, accessed January 25, 2019, *https://health.usnews.com/health-news/health-wellness/articles/2015/04/08/8-myths-about-constipation*.

17. Diane Quagliani and Patricia Felt-Gunderson, "Closing America's Fiber Intake Gap," *American Journal of Lifestyle Medicine* 11, no. 1 (July 07, 2016): 80–85, doi:10.1177/1559827615588079.

18. Ibid.

19. Quagliani and Gunderson, "Closing America's Fiber Intake Gap."

20. Jess White, "Going with the Gut," *Psychology Today*, July/August 2016, 34–38.

21. Elizabeth Lipski, *Digestive Wellness* (New York: McGraw Hill, 2006), 34.

22. Ibid.

23. Hulda Regehr Clark, *The Cure for All Diseases* (Chula Vista, CA: New Century Press, 1995), 45.

24. Ibid.

25. Ibid.

26. Lyle J. Palmer et al., "Ascaris Lumbricoides Infection Is Associated with Increased Risk of Childhood Asthma and Atopy in Rural China," *American Journal of Respiratory and Critical Care Medicine* 165, no. 11 (January 15, 2002): 1489–1493, accessed January 25, 2019, doi:10.1164/rccm.2107020.

27. Anthony William, Medical Medium Liver Rescue: Answers to Eczema, Psoriasis, Diabetes, Strep, Acne, Gout, Bloating, Gallstones, Adrenal Stress, Fatigue, Fatty Liver, Weight Issues, SIBO, and Autoimmune Disease (Carlsbad, CA: Hay House, 2018), 47.

28. Ibid.

29. Kelsey Casselbury, "The Average Fat Intake in SAD," SF Gate, November 19, 2018, accessed March 04, 2019, *https://healthyeating.sfgate.com/average-fat-intake-sad-11370.html*.

30. VegSource, "What the Dairy Industry Doesn't Want You to Know – Neal Barnard, MD," YouTube, January 28, 2017, accessed March 02, 2019, *https://www.youtube.com/watch?v=h3c_D0s391Q*.

31. Mayo Clinic, "Nearly 7 in 10 Americans Are on Prescription Drugs," *Science Daily*, June 19, 2013, accessed February 19, 2019, *http://www.sciencedaily.com/releases/2013/06/130619132352.htm*.

32. William, *Liver Flush*, 82.

33. Clark, The Cure for All Diseases, 553

34. Truman, Feelings Buried Alive Never Die, 256.

35. Hulda Clark, "Cleanse Flowchart" digital image, Self Health Resource Center, accessed January 15, 2019, *https://drclarkstore.com/dr-hulda-clark-kidney-cleanse-vegetarian/*.

36. Ibid.

37. Clark, The Cure for All Diseases, 416.

38. Ibid, 417.

Chapter 9: Habit #3 Hydrate – Am I Thirsty?

1. F. Batmanghelidj, Your Body's Many Cries for Water: You're Not Sick; You're Thirsty: Don't Treat Thirst with Medications, Global Health Solutions, 2008, 6.

2. Ibid, 71.

3. Batmanghelidj, Obesity, Cancer, Depression: Their Common Cause & Natural Cure (Falls Church, VA: Global Health Solutions, 2005), 117.

4. Jessica Cerretani, "Water & Health," Whole Living: Body Soul, July/August 2008, 94–99.

5. Jayne Leonard, "How Often Should You Pee? What's Normal and What's Perfect?" Medical News Today, April 11, 2018, accessed March 04, 2019, https://www.medicalnewstoday.com/articles/321461.php.

6. "5 Steps to Fewer Kidney Stones," Nutrition Action, October 2017, 7.

7. Ibid.

8. Ibid.

9. Caitlin Dow, "Low-Cal Sweeteners," Nutrition Action, September 2017, 7–9.

10. Ibid.

11. Ibid, 32.

12. University Saarland. "Blood is thicker than water – and blood plasma is, too," Science Daily, accessed March 13, 2019, www.sciencedaily.com/releases/2013/02/130218092505.htm.

13. Batmanghelidj, Obesity, Cancer, Depression: Their Common Cause & Natural Cure, 36.

14. Kerry Brandis, "Fluid Physiology," Fluid Physiology: 2.1 Fluid Compartments, accessed March 04, 2019, https://www.anaesthesiamcq.com/FluidBook/fl2_1.php.

15. Mary C. White et al., "Age and Cancer Risk," American Journal of Preventive Medicine 46, no. 3 (March 2014): S7–S15, accessed March 13, 2019, doi:10.1016/j.amepre.2013.10.029.

16. Batmanghelidj, Your Body's Many Cries for Water, 75.

17. Ibid.

18. Kristen Dold, "Healthy-Up Your Blood Pressure," Dr. Oz: The Good Life, 2017, 16–17.

19. Batmanghelidj, Obesity, Cancer, Depression: Their Common Cause & Natural Cure, 171–175.

20. Russell Mariani, "Watercure for a Healthy Body," Well Being Journal, 2014, 22–24.

21. Ibid.

22. Nicholas Bakalar,"37.2 Trillion: Galaxies or Human Cells?" New York Times, June 19, 2015, accessed March 20, 2019, *https://www.nytimes.com/2015/06/23/science/37-2-trillion-galaxies-or-human-cells.html*

23. Mayo Clinic Staff, "Water: How Much Should You Drink Every Day?" Mayo Clinic, September 06, 2017, accessed January 27, 2019, *https://www.mayoclinic.org/healthy-lifestyle/nutrition-and-healthy-eating/in-depth/water/art-20044256.*

24. "Facts on Health Risks of Sugar Drinks," Center for Science in the Public Interest, January 17, 2017, accessed January 28, 2017, *cspinet.org/resource/facts-health-risks-sugar-drinks.*

25. Ibid.

26. Ibid.

27. Isabelle Z., "Pepsi Admits Its Soda Contains Cancer-Causing Ingredients," Natural News, September 15, 2016, accessed March 14, 2019, *https://www.naturalnews.com/055309_Pepsi_carcinogens_4-Mel.html.*

28. Diana Kelly, "21 Ways to Lose a Pound a Week," The Complete Guide to Diets That Work (New York: Centennial Living Media, LLC, 2018), 20–23.

29. Melonie Heron, "Deaths: Leading Causes for 2016," National Vital Statistics Reports, July 26, 2018, 1–77.

30. Batmanghelidj, Your Body's Many Cries for Water, 103–106.

31. Ibid.

32. Ibid.

33. Thomas Foechlich, "7 Drinks That May Affect Your Cancer Risk," UT Southwestern Medical Center, June 29, 2016, accessed March 13, 2019, *https://utswmed.org/medblog/energy-drink-alcohol-cancer/.*

34. Mayo Clinic Staff, "Water: How Much Should You Drink Every Day?" Mayo Clinic, Mayo Foundation for Medical Education and Research, September 06, 2017, accessed January 27, 2019, *www.mayoclinic.org/healthy-lifestyle/nutrition-and-healthy-eating/in-depth/water/art-20044256.*

35.   Batmanghelidj, Your Body's Many Cries for Water, 135.

36.   Ibid.

37.   Batmanghelidj, Your Body's Many Cries for Water, 157–159.

Chapter 10: Habit #4 Sleep – Am I Tired?

1.   Bonnie Liebman, "Short on Sleep," Nutrition Action Healthletter, June 2017, 8–9.

2.   Ibid.

3.   Shawn Stevenson, Sleep Smarter: 21 Essential Strategies to Sleep Your Way to a Better Body, Better Health, and Bigger Success (New York: Rodale Books, 2016), 51.

4.   Diana Kelly, "21 Ways to Lose a Pound a Week," The Complete Guide to Diets That Work (New York: Centennial Living Media, LLC, 2018) 20–23.

5.   Stevenson, Sleep Smarter, 51.

6.   Kelly, "21 Ways to Lose a Pound a Week."

7.   Alexandros N. Vgontzas et al., "Obesity and Self-Reported Short Sleep Duration: A Marker of Sleep Complaints and Chronic Psychosocial Stress," Sleep Medicine Clinics 4, no. 1 (2009): 65–75, accessed April 24, 2018, doi:10.1016/j.jsmc.2009.01.001.

8.   Ibid.

9.   Ibid.

10.   Sara Gottfried, The Hormone Cure: Reclaim Balance, Sleep, Sex Drive, and Vitality Naturally with the Gottfried Protocol (New York: Scribner, 2013) 101.

11.   Liebman, "Short on Sleep," Nutrition Action Healthletter, 8–9.

12.   Brian Tefft, "Asleep at the Wheel: The Prevalence of Drowsy Driving," November 2010, accessed March 4, 2019, *http://www.greylit.org/sites/default/files/collected_files/2012-12/2010DrowsyDrivingReport_1.pdf.*

13.   Shawn Stevenson, Sleep Smarter, 111.

14.   "Americans Are Getting More ZZZZs," Penn Medicine News, January 18, 2018, accessed March 04, 2019, *https://www.pennmedicine.org/news/news-releases/2018/january/americans-are-getting-more-zzzzs.*

15.   Vgontzas et al., "Obesity and Self-Reported Short Sleep Duration: A Marker of Sleep Complaints and Chronic Psychosocial Stress."

16. Liebman, "Short on Sleep," Nutrition Action Healthletter, 8–9.

17. M. Williamson and Anne-Marie Feyer, "Moderate Sleep Deprivation Produces Impairments in Cognitive and Motor Performance Equivalent to Legally Prescribed Levels of Alcohol Intoxication," Occupational and Environmental Medicine 57, no. 10 (2000): 649–655, accessed January 31, 2019, *oem.bmj.com/content/oemed/57/10/649.full.pdf.*

18. Stevenson, Sleep Smarter, 105.

19. Vgontzas et al., "Obesity and Self-Reported Short Sleep Duration: A Marker of Sleep Complaints and Chronic Psychosocial Stress."

20. Teresa Arora et al., "The Impact of Sleep Debt on Excess Adiposity and Insulin Sensitivity in Patients with Early Type 2 Diabetes Mellitus," Journal of Clinical Sleep Medicine 12, no. 05 (May 15, 2016): 673–680, accessed February 11, 2019, doi:10.5664/jcsm.5792.

21. Vgontzas et al., "Obesity and Self-Reported Short Sleep Duration: A Marker of Sleep Complaints and Chronic Psychosocial Stress."

22. Liebman, "Short on Sleep," Nutrition Action Healthletter, 8–9.

23. Shahrad Taheri et al., "Short Sleep Duration Is Associated with Reduced Leptin, Elevated Ghrelin, and Increased Body Mass Index," PLoS Medicine 1, no. 3 (December 07, 2004), accessed January 31, 2019, doi: 10.1371/journal.pmed.0010062.

24. Liebman, "Short on Sleep," Nutrition Action Healthletter, 8–9.

25. Celeste McGovern, "Smash Your Addictions," What Doctors Don't Tell You: Helping You Make Better Health Choices, May 2018, 28–37.

26. Ibid.

27. Proceedings of the European Society of Cardiology Congress, Munich, Germany, August 26, 2018, ed. "Sleep Sweet Spot Is Six to Eight Hours a Day," What Doctors Don't Tell You: Helping You Make Better Health Choices, January 2019, 12.

28. Hulda Regehr Clark, The Cure for All Diseases (Chula Vista, CA: New Century Press, 1995), 244.

29. Helen Messina, "Detoxifiers for High Ammonia Levels Due to Liver Diseases," Livestrong, accessed March 04, 2019, *https://www.livestrong.com/article/351568-detoxifiers-for-high-ammonia-levels-due-to-liver-diseases/.*

30. Clark, The Cure for All Diseases, 244.

31. Ann Miller-Cohen, "The Art of Cooking Green Gourmet Foods," Well Being Journal, May/June 2006, 14–18.

32. Fumito Naganuma et al., "Histamine N-methyltransferase Regulates Aggression and the Sleep-wake Cycle," Scientific Reports 7, no. 1 (November 21, 2017), doi:10.1038/s41598-017-16019-8.

33. Stephen Cherniske, Caffeine Blues: Wake up to the Hidden Dangers of Americas #1 Drug (New York: Warner, 1998), 98.

34. Ibid.

35. Pauline Harding, "Eat Your Way to Better Sleep," Well Being Journal, March/April 2008, 5–10.

36. Ibid.

37. "Curb Carbs at Dinner," Nutrition Action Healthletter, May 2017, 8.

38. Harding, "Eat Your Way to Better Sleep," 5–10.

39. Ibid.

40. Jason Fung, The Obesity Code: Unlocking the Secrets of Weight Loss (Vancouver: Greystone Books, 2016), 94.

41. Ibid.

42. Pauline Harding, "Eat Your Way to Better Sleep," 5–10.

43. Sara Gottfried, The Hormone Cure,134.

44. Abbasi et al., "The Effect of Magnesium Supplementation on Primary Insomnia in Elderly: A Double-blind Placebo-controlled Clinical Trial," Current Neurology and Neuroscience Reports, December 17, 2012, accessed March 06, 2019, *https://www.ncbi.nlm.nih.gov/pubmed/23853635.*

45. Michael J. Breus, "Magnesium – How It Affects Your Sleep," Psychology Today, May 2, 2018, accessed March 06, 2019, *https://www.psychologytoday.com/us/blog/sleep-newzzz/201805/magnesium-how-it-affects-your-sleep.*

46. Chris Gilbert, "Repressed Emotions and Physical Illness," Well Being Journal, April/May 2018, 20–23.

47. Liebman, "Short on Sleep," Nutrition Action Healthletter, 8–9.

48. Sara Gottfried, The Hormone Cure, 101.

49. Vyga Kaufmann, TEDx Talks, YouTube, October 22, 2015, accessed January 05, 2019, *https://www.youtube.com/watch?v=WNj1Y11t_x8.*

50. Ibid.

51. Dave Asprey, "Bulletproof Your Sleep with vitamin D | When to Take vitamin D," Bulletproof, June 04, 2018, accessed January 27, 2019, *https://blog.bulletproof.com/bulletproof-your-sleep-with-vitamin-d/#ref-5.*

52. Michael Breus, "The Latest on Blue Light and Sleep," The Sleep Doctor: Your Guide to Better Sleep, November 06, 2017, accessed March 06, 2019, *https://thesleepdoctor.com/2017/11/06/latest-blue-light-sleep/.*

53. Borge Sivertsen et al., "Use of Sleep Medications and Mortality: The Hordaland Health Study," Drugs – Real World Outcomes 2, no. 2 (May 05, 2015): 123–128, doi:10.1007/s40801-015-0023-8.

54. Ibid.

Chapter 11: Habit #4 Exercise – Am I Inactive?

1.   Steven C. Moore et al., "Association of Leisure-Time Physical Activity with Risk of 26 Types of Cancer in 1.44 Million Adults," *JAMA Internal Medicine* 176, no. 6 (June 01, 2016): 816–25, doi:10.1001/jamainternmed.2016.1548.

2.   Alexandra Sifferlin, "The Truth about Running," *The Science of Exercise, Special ed.* (New York: Time Books, Inc., 2017), 68–69.

3.   Dr. Mercola, "The Right Dose of Exercise for a Longer Life," mercola.com, accessed January 02, 2019, *https://fitness.mercola.com/sites/fitness/archive/2015/05/01/right-dose-exercise-for-long-life.aspx.*

4.   Dr. Mercola, "How Short Bursts of Exercise Help Decrease Disease and Risk of Death," mercola.com, April 6, 2018, accessed March 06, 2019, *https://fitness.mercola.com/sites/fitness/archive/2018/04/06/short-bursts-exercise-may-prevent-death.aspx.*

5.   Sifferlin, "The Truth about Running," 68–69.

6.   Many Oaklander, "The Power of Strength Training," *The Science of Exercise, Special ed.* (New York: Time Books, Inc., 2017), 40–45.

7.   Oaklander, "The Power of Strength Training," 40–45.

8.   Alyssa Shaffer, "The Truth about Weight Loss," *The Science of Exercise* Special ed. (New York: Time Books, Inc., 2017), 36–37.

9.   Markham Heid, "The Truth about Walking," *The Science of Exercise* Special ed. (New York: Time Books, Inc., 2017), 92–93.

10. Heid, "The Truth about Walking," 92–93.

11. Alexandra Sifferlin, "How to Exercise When You Have No Time," *The Science of Exercise* Special ed. (New York: Time Books, Inc., 2017), 82–85.

12. Ibid.

13. Ibid.

14. Ibid.

15. Caitlin Dow, "Exercise: Can You Trust the Latest Buzz?" *Nutrition Action Healthletter*, April 2017, 9–11.

16. Alice Park, "How Exercise Keeps You Young," *The Science of Exercise, Special ed.* (New York: Time Books, Inc., 2017), 24–27.

17. D. Reimers et al. "Does Physical Activity Increase Life Expectancy? A Review of the Literature," *Journal of Aging Research* 2012, July 1, 2012, 1–9, doi:10.1155/2012/243958.

18. Kristen Dold, "Healthy-Up Your Blood Pressure," *Dr. Oz: The Good Life*, 2017, 16–17.

19. Caitlin Dow, "Exercise: Can You Trust the Latest Buzz?" *Nutrition Action Newsletter*, April 2017, 9–11.

20. Camille Noe Pagan, "The Fitness Rx," *The Science of Exercise* Special ed. (New York: Time Books, Inc., 2017), 18–21.

21. Ibid.

22. Mandy Oaklander, "The Power of Strength Training," *The Science of Exercise* Special ed. (New York: Time Books, Inc., 2017), 40–45.

23. Mandy Oaklander, "The New Science of Exercise," *The Science of Exercise* Special ed. (New York: Time Books, Inc., 2017), 10–17.

24. Jacques Steinberg, "Anyone Can Be an Ironman," *The Science of Exercise* Special ed. (New York: Time Books, Inc., 2017), 86–91.

25. "Physical Activity and Adults," World Health Organization, June 19, 2015, accessed March 05, 2019, *https://www.who.int/dietphysicalactivity/factsheet_adults/en/*.

26. "Reality Bites," *The Complete Guide to Diets That Work* (New York: Centennial Living Media, 2018), 96.

27. Ellie Zolfagharifard, "You Should Be Working Out for More than an Hour a Day, Claim Scientists," Daily Mail Online, April 15, 2015, accessed January 02, 2019, *https://www.dailymail.co.uk/sciencetech/article-3040911/Forget-doing-150-minutes-exercise-week-working-HOUR-day-claim-scientists.html*.

28. Caitlin Dow, "Exercise: Can You Trust the Latest Buzz?" *Nutrition Action Healthletter*, April 2017, 9–11.

29. Diana Kelly, "21 Ways to Lose a Pound a Week," *The Complete Guide to Diets That Work* (New York: Centennial Living Media, 2018), 20–23.

30. Dow, "Exercise: Can You Trust the Latest Buzz?" 9–11.

31. Ibid.

32. Heid, "The Truth about Walking," 92–93.

33. Camille Noe Pagan, "The Fitness Rx," *The Science of Exercise* Special ed. (New York: Time Books, Inc., 2017), 18–21.

34. Park, "How Exercise Keeps You Young," 24–27.

35. Ibid.

36. Oaklander, "The New Science of Exercise," 15.

37. Dow, "Exercise: Can You Trust the Latest Buzz?" 9–11.

38. Oaklander, "The New Science of Exercise," 15.

39. Dow, "Exercise: Can You Trust the Latest Buzz?" 9–11.

40. Kristin J. Homan et al., "Appearance-based Exercise Motivation Moderates the Relationship between Exercise Frequency and Positive Body Image," *Body Image* 11, no. 2 (March 2014): 101–108, doi:10.1016/j.bodyim.2014.01.003.

41. Mandy Oaklander, "7 Ways to Motivate Yourself to Exercise," *The Science of Exercise* Special ed. (New York: Time Books, Inc., 2017), 72–77.

42. James Clear, "How the 'Seinfeld Strategy' Can Help You Stop Procrastinating," Entrepreneur, January 27, 2014, accessed March 05, 2019, *https://www.entrepreneur.com/article/231023*.

43. "Camino De Santiago," Wikipedia, February 25, 2019, accessed March 14, 2019, *https://en.wikipedia.org/wiki/Camino_de_Santiago*.

44. Ibid.

45. Oaklander, "7 Ways to Motivate Yourself to Exercise."

Chapter 12: Habit #6 Balance – Am I Hormonal?

1. Sara Gottfried, The Hormone Cure: Reclaim Balance, Sleep, Sex Drive, and Vitality Naturally with the Gottfried Protocol (New York: Scribner, 2013), 101.

2. Ibid.

3.   Gary Donovitz, Age Healthier, Live Happier: Avoiding Over-Medication through Natural Hormone Balance (Orlando: Celebrity Press, 2015), 87.

4.   Ibid, 57.

5.   Gottfried, *The Hormone Cure*, 46.

6.   Gary Taubes, *Why We Get Fat: And What to Do about It* (New York: Anchor Books, 2011), 134.

7.   Carina Wolff, "Does Exercising Affect Your Homones? You Might Feel These 8 Changes," Bustle, August 16, 2018, accessed February 19, 2019, *https://www.bustle.com/p/does-exercising-affect-your-hormones-you-might-feel-these-8-changes-10127007.*

8.   Gottfried, *The Hormone Cure*, 135.

9.   "Sperm Counts on the Decline," *Nutrition Action Healthletter*, November 2017, 3.

10.   Mary Shomon, "Why Is Cortisol So Controversial for Weight Loss?" Verywell Health, October 8, 2018, accessed February 11, 2019, *https://www.verywellhealth.com/the-cortisol-weight-loss-controversy-3233036.*

11.   Leonardo Trasande, Sicker, Fatter, Poorer: The Urgent Threat of Hormone-Disrupting Chemicals on Our Health and Future . . . and What We Can Do about It (Boston: Houghton Mifflin Harcourt, 2019), 139.

12.   Juliet Wilkinson, "Are Hormones in Meat Affecting Humans?" Livestrong, accessed March 09, 2019, *https://www.livestrong.com/article/464430-are-hormones-in-meat-affecting-humans/.*

13.   Nick Garcia, "4 Hormone Imbalances Preventing You from Losing Weight," Upgraded Health, January 14, 2019, accessed March 06, 2019, *https://upgradedhealth.net/4-hormone-imbalances-preventing-you-from-losing-weight/.*

14.   Gottfried, *The Hormone Cure,* 163.

15.   Garcia, "4 Hormone Imbalances Preventing You from Losing Weight."

16.   Center for Veterinary Medicine, "Product Safety Information – Steroid Hormone Implants Used for Growth in Food-Producing Animals," US Food and Drug Administration Home Page, accessed March 10, 2019, *https://www.fda.gov/animalveterinary/safetyhealth/productsafetyinformation/ucm055436.htm.*

17. Juliet Wilkinson, "Are Hormones in Meat Affecting Humans?" Livestrong, accessed March 09, 2019, *https://www.livestrong.com/article/464430-are-hormones-in-meat-affecting-humans/*.

18. "Recombinant Bovine Growth Hormone," American Cancer Society, September 10, 2014, accessed March 10, 2019, *https://www.cancer.org/cancer/cancer-causes/recombinant-bovine-growth-hormone.html*.

19. Interview with Vegan Outreach, August 18, 2018, accessed August 18, 2018, *https://www.facebook.com/jendayi.harris/videos/2225625044133579/*.

20. Carina Storrs, "Hormones in Food: Should You Worry?" Health, October 22, 2011, accessed March 10, 2019, *https://www.health.com/health/article/0,,20458816,00.html*.

21. "Recombinant Bovine Growth Hormone."

22. "Sperm Counts on the Decline."

23. Juliet Wilkinson, "Are Hormones in Meat Affecting Humans?" Livestrong.com, accessed March 09, 2019, *https://www.livestrong.com/article/464430-are-hormones-in-meat-affecting-humans/*.

24. Josh Axe, "High-Estrogen Foods to Avoid (Some Mess with Breast Cancer Treatment!)," Dr. Axe, October 15, 2018, accessed February 12, 2019, *https://draxe.com/5-high-estrogen-foods-avoid/*.

25. "The FoodPrint of Beef," FoodPrint, accessed March 10, 2019, *https://foodprint.org/reports/the-foodprint-of-beef/?cid=258*.

26. Jason Fung, *The Obesity Code: Unlocking the Secrets of Weight Loss* (Vancouver: Greystone Books, 2016), 87.

27. Dr. Jason Fung, "Insulin and Weight Gain – Hormonal Obesity," Intensive Dietary Management (IDM), May 26, 2018, accessed March 09, 2019, *https://idmprogram.com/insulin-causes-weight-gain-hormonal-obesity-iv/*.

28. Laura Dolson, "Insulin Resistance Symptoms, Causes, and Treatment," Very Well Health, January 03, 2019, accessed February 7, 2019, *https://www.verywellhealth.com/what-is-insulin-resistance-2242260*.

29. Integrated Diabetes Services, Gary Scheiner, "Insulin & Weight Gain: Does Tighter Control Make You Loosen Your Belt?" Diabetes Strong, January 20, 2018, accessed February 10, 2019, *https://diabetesstrong.com/insulin-weight-gain-does-tighter-control-make-you-loosen-your-belt/*.

30. Fung, "Insulin and Weight Gain – Hormonal Obesity."

31. Fung, *The Obesity Code*, 175.

32. Franziska Spritzler, "12 Natural Ways to Balance Your Hormones." Healthline, May 15, 2017, accessed February 12, 2019, *https://www.healthline.com/nutrition/balance-hormones#section12*.

33. Taubes, *Why We Get Fat*, 90–95,105.

34. Ibid, 136–139.

35. D. Anton et al., "Flipping the Metabolic Switch: Understanding and Applying the Health Benefits of Fasting," *Obesity* 26, no. 2 (October 31, 2017): 254–268, doi:10.1002/oby.22065.

36. Hiliary Parker, "A Sweet Problem: Princeton Researchers Find That High-fructose Corn Syrup Prompts Considerably More Weight Gain," Princeton University, March 22, 2010, accessed March 09, 2019, *https://www.princeton.edu/news/2010/03/22/sweet-problem-princeton-researchers-find-high-fructose-corn-syrup-prompts*.

37. Fung, *The Obesity Code*, 164.

38. Ibid.

39. Parker, "A Sweet Problem: Princeton Researchers Find That High-Fructose Corn Syrup Prompts Considerably More Weight Gain," 1.

40. Fung, *The Obesity Code*, 246–247.

41. Ibid, 120.

42. D. Anton et al., "Flipping the Metabolic Switch: Understanding and Applying the Health Benefits of Fasting."

43. Fung, The Obesity Code, 92–94.

44. Gottfried, *The Hormone Cure*, 331.

45. Ibid, 24–25.

46. Ibid, 86.

47. Fung, The Obesity Code, 92.

48. Ibid, 94.

49. Taubes, *Why We Get Fat*, 124.

50. Dr. Len Lopez, "Stress and Hormone Imbalances," The Christian Post, accessed March 09, 2019, *https://www.christianpost.com/news/stress-and-hormone-imbalances.html*.

51. Josh Axe, "Adrenal Fatigue Symptoms, Diet & Remedies," Dr. Axe, November 01, 2018, accessed March 08, 2019, *https://draxe.com/3-steps-to-heal-adrenal-fatigue/*.

52. Dave Korsunsky, "Basal Body Temperature Tracking – Part One – Thyroid," Heads Up Health, September 17, 2017, accessed March 10, 2019, *https://www.headsuphealth.com/blog/self-tracking/basal-body-temperature-tracking-part-one-thyroid/*.

53. Gottfried, *The Hormone Cure*, 333.

54. Broda Otto Barnes and Lawrence Galton, *Hypothyroidism: The Unsuspected Illness* (New York: Harper & Row, 1976), 23–24.

55. Ibid.

56. Dave Korsunsky, "Basal Body Temperature Tracking – Part One – Thyroid."

57. Ibid.

58. N. Walter et al., "Elevated Thyroid Stimulating Hormone Is Associated with Elevated Cortisol in Healthy Young Men and Women," *Thyroid Research* 5, no. 1 (October 30, 2012): 13, doi:10.1186/1756-6614-5-13.

59. Gottfried, *The Hormone Cure*, 242.

60. Walter, "Elevated Thyroid Stimulating Hormone Is Associated with Elevated Cortisol in Healthy Young Men and Women."

61. Jacqueline Jacques, "The Role of Your Thyroid in Metabolism and Weight Control," Obesity Action Coalition, accessed March 09, 2019, *https://www.obesityaction.org/community/article-library/the-role-of-your-thyroid-in-metabolism-and-weight-control/*.

62. American Thyroid Association, "Thyroid and Weight," American Thyroid Association, accessed March 09, 2019, *https://www.thyroid.org/thyroid-and-weight/*.

63. Ibid.

64. Anthony William, Medical Medium Thyroid Healing: The Truth behind Hashimotos, Graves, Insomnia, Hypothyroidism, Thyroid Nodules & Epstein-Barr (Carlsbad, CA: Hay House, 2017), 29.

65. Anthony William, "Epstein Barr Virus Revealed," Medical Medium, accessed March 9, 2019, *http://www.medicalmedium.com/blog/epstein-barr-virus-revealed*.

66. William, *Thyroid Healing*, 99.

67. Dana Trentini, "Hypothyroidism Symptoms," Hypothyroid Mom, accessed February 12, 2019, *https://hypothyroidmom.com/category/hypothyroidism-symptoms/*.

68. Ibid.

69. Ibid.

70. Izabela Wentz, "Fluoride and Your Thyroid," Thyroid Pharmacist, March 15, 2018, accessed March 10, 2019, *https://thyroidpharmacist. com/articles/fluoride-and-your-thyroid/*.

71. Anna Cabeca, "What Men Need to Know about Healthy Testosterone Levels," Dr. Anna Cabeca, date written, accessed February 12, 2019, *https://drannacabeca.com/blogs/mens-health/ what-men-need-to-know-about-healthy-testosterone-levels*.

72. Ibid.

73. Mary Elizabeth Dallas, "The Link Between Low Testosterone and Diabetes," Stroke Center – Everyday Health, January 16, 2014, accessed February 12, 2019, *https://www.everydayhealth.com/hs/ low-testosterone-guide/low-testosterone-diabetes/*.

74. Ibid.

75. Gottfried, *The Hormone Cure*, 345.

76. Anna Cabeca, "What Men Need to Know about Healthy Testosterone Levels."

77. Donovitz, Age Healthier Live Happier, 87.

78. Gottfried, *The Hormone Cure*, 182.

79. Andre Harris, TEDx Talks, YouTube, December 05, 2018, accessed January 2, 2019. *https://www.youtube.com/ watch?time_continue=1&v=ZiDfZLJZTGU*.

80. Jade Teta, "Female Hormones: Estrogen (Oestrogen) & Weight Loss," Metabolic Effect, June 10, 2013, accessed February 11, 2019, *https:// www.metaboliceffect.com/female-hormones-estrogen/*.

81. Axe, "High-Estrogen Foods to Avoid."

82. Taubes, *Why We Get Fat*, 90.

83. Laura Paris and Anita Sadaty. "4 Causes of Hormone Imbalance and 5 Ways to Fix It," My Hormone Answers, January 18, 2019, accessed March 11, 2019, *https://myhormoneanswers. com/4-causes-of-hormone-imbalance-and-5-ways-to-fix-it/*.

84. Debra Rose Wilson, "Signs and Symptoms of High Estrogen," Healthline, February 20, 2018, accessed February 7, 2019, *https://www. healthline.com/health/high-estrogen#outlook*.

85. Gottfried, *The Hormone Cure*, 163.

86. Cabeca, "What Men Need to Know about Healthy Testosterone Levels."

87. Gottfried, *The Hormone Cure*, 27.

88. Wilson, "Signs and Symptoms of High Estrogen."

89. Marion Gluck, "Estrogen Dominance and Hypothyroidism," Marion Gluck Clinic, April 23, 2018, accessed February 12, 2019, *https://www.mariongluckclinic.com/blog/estrogen-dominance-hypothyroidism.html*.

90. Carrie Drzyzga, "Signs of Estrogen Deficiency," The Functional Medicine Radio Show with Dr. Carrie, February 24, 2016, accessed March 11, 2019, *https://www.drcarri.com/signs-of-estrogen-deficiency/*.

91. James, "High Estrogen vs. Low Estrogen Symptoms (For Men)," Dosage May Vary, August 23, 2017, accessed February 11, 2019, *https://dosagemayvary.com/high-estrogen-vs-low-estrogen-symptoms-for-men/*.

92. Drzyzga, "Signs of Estrogen Deficiency."

93. Gottfried, *The Hormone Cure*, 179.

94. Ibid.

95. Taubes, *Why We Get Fat*, 90.

96. Ibid.

97. Wilson, "Signs and Symptoms of High Estrogen."

98. Gottfried, *The Hormone Cure*, 345.

99. Taubes, *Why We Get Fat*, 90.

100. Lindsay Wilson. *Genetically-Modified Foods: Your Right to Know* (Lakewood, CO: Natural Grocers, 2013).

101. Natural News. "'Most Thorough Research' to Date Links GMO Corn to Tumors, Organ Damage, and Premature Death in Rats," Food Matters®, July 12, 2018, accessed March 10, 2019, *https://www.foodmatters.com/article/gm-corn-linked-to-cancer-tumors*.

102. Axe, "High-Estrogen Foods to Avoid."

103. Ibid.

104. Josh Axe, "How to Balance Hormones Naturally," Dr. Axe, February 04, 2019, accessed March 07, 2019, *https://draxe.com/10-ways-balance-hormones-naturally/)*.

105. Donovitz, Age Healthier Live Happier, 132–133.

106. Aaron Kandola, "10 Health Benefits of Maca Root," Medical News Today, July 18, 2018, accessed February 11, 2019, *https://www.medicalnewstoday.com/articles/322511.php*.

107. The Maca Team, "What Is Maca," The Maca Team, LLC, accessed March 10, 2019, *https://www.themacateam.com/what-is-maca.*

108. Axe, "How to Balance Hormones Naturally."

109. Carina Wolff, "Does Exercising Affect Your Hormones? You Might Feel These 8 Changes," Bustle, August 16, 2018, accessed February 18, 2019, *https://www.bustle.com/p/does-exercising-affect-your-hormones-you-might-feel-these-8-changes-10127007.*

110. Ibid.

111. Women's Health, "PMS," Women's Health, March 16, 2018, accessed March 10, 2019, *https://www.womenshealth.gov/menstrual-cycle/premenstrual-syndrome.*

Chapter 13: Prioritize Body Stewardship

1. Nadine Roberts Cornish, *Tears in My Gumbo*, Book 1 (Denver: Caregivers Guardian Publishing House, 2017), 6.

2. Dwayne Johnson, "Dwayne Johnson's Insane Diet and Workouts That Make Him Ripped," YouTube, October 30, 2018, accessed March 09, 2019, *https://www.youtube.com/watch?v=xkY45e5k9sw.*

Chapter 14: Grubbology – Say Hello to Your Inner Glutton

1. Chris Isidore and Tami Luhby, "Turns out Americans Work Really Hard ... but Some Want to Work Harder," CNNMoney, Cable News Network, July 9, 2015, *http://money.cnn.com/2015/07/09/news/economy/americans-work-bush/index.html.*

2. John Bradshaw, *Healing the Shame That Binds You* (Deerfield Beach, FL: Health Communications, Inc., 2005).

3. Mark E. Koltko-Rivera, "Rediscovering the Later Version of Maslows Hierarchy of Needs: Self-Transcendence and Opportunities for Theory, Research, and Unification," *Review of General Psychology* 10 (4) (2006): 302–317, https://doi.org/10.1037/1089-2680.10.4.302.

4. Ibid.

Chapter 15: The Fear of the Whole Self

1. "Torment," Merriam-Webster, *www.merriam-webster.com/dictionary/torment, accessed March 19, 2019.*

2. Marianne Williamson, A Return to Love: Reflections on the Principles of a Course in Miracles (New York: HarperOne, 2012).

3. Pastor Chad Dedmon, BridgeWay Church Denver, YouTube, January 21, 2018, *https://www.youtube.com/watch?v=kHWeCLPhLuA&t=3s.*

4. John Bradshaw, *Healing the Shame That Binds You* (Deerfield Beach, FL: Health Communications, Inc., 2005).

5. Cancer Treatment Centers of America, "More New Cancer Cases Linked to Obesity," Cancers Treatment Center of America, accessed July 1, 2018, *https://www.cancercenter.com/.*

Chapter 16: Chubbology – Why We're Super Scared to Drop the Weight

1. Child Sexual Abuse Statistics, National Center for Victims of Crime, accessed March 21, 2019, *http://victimsofcrime.org/media/reporting-on-child-sexual-abuse/child-sexual-abuse-statistics.*

2. Olga Khazan, "Abused as Children, Obese as Adults," *The Atlantic,* Atlantic Media Company, December 15, 2015, *https://www.theatlantic.com/health/archive/2015/12/sexual-abuse-victims-obesity/420186/.*

3. Amber Smith, "Experts See Strong Link between Sexual Abuse and Obesity," syracuse.com, July 25, 2010, *https://www.syracuse.com/news/2010/07/linking_sexual_abuse_to_obesit.html.*

4. Ibid.

5. Kanaklakshmi Masodkar, Justine Johnson, and Michael J. Peterson, "A Review of Posttraumatic Stress Disorder and Obesity," *The Primary Care Companion for CNS Disorders*, January 2016, *https://doi.org/10.4088/pcc.15r01848.*

6. Jendayi Harris, "Whole and Free Health Course Survey," The Potter's House Church Denver, June 15, 2018.

7. "Vulnerable," Merriam-Webster, accessed March 21, 2019, *https://www.merriam-webster.com/dictionary/vulnerable.*

8. Saul McLeod, "Saul McLeod," Simply Psychology, January 1, 1970. *https://www.simplypsychology.org/self-concept.html.*

9. Barbra E. Russell, *Yes! I Said No!* (Aurora, CO: Noble House Press, 2017), 23.

Chapter 17: Adopt the Freedom Mindset – Mental Freedom

1. "U.S. Weight Loss Market Worth $60.9 Billion," PRWeb, May 9, 2011, *http://www.prweb.com/releases/2011/5/prweb8393658.htm.*

2. Katherine Schreiber and Diana Kelly, "Don't Fall for It Dietary Fads over the Decades," essay in *The Complete Guide to Diets That Work* (New York: Centennial Living Media, 2018), 20–23.

3. Ibid, "U.S. Weight Loss Market Worth $60.9 Billion."

4. Caroline Leaf, Who Switched off My Brain?: Controlling Toxic Thoughts and Emotions (Southlake, TX: Inprov, Ltd., 2009).

5. Albert Einstein, "Albert Einstein Quotes," BrainyQuote, Xplore, accessed March 19, 2019, *https://www.brainyquote.com/quotes/albert_einstein_121993.*

6. "How Many Thoughts Do We Have Per Minute?" IAC Publishing, accessed March 25, 2019, *https://www.reference.com/world-view/many-thoughts-per-minute-cb7fcf22ebbf8466.*

7. Brian Wansink, "Why Dieters Are Doomed on Tuesdays," NBCNews.com, NBCUniversal News Group, May 14, 2007, *http://www.nbcnews.com/id/16472344/ns/health-diet_and_nutrition/t/why-dieters-are-doomed-tuesdays/#.XJi45rhMGUk.*

8. Sharon Fruh et al., "Meal-Planning Practices with Individuals in Health Disparity Zip Codes." *The Journal for Nurse Practitioners* 9 (6) (2013): 344–349, *https://doi.org/10.1016/j.nurpra.2013.03.016.*

9. Laura Pratt and Debra Brody, "National Center for Health Statistics," Centers for Disease Control and Prevention, October 16, 2014, *https://www.cdc.gov/nchs/products/databriefs/db167.htm.*

10. David Engstrom, "Obesity and Depression," Obesity Action Coalition, accessed March 19, 2019, *https://www.obesityaction.org/community/article-library/obesity-and-depression/.*

11. Marci Shimoff and Carol Kline, *Happy for No Reason: 7 Steps to Being Happy from the Inside Out* (New York: Atria Paperback, 2013), 36.

Chapter 18: Enact an Emotional Strength Training Plan – Emotional Freedom

1. "Emotions," Merriam-Webster, accessed March 22, 2019, *https://www.merriamwebster.com/dictionary/emotions.*

2. Peter Scazzero, Emotionally Healthy Spirituality: It's Impossible to be Spiritually Mature while Remaining Emotionally Immature. (Nashville: Thomas Nelson, 2014), 1.

3. Robert Plutchik, "Emotion Wheel," ToolsHero, July 18, 2018, *https://www.toolshero.com/psychology/personal-happiness/emotion-wheel-robert-plutchik/*.

4. Otto Kroeger and Janet M. Thuesen, Type Talk: The 16 Personality Types That Determine How We Live, Love, and Work (New York: Dell Trade Paperbacks, 1998), 70.

5. Wendy Backlund, *Victorious Emotions* (Redding, CA: Igniting Hope Ministries, 2017), 67.

6. Scazzero, Emotionally Healthy Spirituality, 24.

7. Ibid, 25.

8. "Release," Merriam-Webster, accessed March 22, 2019, *https://www.merriam-webster.com/dictionary/release*.

9. Peggy A. Hannon et al., "The Soothing Effects of Forgiveness on Victims and Perpetrators Blood Pressure," Personal Relationships 19 (2) (2011): 279–28, https://doi.org/10.1111/j.1475-6811.2011.01356.x.

10. Mayo Clinic Staff, "Why Is It So Easy to Hold a Grudge?" Mayo Clinic, Mayo Foundation for Medical Education and Research, November 4, 2017, *https://www.mayoclinic.org/healthy-lifestyle/adult-health/in-depth/forgiveness/art-20047692*.

11. Susan McQuillan, "A New Approach to Weight Loss," *Psychology Today*, Sussex Publishers, October 3, 2016, *https://www.psychologytoday.com/us/blog/cravings/201610/new-approach-weight-loss*.

12. Lucene Wisniewski and Denise D. Ben-Porath, "Dialectical Behavior Therapy and Eating Disorders: The Use of Contingency Management Procedures to Manage Dialectical Dilemmas," American Journal of Psychotherapy 69 (2) (2015): 129–140, *https://doi.org/10.1176/appi.psychotherapy.2015.69.2.129*.

13. Carlos M. Grilo et al., "Cognitive-behavioral therapy, behavioral weight loss, and sequential treatment for obese patients with binge-eating disorder: a randomized controlled trial," Journal of Consulting and Clinical Psychology 79 (5) (2011): 675–685, accessed November 18, 2018, *http://commonweb.unifr.ch/artsdean/pub/gestens/f/as/files/4660/33127_093048.pdf*.

14. Sue Popkess-Vawter, "Holistic Self-Care Model for Permanent Weight Control," *Journal of Holistic Nursing* 11 (4) (1993): 341–355, *https://doi.org/10.1177/089801019301100404.*

Chapter 19: Supersize Your Power Source – Spiritual Freedom

1. "Intention," Merriam-Webster, accessed March 20, 2019, *https://www.merriam-webster.com/dictionary/intention.*

2. Chris Tracy, Chris Tracy – Wm. Paul Young, Facebook, May 7, 2018, *https://www.facebook.com/christine.tracy.357/videos/10214366273623346/UzpfSTE2MTI3NjQ0MDY6Vks6MTYyNzEzNTQzNzM5OTM3NQ/.*

3. Jendayi Harris, Jendayi Harris – Talking with Wm. Paul Young, Facebook, May 5, 2018, *https://www.facebook.com/jendayi.harris/videos/2068970349799050/UzpfSTEwMDAwMDU4MzE0NDQxODpWSzox ODEzMjg5NDk4NzI3Nzc3/?q=fb lives jendayi harris&epa=FILTERS&filters=eyJycF9hdXRob3JiOiJ7XCJuYW1lXCI6XCJhdXRob3Jfb WVclixcImFy Z3NcIjpcIlwifSIsInJwX2NyZWF0aW9uX3RpcWUiOiJ7XCJuYW1lXCI6 XCJjcmVhdGlvbl90aW1lXCIsXCJhcmdzXCI6XCJ7XFxcInN0YXJ0X3llY XJcXFwiOlxcXCIyMDE4XFxcIixcXFwic3RhcnRfb W9udGhcXFwiOlxcXC IyMDE4LTFcXFwiLFxcXCJlbmRfeWVhclxcXCI6XFxcIjIwMThcXFwiLF xcXCJlbmRfbW9udGhcXFwiOlxcXCIyMDE4LTEyXFxcIixcXFwic3RhcnR fZGF5XFxcIjpcFwiMjAxOC0xLTFcXFwiLFxcXCJlbmRfZGF5XFxcIjpc XFwiMjAxOC0xMi0zMVxcXCJ9XCJ9In0=.*

4. Jendayi Harris, "Interview with Dr. Timothy Johns" (Denver: BridgeWay Church, 2019).

5. Matthew Kelly, *The Seven Levels of Intimacy: The Art of Loving and the Joy of Being Loved* Fireside ed. (New York: Beacon Publishing, 2007), 39.

6. Jack O. Balswick and Judith K Balswick, *The Family* Third ed. (Grand Rapids, MI: Baker Academic, 2007), 33.

7. Balswick and Balswick, *The Family* Third ed., 35.

8. Pastor Peter Young, BridgeWay Church Denver, YouTube, March 24, 2019, *https://www.youtube.com/watch?v=JCUCdYqpEMY.*

9. Myles Munroe, The Purpose and Power of the Holy Spirit: God's Government on Earth (New Kensington, PA: Whitaker House, 2007), 153.

10. Ibid, 230.

11. Karen McNeil, Are You Really Saved? – Common Christian Fables about Salvation, (Phoenix: Joshua Generation Press, 2016).

12. Laura Woodard, Letter to Jendayi Harris, "Re: Encouragement [Quote]," December 31, 2018.

13. Steve Wohlberg, End Times Health War: How to Outwit Deadly Diseases through Super Nutrition and Following God's Eight Laws of Health (Shippensburg, PA: Destiny Image Publishers, Inc., 2014), 19.

14. Michael Moss, *Salt, Sugar, Fat: How the Food Giants Hooked Us* (New York: Random House, 2013), xxvii.

15. Ibid.

16. Michael Moss, Salt, Sugar, Fat: How the Food Giants Hooked Us, 109.

17. Gene B. Moody, *Deliverance Manual* (Baton Rouge, LA: Deliverance Ministries, 1970), 5.

18. Ibid.

19. Ibid.

20. Moody, Deliverance Manual, 235.

21. "Placebo," YouTube, February 19, 2017, *https://youtu.be/FoH8inFoFAo.*

Chapter 20: Coming Right Up, An Order to Win

1. Beatrice Bruno, *How to Get Over Yourself and Let Go of the P.A.S.T.* (Aurora, CO: Heard Word Publishing, 2012), 37.

Invitation to Christ

1. Douglas Groothuis, *Christian Apologetics: A Comprehensive Case for Biblical Faith* (Downers Grove, IL: IVP Academic, 2011), 503.

2. Ibid, 500–501.

3. "Know Jesus," Daystar Television, accessed March 26, 2019. *http://www.daystar.com/prayer/know-jesus/.*

Made in the USA
Las Vegas, NV
03 January 2022